Discovering
Great Singers of
Classic Pop

THE NEWMARKET DISCOVERING GREAT MUSIC SERIES

Discovering Great Jazz

Discovering Great Music

Discovering Great Singers of Classic Pop

Discovering Great Singers of Classic Pop

*A New Listener's Guide to the Sounds
and Lives of the Top Performers and
Their Recordings, Movies, and Videos*

ROY HEMMING
DAVID HAJDU

NEWMARKET PRESS
New York
A Newmarket Discovering Great Music Series Book

91 92 93 94   10 9 8 7 6 5 4 3 2 1

Library of Congress Cataloging-in-Publication Data

Hemming, Roy.
Discovering great singers of classic pop : a new listener's guide
to the sounds and lives of the top performers and their recordings,
movies, and videos / Roy Hemming, David Hajdu.
p.   cm.
Includes bibliographical references and index.
ISBN 1-55704-072-9
1. Singers—Biography.   2. Popular music—History and criticism.
I. Hajdu, David.   II. Title.
ML400.H43   1991
782.42164'092'2—dc20   90-27452
[B]   CIP
                                          MN

QUANTITY PURCHASES
Companies, professional groups, clubs, and other organizations
may qualify for special terms when ordering quantities of this title.
For information, write Special Sales, Newmarket Press,
18 East 48th Street, New York, N.Y. 10017, or call (212) 832-3575.

Manufactured in the United States of America

First Edition

For Angelina and Charles Hajdu,
who used to rock on the back porch to the music of
WNEW as their son watched through the screen door,
listened, and learned.

And for Anna J. and Benjamin Whitney Hemming,
who, after hearing their eight-year-old son sing in
Madame Annette's Annual Review, wisely encouraged him
to write about popular music rather than perform it.

ACKNOWLEDGMENTS

For their generous assistance, counsel, or advice on parts of this book in progress, the authors are deeply grateful to Jeff Austin, Richard Rodney Bennett, Steven Davis, Gary Giddins, Genevieve A. Kazdin, Thomas McNulty, Jeff Menell, Mary Kate Rodman, Daryl Sherman, Arthur Siegel, Stephen I. Simon, Suzanne Smith, Billy Stritch, Christopher Vaughn, John S. Wilson, and, most especially, Seth Fahey and Richard M. Sudhalter.

For their help in locating and verifying information for some of the chapters or making useful materials available, the authors thank Jane Ayer, Buddy Barnes, Danny Bennett, Charles Bourgeois, Larry Carr, Didier C. Deutsch, Charles DeForest, Wendell Echols, George Feltenstein, Michael Finnegan, Alyse Fisher, Fritz Friedman, Janet Gari, Bill Goodwin, Stanley Green, Michael Kerker, Taehee Kim, Miles Kreuger, Maurice Levine, Ros Lipps, John Meyer, Richard Pasqual, Susan Reynolds, Joe Savage, Berte Schuchat, Donald Smith, George Sponhaltz, David Weiner, and the staffs of the Library of Congress, the Elmer Holmst Bobst Library at New York University, the Institute for Jazz Studies at Rutgers University, the Louis Armstrong Archives at Queens College in New York, and, most especially, the Library for the Performing Arts at Lincoln Center in New York.

Special thanks must also go to Esther Margolis and Keith Hollaman of Newmarket Press for their enthusiastic support and knowing guidance of the book from its planning stages to the presses.

Finally, for her selfless and invaluable labor throughout the course of the preparation of this book, deepest thanks to Joanne Simbal Hajdu.

CONTENTS

PART TWO: THE CHANGING SCENE—
THE SECOND WAVE

INTRODUCTION

This book is about some fifty outstanding men and women who have enriched the lives of generations of music lovers with a specific type of singing of a specific type of music. In their different and individual ways, each of these singers has influenced both the development of popular music and its substantial role in America's cultural history from the 1920s up to the present day.

Most importantly, these singers continue their influence today, not merely as nostalgia for "old-timers" but also as the foremost exponents of a type of music that people of all ages keep discovering and rediscovering to be a treasure chest unlike any other in American music.

Some people now call the genre "vintage pop" or "standard pop." Some reverse the latter tag and call the songs "pop standards." In any case, this type of music has never had a commonly agreed-upon name the way jazz and rock 'n' roll do. Yet it has graced American popular music for most of the twentieth century—and at least three generations of singers have kept its songs in the mainstream through theatrical productions, movies, radio, television, supper clubs, cabaret, the concert hall, videos, and, most far-reaching of all, recordings. We prefer the name that New York disc jockey Rich Conaty was among the first to popularize: *classic pop*. It fits because this type of music has survived just about every other musical development or fad in this century, from ragtime to rap, and shows every sign of continuing to flourish into the next century, just as the symphonic and operatic classics of previous centuries have survived into ours.

EXACTLY WHAT IS CLASSIC POP?

At the risk of oversimplification, classic pop is usually highly melodic, with tunes that are memorable *without* the words. Classic-pop melodies are more likely to be lilting or lyrical than singsongy. But classic pop can also be rhythmic music, with an underlying swing that makes it ideal for dancing—without being dependent on a hard, driving beat. Classic-pop lyrics, meanwhile, are generally romantic in theme and sophisticated in language, with conspicuous touches of intimacy, wit, and honesty in the best of them. Within that framework, there can be the most complex and occasionally even profound interplay of music and lyrics. Moreover, the best of the songs lend themselves to varying musical arrangements and interpretations by different singers.

Many of these songs were originally written for Broadway shows, Hollywood movies, nightclub acts, or specific singers' or orchestras' recordings—by such well-known songwriters as George and Ira Gershwin, Jerome Kern, Cole Porter, Irving Berlin, Harold Arlen, Richard Rodgers, Lorenz Hart, Oscar Hammerstein II, Dorothy Fields, and Johnny Mercer—*and* by such lesser-known but equally durable songwriters as Ralph Rainger, Richard Whiting, Harry Warren, Jimmy McHugh, Jimmy Van Heusen, Frank Loesser, Arthur Schwartz, Hoagy Carmichael, and Herman Hupfeld, to name just a few.

Through radio (and later television), recordings, and the live engagements of individual singers and dance bands, these songs reached—and touched—millions of listeners far and wide. Most significantly, although some of these songs became primarily identified with specific singers, the best of them were taken up by many other performers as well (unlike most of the songs of recent years, which become almost the exclusive property of one artist or group). As a result, the songs have continued to be a standard part of the repertories of many singers throughout the country, especially in clubs and cabarets, and to some extent on television. What's more, they continue to be *loved* by young and old alike.

THE CLASSIC-POP SINGING STYLE

Much has been written about most of the great songwriters of classic pop. But what about the singers? Unlike the leading rock performers of the past few decades (whose professional and private lives are grist for all sorts of magazine, book, TV, and video coverage), the major singers of the '20s, '30s, '40s, and '50s did not usually get the kind of media coverage that movie stars of the same period got—unless, of course, they found themselves embroiled in a juicy scandal. With few exceptions, most music lovers today know the names and perhaps a few recordings of the great singers of the Golden Age of classic pop, but not much about the singers themselves or what has made them significant.

Yet it is the singers who have given classic pop its life—a life that goes beyond the notes and words on the sheet music. A listener must relate to a singer one-to-one in some way—whether as a lover, a confidant, a soldier-in-arms, a brother, or a sister. Through the singer's art, the listener connects with a song and draws emotional meaning from it. And that art is not an entirely technical one, although musical skill is the most obvious ingredient. Equally important are all the intangibles that make certain performers so appealing and important to us—the personalities *behind* the voices. The singer's life, then, infuses the life he or she gives the song and, in turn, the way the song touches the life of each listener.

Like the music itself, the classic-pop singing style is mostly rooted in the dual tenets of urbanity and accessibility. Classic-pop singing is not necessarily perfect technically. But it can be deeply touching and emotional. It can be infused with either warm sentiment or cool sophistication, or be highly individualistic. Above all, unlike operatic or theatrical singing, the classic-pop style is naturalistic, sung in the singer's ordinary voice. And unlike blues or rock 'n' roll, it is conversational, sung for the most part at a speaking level. You can't shout out or wail lyrics such as "A kiss is just a kiss, a sigh is just a sigh." In short, a classic-pop song, like a vintage Bordeaux, is best when served for two, at room temperature.

CHOICES, LIMITS, AND QUALIFICATIONS

Putting a numerical limit on the choices for coverage in this book has inevitably created problems—and risked discord among authors and publishers as well as readers. So let us admit right from the start that selecting the singers we have included was harder than actually writing any of the individual chapters. We finally agreed to include only those singers who have been *primarily* identified with singing classic pop through the years. This, of course, eliminates many great singers who have *sometimes* sung pop standards but who were or are essentially jazz singers, rhythm-and-blues singers, country-and-western singers, or other genre specialists. That's why you won't find Alberta Hunter,

Ivie Anderson, Billy Eckstine, Anita O'Day, June Christy, Chris Connor, Aretha Franklin, Ray Charles, or Loretta Lynn. It also eliminates later singers who have specialized in contemporary pop and only occasionally have delved into the classic pop repertory, such as Bobby Darin, Paul Anka, Diana Ross, Dionne Warwick, Linda Ronstadt, or Carly Simon. And in classic pop, our focus has remained on only the very best and the most popular. In a few cases, our personal tastes have also inevitably come into play.

The singers profiled in our main chapters are arranged in a loose chronological order, even though many of them overlap or crisscross different time periods. We feel that even an imperfect chronological order places each singer in a more useful historical perspective for most readers than alphabetical order would.

These profiles are not intended to "tell all" (the Bibliography, at the end of the book, lists other sources for that). Instead, we have sought to pull together a meaningful overview of all these singers' lives, work, and achievements. Similarly, our critical assessments of their singing are meant to be not exhaustive musicological analyses (that we leave to the academicians), but rather a guide to characterizing each singer's distinctiveness in terms that nonmusically trained, average listeners can easily understand.

At the end of the book there is a selective discography of each singer's most representative recordings, plus a selective listing of movies, documentaries, or other types of programs available on home-video cassettes and videodiscs. The emphasis in these listings is on the most representative of their discs and tapes now available in record or video stores, or likely to be found in public or college libraries. For easy reference, these discographies and videographies are arranged alphabetically by singer.

We feel strongly, furthermore, about these record and video guides as essential components to any complete appreciation of these singers, for the written word can tell you only part of these singers' individual stories or at best throw a partial light on their great talents. In the final analysis, singers must be seen and heard. It is our hope that this volume will encourage just that.

ROY HEMMING AND DAVID HAJDU
New York City, 1991

PART ONE

Setting the Scene— The First Wave

So many great singers of classic American pop have been part of our musical life for so long that we forget that there was a time when neither a Top 40 nor a *Hit Parade* existed, and when the idea of making a career singing popular songs was taken seriously by very, very few.

That certainly doesn't mean that popular music itself didn't exist before our century turned it into a megaforce whose influence now extends far beyond our national borders. For generations long before us, however, an era's popular music was primarily folk music handed down orally. Eventually some of these songs managed to get written down and then printed. In this country, the American Revolution spurred the printing of patriotic tunes such as "Yankee Doodle" (which were sold in the streets for a penny a copy). By the end of the nineteenth century the publishing of songs had become a major industry whose sales reached into cities and towns of virtually every size throughout the country. Most of the songs that got published were sentimental ballads or novelty tunes to be sung by families around the parlor piano, or by entertainers in local vaudeville theaters and saloons.

In the early decades of this century, sweeping technological developments—most particularly the phonograph and radio—played decisive roles in turning pop music into a major industry. So did a number of interconnected social and economic factors, chief among them the eagerness of more and more men and women to dedicate themselves to being a part of popular music as songwriters, instrumental players, and singers.

For the first third of the twentieth century, those men and women were generally said to be linked to Tin Pan Alley. No such street ever existed literally, of course. The name arose around the turn of the century to describe the din that usually surrounded the offices of the major New York music publishers (first located in the Union Square area around Fourteenth Street, then on Twenty-eighth Street, and still later farther uptown, in the Broadway theater district). Row upon row of these offices would be filled with people trying to peddle or buy songs, with the sounds from one office frequently overlapping with those of another or even flowing into the street in those days of open windows, no air conditioning, and nonsoundproof walls. "It always reminded me of kitchen clatter, just like tin pans," composer Harry von Tilzer ("Wait Till the Sun Shines, Nellie," "I Want a Girl Just Like the Girl That Married Dear Old Dad") is reputed to have said, and the name Tin Pan Alley stuck.

By the decade preceding World War I, the publishers of Tin Pan Alley had pretty much set the patterns that would endure in American popular music for the first half of this century. The singers, pianists, and others who bought their tunes, whether for professional stage use or for amateur use, favored romantic or sentimental ballads with easy-to-play, hummable melodies and easy-to-remember rhymes in the lyrics (the "moon, June, spoon" syndrome). Most songs consisted of a brief verse that set up the premise of the song, followed by a thirty-two-bar melodic refrain.

With the 1920s, however, came several developments that brought the flowering of the Tin Pan Alley–style tune into what we can now call classic pop—and the rise of singing stars who specialized in it. The first was an extraordinary upgrading of the standards of Broadway musicals, spearheaded by Jerome Kern; Irving Berlin; Cole Porter; the Gershwin brothers, George and Ira; and the team of Richard Rodgers and Lorenz Hart. Rejecting both the operetta-style songs that Broadway had inherited from European musical models *and* the prevailing simplicities of vaudeville pop songs, these young American songwriters wrote scores that grew increasingly sophisticated in introducing more personal concepts of melody, rhythm, and harmony into the song form, even breaking away from the thirty-two-bar refrain on occasion. The music publishers of Tin Pan Alley, for whom many of these songwriters had worked while waiting for their Broadway breaks, were quick to publish and publicize the best songs from the latest Broadway shows—and to help the country's growing number of professional singers and instrumentalists turn them into hits performed in all parts of the country.

In doing that, they interacted with several other major developments of the 1920s. Chief among them: the rise of popular dance orchestras and their need for a continual supply of fresh songs. The leading hotels and clubs in virtually every city vied with each other for good dance bands as dance craze after dance craze swept the country. Social dancing, which prior to World War I (in polite white society, at least) had been relegated primarily to chaperoned balls or parties, and to such formal dance forms as the waltz, grew increasingly looser and more popular. "Jass" syncopations, including ragtime, spread quickly from small black bands to white ones. So, too, did the so-called animal dances that had developed out of old plantation dances (such as the Cakewalk) and had turned the Turkey Trot, the Monkey Glide, the Kangaroo Dip, the Buzzard Lope, the Grizzly Bear, and the Bunny Hug into prewar vaudeville staples for both blacks and whites (scandalizing proper society along the way). At any rate, "going out dancing" became millions of Americans' most passionate pastime in the 1920s, especially among young people, who delighted in dance fads as a form of rebellion against the straitlaced norms and tastes of their elders.

Especially popular were the sweet bands, which emphasized sentimental or romantic ballads for dancing cheek to cheek. In most of these bands, at first, instrumental players doubled as vocalists for certain songs, sometimes solo but more often in vocal trios or quartets. Among the best-known leaders of such bands were Art Hickman, Isham Jones, Leo Reisman, Abe Lyman, George Olsen, Roger Wolfe Kahn, Guy Lombardo, and, the most famous of them all, Paul Whiteman. Coinage of the term "sweet band," incidentally, is generally attributed to Broadway showman Florenz Ziegfeld, who used it to promote his Ziegfeld Roof nightclub in the early 1920s distinguishing his orchestras' musical style from that identified with more "lowdown" jazz groups. And so another link was forged between the music of Broadway and the music that mainstream America was dancing to.

Even those couples who couldn't always get out to where the dance bands were playing could hear their music almost any night of the week, thanks to two other developments: the rapid growth of radio as an entertainment medium and improvements in electrical recordings for home phonographs. Among the most listened-to early radio shows were dance-band remotes, on which the announcer's voice would proclaim: "And now, direct from the Astor Roof in the heart of Times Square, it's the music of Freddy Rich and his orchestra . . . " or "From the Cocoanut Grove in the Hotel Ambassador in Los Angeles, it's the music of Gus Arnheim and his orchestra. . . ." Radios and phonographs were quickly replacing parlor pianos as the home entertainment center of the time. Sales of sheet music for amateur performing also declined as the popularity of a growing number of professional singers flourished through radio and records.

Both radio and records also brought stardom to a new type of singer—the kind of stardom that had previously been possible only with a successful Broadway show or vaudeville act. Significantly, these new singers didn't need the kind of vocal chords that could reach the last row of a theater's balcony without leaving them hoarse by the end of a number. With radio and recording microphones, a new type of more intimate popular singer sprang up. Among the earliest and most popular of this type were Gene Austin, Blossom Seeley, Vaughn DeLeath, Marion Harris, Johnny Marvin, Nick Lucas, Annette Hanshaw, and Smith Ballew. But for all the individual qualities of their voices and their conversational stylings, each of these singers was to be quickly outshone by others who came up in the years right after them. They should not be forgotten, however, for the pivotal roles they played in paving the way for the bigger impact of Ruth Etting, Helen Morgan, Ethel Waters, Rudy Vallee, and, most especially, Bing Crosby in the late 1920s.

Because these singers relied on a more evenly modulated style of singing for the microphones than the more bravura style required of their predecessors on operetta or vaudeville stages, the men came to be called "crooners" and the women "canaries" in the slang of the day. At first the terms were not always meant complimentarily. But after Bing Crosby began calling himself a crooner unashamedly, that one became a more neutral and acceptable designation. Canary, meanwhile, was most commonly used for female band singers, with "thrush" or "songbird" the terms for nonband alternates. Virginia-born Kate Smith even billed herself in the 1930s as "The Songbird of the South."

All of these singers usually concentrated on the best songs from Broadway or on similar songs written especially for them to introduce on radio or in nightclubs. And in the competition among songwriters to get the top singers to introduce their latest tunes and, hopefully, start them on the road to becoming hits, the singers could be choosy and hold out for only the best material—thereby helping to raise the general standards of what was (unknown to them, of course) becoming the Golden Era of classic pop.

By the late 1920s, talking pictures had also revolutionized the movie industry. Hollywood suddenly needed singers and dancers—and songs for them to sing and dance to. Quite naturally, the studios turned to Broadway and radio, and raided its musical talent for screen adaptations. Not only performers headed West but so, too, did the top songwriters. As a result, from the start, Hollywood's musicals took on the basic song style of what is now classic pop. The relationship was cemented when, after the 1929 stock market crash and the beginning of the Great Depression, the relatively well-to-do major studios bought out most of the economically hard-pressed New York music publishers, getting ongoing access to their extensive and valuable music libraries. In addition, by controlling the music-publishing firms and all their licenses, the studios could pressure the growing number of dance-band leaders as well as the producers of records and radio programs into promoting the songs from their latest movies, in some cases turning them into hits even before a movie opened in theaters across the country.

That situation continued essentially throughout the 1930s and into the early 1940s—as American popular music dominated by Broadway, Hollywood, Tin Pan Alley, and the dance bands swept the land. Out of it came the first wave of great singers whose work survives to this day on records and film—the first, and in many cases still influential, singers of classic American pop.

AL JOLSON

*Jolson is the greatest singer of all
time. He said so himself.*
—GEORGE BURNS

In a loopy, accidental way, Al Jolson helped start the sophisticated, intimate style of singing that's so integral to classic pop. He didn't sing that way himself, of course. Quite the contrary, the Jolson style was pure pizzazz—as big and brash and unabashedly sentimental as America felt in the era of the First World War. But Jolson sang the way he sang so successfully and so definitively that subsequent singers had no choice but to invent another way to sing. In this sense, crooning was a reaction *against* the Jolson style, just as Jolson's razzmatazz was a rejection of the prim formality of the operetta-influenced romantic singers who dominated Broadway and vaudeville before him.

This is not to say that Al Jolson is just an outdated artifact of a bygone time, as he has often been depicted in recent years. In truth, Jolson is such a seminal figure in popular entertainment that his influence continues to permeate the pop scene today. After all, he virtually invented the role of pop music superstar, as well as the superstar ego. Jolson was also the first pop singer to become a national symbol of youthful rebellion against parental tastes and tradition, and the first star to delve into national political issues—all in addition to his groundbreaking role as the star of the movie widely regarded as the first talkie, *The Jazz Singer*.

To this day, there's a little Jolson in every singer who pulls out all the show-biz stops and delivers a number like it's the only thing in the world that matters. He showed the crooners what to do when it's not the right time to croon. Sinatra, crowing "That's Life"; Streisand, barking "Don't Rain on My Parade"; Minnelli, belting out "New York, New York"—they're all doing Jolson.

"He sang every song as if he was going to drop dead at the end of it," said Larry Parks, who mimicked the technique well enough to earn an Oscar nomination for his starring role in the 1946 movie *The Jolson Story*. That's the essence of Jolson: death by schmaltz. He put so much life into a song that he always seemed on the verge of using up his own supply.

At one point, performing actually made Jolson ill, according to backstage legend. As a result of dancing too strenuously in stage shoes, he developed an ingrown toenail, which hurt so much during one show that he had to take the weight off his foot to relieve the pain. Bending on one knee, grimacing in pain, Jolson decided he might as well work the whole effect into his act, and it went over so well he did it at every show for the next thirty-five years. At least that's how the legend goes.

Ingrown toenail or not, the one-knee shtick and the mugging fit the highly emotive singing style Jolson developed over the years. The Russian-born son of a cantor, Asa Yoelson was reared on an emotionally charged mix of the heartfelt music of the Judaic liturgy, the colorful folk tunes of his parents' homeland, and the bouncy, Southern-style popular songs he picked up while growing up in Washington, D.C. Breaking an age-old line of Yoelson cantors, against vehement parental objections, Asa drew from these rich and diverse musical traditions to become the unique popular singer Al Jolson. As he explained late in his career, with characteristic humility, "When I sing, I want to give the people a feeling in their hearts they never had before."

He was gifted with a strong tenor (which dropped to a baritone late in his career), good range, and a distinctive, brassy vocal timbre. More important, as a singer Jolson was a great actor. Like many popular performers at the time, he frequently sang in "blackface"—a stylized black makeup used by many white entertainers (including Eddie Cantor and Jack Benny) as well as blacks (such as Bert Williams), dating back to the days of "minstrel" shows. "Jolie was a cantor's son, and everybody thought his mother was a mammy," George Burns told us. "That's how good an actor Jolson was." Rolling his eyes mischievously, clasping his hands together hopefully, stretching out his arms pleadingly, Jolson made every song a playlet in thirty-two bars.

There has rarely been a better match of singer and songs. Jolson's repertoire included many of the liveliest, catchiest songs of the vaudeville era and very early Tin Pan Alley, including "Toot, Toot Tootsie (Goo'bye)," "California, Here I Come," "My Mammy," and "Swanee." Not quite Cole Porter selections, this stuff doesn't even bother with the brain and goes straight to the autonomic nervous system. Your feet are tapping and your heart pounding as soon as the notes hit you, even if you *think* you don't like this sort of music. Jolson knew what people really liked, and he had most of his hits written or adapted to his specifications—or he wrote them himself. (He is credited as the writer or cowriter of dozens of songs, including "Me and My Shadow," "There's a Rainbow 'Round My Shoulder," and "Don't Mind the Darkness, Morning Will Come.")

To Jolson, every number had to be a showstopper. In fact, the very term has been attributed to him, because he was known literally to stop a Broadway show in the midst of a scene if he thought it could be impoved by being cut. Stepping out of character, he'd turn to the audience and stage-whisper something like, "You know what happens in this play, don't you, folks? Well, would you rather see more of it . . . or would you rather hear Jolson sing?" A rhetorical question, given the hackneyed quality of some of the Jolson-featured Broadway "plays," such as *La Belle Paree, Big Boy, Bombo, Robinson Crusoe, Jr.*, and *Sinbad*. Most were essentially disposable vehicles for Jolson to be Jolson, and he wouldn't hesitate to dispose of them—at which point the entire cast would come out from behind the curtain, sit on the stage floor, and watch the real show, Jolson, for an hour or so.

As he once revealed, Jolson's "secret" was "taking the audience in confidence" by using little conspiratory devices like throwing away the third act. Jolson had a few other extraordinary techniques, including a couple of real secrets, to help him come as close to his audience as he could. Sometimes he would go to the box office half an hour before show time and chat with ticket-buyers, venturing out to the sidewalk to drum up business if necessary. At other times he'd lounge around the theater lobby anonymously as the audience milled in, to develop a firsthand feel for that night's crowd. Or he'd sit in with the orchestra and play the clarinet until his cue was coming, to be able to watch the audience in their seats and catch their mood.

If Jolson couldn't get enough of his audiences, they certainly returned the sentiment. His fans packed the Winter Garden Theater on Broadway, Jolson show after Jolson show, eight shows a week most weeks, from 1911 to 1925. The singer was far and away the greatest phenomenon ever to hit the stage at a time when popular music *was* the stage. Though recording wasn't yet very big, Jolson had the first million-selling hit anyway, with George Gershwin's and Irving Caesar's "Swanee." (The song peaked with sales of 2.5 million, including both records and sheet music.) In short, Jolson was to pop music what

Charlie Chaplin was to film and Babe Ruth was to sports: the first superstar.

The term hadn't been coined yet, though it's amazing Jolson never thought of it. Despite his gushily ingratiating manner onstage, Jolson was known for having something of an attitude problem outside of the public eye. Or, as a *Variety* critic once said, "He's arrogant, ruthless, rude, impatient, impetuous, cruel, shrewd, thoughtless, and ignorant." Naturally, some members of his family disagreed; a few of his four wives, including movie-musical star Ruby Keeler (wife number three, 1929–39), said Jolson wasn't really quite that nice.

Whatever Jolson's private problems may have been, they never interfered significantly with his professional success. The public eventually rejected him for purely artistic reasons. Jolson was a stage artist—he didn't need a thirty-foot movie-house screen to be larger than life, nor the imaginary world of radio to transport audiences to another time and place. He did it all alone, in person, and using only one knee. When radio and sound movies came and changed popular entertainment, however, Jolson didn't change with them. He stuck with the same big, broad, theatrical style and much of the same simplistic material, and he was stuck with them, indeed.

It's ironic that Jolson's best-known achievement was in motion pictures, as the star of the first successful feature-length film with sound, *The Jazz Singer*, in 1927. With a plot somewhat similar to Jolson's own life story, the movie proved that as an actor Jolson could really deliver a song. His acting style proved to be too big and broad for the subtle demands of the screen, though he starred or costarred in ten features and made cameo appearances in another six. After his first bad reviews and critical counsel from his studio, Warner Bros., Jolson learned to adapt to film, to some extent, and made a few decent movies, notably *The Singing Fool* in 1928, *Mammy* in 1930, and *Go Into Your Dance* in 1935. But Jolson's career as a film star was over less than a decade after it began.

The singer had similar problems on radio, which he pioneered with a show of his own in 1927, the same year *The Jazz Singer* premiered. In interviews, Jolson admitted that he was never comfortable on radio. "When I have to stick to a script, my hands are tied, my mouth is tied, my keister is tied," he complained. Still, Jolson tried his hand at four different radio shows over the course of the 1930s, and one (*The Lifebuoy Show* costarring Jolson, Martha Raye, and the radio comedian Parkyakarkus, father of filmmaker Albert Brooks) reached the number-five spot in the ratings at one point.

In his last years, he did get to play to the largest audiences of his career—the millions of soldiers he entertained as a volunteer during both the Second World War and the Korean War. And a few years before his death, he enjoyed a resurgence in public interest in his work, thanks to both the highly acclaimed hit movie *The Jolson Story* and its sequel *Jolson Sings Again*. Still, when he died of a heart attack at age sixty-four in 1950, shortly after returning from a Korean War tour, Jolson had become little more than a memory to most of the ticket-buying public. Indeed, it's been said that Jolson performed so much during the war years in part to hear the applause he could no longer get from paying audiences.

To this day, Jolson is vastly underappreciated. The fact is that Jolson's greatest legacy is lost. The stage performances that made him an almost mythic figure in the first third of this century were never preserved on film—not that they could convey the impact of his live appearances. He never appeared on television, his radio broadcasts exist only in archival copies of air checks, and his relatively few notable movies are practically unknown to modern-day audiences. As a matter of fact, the generations of music fans born in the second half of the century, after his death, know Al Jolson primarily from TV impressionists and cartoon caricatures; their conceptions of the man are founded on jokes, and they can't help but think of Jolson himself as a joke.

Jolson's image as a blackface performer has also damaged his reputation, perhaps beyond repair. As the best-known singer to have worked in "minstrel" style, Jolson is sometimes disparaged as a symbol of racism. Indeed, Jesse Jackson has depicted government insensitivity to the African-American underclass as "the Al Jolson syndrome," despite the fact that blackface was popular long before Jolson—and Jolson steered clear of it for the last twenty years of his career.

Fortunately, as the first major pop recording artist, Jolson left a rich legacy of recordings made over the course of some thirty years. As this legacy emerges in restored form on CD, listeners have a new opportunity to rediscover and reassess Jolson, the first superstar of classic pop.

ETHEL WATERS

Ethel Waters was the mother of us all.
—LENA HORNE

The first black pop singer to become a major American star, Ethel Waters has a pivotal place in both the history of popular music and the history of African-American culture. Before her there were Edith Wilson, Sara Martin, Clara Smith—gifted black singers whose gifts were virtually unknown to most listeners outside of the artists' almost exclusively black society of devotees. With few exceptions, they performed to black audiences and sold records in black record shops in black neighborhoods. In the eyes of the white audience at the time, black singers were still seen as blacks who happened to sing. But after Ethel Waters, there were Louis Armstrong, Ella Fitzgerald, Lena Horne—giants who got the giant audiences they deserved. They were recognized, finally, as singers who happened to be black. The difference is a big one, and the one who made the difference is Ethel Waters.

Over the years, the cross-pollination of African and Anglo influences has played a critical role in the development of popular American singing. Yet Ethel Waters' unique place in this process often seems to be understated or misinterpreted. Ever since the 1940s, when Waters parlayed her enormous success as a Broadway and nightclub singer into a film acting career, the press has rarely mentioned her singing. By the time of her death at age eighty in 1976, many of Waters' obituaries described her only as an actress or as a strictly blues singer, which she was not. Compounding the issue, Ethel Waters was always a complex figure, impossible to categorize. Onetime thief and longtime evangelist, aristocrat, mother figure, civil-rights booster, and political conservative, Ethel Waters may have a popular image that contradicts her true legacy because she lived a life of contradictions.

Ethel Waters spent much of her life—and her creative energy—fighting to shake the shadow of her own past. And there was much to fight. Her mother was practically a child herself, a thirteen-year-old rape victim, when Ethel Waters was born on October 31, 1896. Raised on the streets of the red-light district in South Philadelphia, young Waters took to stealing food for both sustenance and relatively harmless kicks, considering the graver crimes all around her. By ten, she was leading her own gang, a certain mark of honor. Her street name was Chip, which she later said was based on her emerging ability to sing (or chirp), although women with reputations for sexual promiscuity have often been nicknamed "chippies."

By the time Waters herself was thirteen, she was married—and not happily. Her husband, a twenty-three-year-old neighborhood roustabout named Merritt ("Buddy") Purnsfly, neither loved nor honored his wife. "He spent more time with other women than me," she recalled in later years, "and when I protested, he beat me."

The scars were not all physical. Separated within a year of her marriage and never happily married in her life, Waters freely admitted her distaste for romance in general and sex in particular. As she explained in a magazine article she wrote in the 1950s, the strongest love she ever had for a man was in a brief, purely platonic relationship with a prizefighter with whom she enjoyed sparring.

Upon discovering religion in a mixed-race Catholic school in Philadelphia, Waters channeled her love toward God. She became devoutly faithful as a young woman, embracing Christianity as a formal means of rejecting the sins associated with her circumstances of birth, her youth in the streets, and her brief, failed marriage. Later in life, as a successful singer and actress, Waters would become increasingly dedicated to her faith, having her screen parts rewritten to incorporate Scripture and religious themes. By her final years, Waters would dedicate most of her working hours to the Billy Graham Crusades.

Steel-willed, mature beyond her seventeen years, and sternly opposed to sin, Ethel Waters brought an uncommon discipline and restraint to her work when she began singing publicly in 1913. At places like Jack's Rathskeller in South Philly, where she made her first public appearance, young female singers were expected to take full advantage of, rather than defiantly ignore, their sexuality. Waters chose to perform a plaintive ballad, "When You're a Long, Long Way from Home," in what she later described as "my low, sweet, and then new way of singing."

It is that genuinely "then new" style that served to distinguish Ethel

Waters among young black singers of the day. Graduating from her neighborhood haunts to the New York club circuit, Waters developed a distinctively elegant and sophisticated style distinct from the energetically emotional blues singing popular in Manhattan night spots such as Edmond Johnson's Cellar and the Plantation Club, where Waters was appearing in the early 1920s. As a matter of fact, she later explained that although she recorded some blues *material*, she disliked blues *singing*, with "those unladylike shouts and growls," as much as she disliked sex.

In her earliest recordings, made with Fletcher Henderson in New York in the early 1920s, the components of the Waters singing style were already evident. Though she couldn't read music, her intonation was excellent. Her phrasing emphasized the lyric over the beat; she didn't swing. And, most strikingly, her elocution was impeccable, indeed formal—open vowels, crisp consonants, even rolling *r*'s.

Indeed, her strongly Anglicized enunciation enabled Waters to break racial barriers as a pop singer. She was the first black singer to perform on major radio programs in the South, and she was the first black singer to receive top billing at a "white" theater. In the process, and despite her critics' claims of musical Uncle Tomism, Waters cracked open the door for future black performers such as Louis Armstrong and Billie Holiday, who would begin to stretch white listeners' ears with music in the African-American tradition. In a sense, then, Ethel Waters is contrapuntal to Bing Crosby in the evolution of classic-pop singing. While Crosby drew upon African-American musical techniques as a white artist, Waters adopted white musical techniques to help advance African-American artists.

Moreover, Waters' vocal precision and stylistic formality influenced generations of singers who followed her, black and white, including Mabel Mercer, Lee Wiley, Ivie Anderson, Lena Horne, Frances Wayne, and Bobby Short, among others. In a most exceptional effort to emulate Waters, Sophie Tucker outright hired her for vocal lessons. There are even traces of Waters' style in the earliest recordings of Billie Holiday, despite the fact that Holiday never publicly acknowledged any debt to Waters.

As the 1920s ended, Waters moved on from recording and nightclub performing to the second phase of her career, as a Broadway and film star. She appeared in her first Broadway revue, *Africana*, in 1927 and her first film, *On with the Show* (in which she appeared in two numbers), two years later. A long series of similar singing performances on both stage and screen followed over the course of the 1930s.

Plump and plain-featured—and, of course, black, in an era when African-Americans were usually ignored or caricatured in mainstream stage and screen productions—Ethel Waters wasn't offered an enormous range of roles. Although she showed a natural presence onstage from her earliest revue appearances, it wasn't until 1939 that Waters landed her first substantial role on Broadway, starring in the melodrama *Mamba's Daughters*. It took more than a decade for the actress to achieve what was certainly the critical high point of her Broadway career, her highly acclaimed performance in the drama *The Member of the Wedding* (in which she also starred on-screen).

On film, Ethel Waters was relegated to a seemingly countless string of "mammy" roles, denied a role substantial enough to showcase her skills as an actress until *Cabin in the Sky* in 1943. Even so, by 1949 her acting had progressed to the point at which she was able to bring considerable depth to a role that was little more than an emotionally complex "mammy," in *Pinky*—and win an Academy Award nomination for her performance.

When television emerged in the 1950s, Waters made the record books once again as the first black woman to star in her own network series. Yet the show, called *Beulah*, cast her stereotypically as a happy-go-lucky domestic worker—little more than a *funny* "mammy." In the last two decades of Waters' career, however, TV turned out to be the source of some of her most diverse roles. From the late 1950s to the early 1970s, Waters appeared in a wide range of programs, playing dramatic parts in such shows as *Route 66, The Whirlibirds, Daniel Boone,* and *Owen Marshall, Counsellor at Law*. She was, as always, consummately ladylike and professional.

In her final years, Ethel Waters dedicated her mature resources to touring with the evangelist Billy Graham in his inspirational tent show, the Billy Graham Crusades. Though this phase of her career is generally dismissed by musicologists, we tend to feel that the Crusades featured some of Ethel Waters' most compelling work. She was clearly in her element at these performances, many of which were televised live. She gave speeches, and her conviction cut through all the predictable polemic. Most importantly, her long-seasoned singing voice had so much majesty; there was wisdom in her phrasing and a twinkle of vigor in her tone. This was Ethel Waters as she wanted to be—strong and good and close to her God.

LOUIS ARMSTRONG

*Ask any singer. They know how great
Pops was—as a singer.*
—TONY BENNETT

Like Picasso's sculpture or Chaplin's music, Louis Armstrong's pop singing has always been upstaged by the performer's more critically acclaimed work—his incomparable trumpet playing. This is easy to understand, considering that Armstrong has frequently been regarded as the single greatest jazz instrumentalist of all time. Yet it does not detract from Armstrong's genius as a trumpet player to give his gifts as a vocalist the attention they deserve. He may not have been the single greatest vocalist of all time, but Satchmo was a merely great one.

Although his singing is usually glossed over in summaries of his life and work, Louis Armstrong was as much a singer as an instrumentalist throughout most of his career. He started out as a vocalist, he sang on the vast majority of his recordings, he had his biggest hits with vocal numbers, and he capped his career with predominantly vocal performances. Moreover, while he was always a *jazz* trumpeter, he was essentially a *pop* singer. He worked almost exclusively in the pop repertoire, especially in the second half of his career, when his singing was often backed by pop arrangements and orchestras.

Had he done nothing else but sing as he did, Armstrong would have earned his place in the history of classic pop. As a vocal innovator he played a key role in pioneering two important components of the classic-pop singing style—natural vocal color and the distinctive rhythmic underpinning called swing. No other singer has ever tried to sing exactly like him (although practically everybody can do an impersonation of him). He's original and unique to this day, yet there's a whole lot of Louis in all pop singers who sing in their natural voices or know how to swing.

Armstrong never learned how to swing. He practically invented it. Born at the same time in the same town, Louis Armstrong and jazz grew up together in New Orleans. He always gave his birth date as the Fourth of July 1900, which is the date listed in all the standard reference books and which seems so perfect for the man who symbolizes the American music of the twentieth century—but which is apparently a fabrication, as jazz critic and historian Gary Giddins discovered in a search through the New Orelans town records. May Ann Armstrong, a domestic worker, and her husband, Willie Armstrong, a laborer in a turpentine factory, had their son David Louis on August 4, 1901. His mother took to calling him Little Louis, which stuck and became his first professional name.

By age twelve, Little Louis was singing well enough to average a dollar a day in tips on the streets of New Orleans, he later recalled. He put together a boy harmony quartet and tackled the tenor parts, although his ambition at the time was to grow up to be a bass singer.

Louis Armstrong's instrumental training began at a conservatory called the Colored Waif's Home for Boys, a local reform school where Armstrong was sent for shooting a handgun into the air in celebration of New Year's Eve. There, where Armstrong received his only formal education, he was taught the basics of the drums, the bugle, and the cornet. Upon his graduation, New Orleans cornetist Bunk Johnson took Armstrong under his wing, eventually letting him sit in when he missed gigs.

At age eighteen, Armstrong married Daisy Parker, a prostitute who, to his surprise, preferred to continue her career after their marriage. It was brief.

A natural player with a strong, clear intonation and a seemingly boundless musical imagination, Armstrong rose quickly up the ranks of the New Orleans ballrooms and dance halls, where what we now know as jazz was undergoing spontaneous generation. Within a few years he was playing occasionally with King Oliver, leader of one of the top New Orleans dance bands of the time. It was Oliver who in the early 1920s brought Armstrong to Chicago, which became the new center of jazz after New Orleans' economy declined.

Chicago was the home of Louis Armstrong's creative coming of age. Under the guidance of a strong new mentor—his second wife, pianist Lillian Hardin—Armstrong was soon being billed as "The World's Greatest Jazz Cornetist" (later changed to "The World's Greatest

Trumpeter," when he switched instruments). The bandleader, Lillian Hardin, wrote the billing—and encouraged Armstrong to return to his first love, singing, for a few numbers each night. Within months, Hardin had helped Armstrong put together the Hot Five (later the Hot Seven), which made music history in Chicago with a series of recordings that set the standards for generations of jazz performers. (Though Hardin and Armstrong divorced in 1932, they remained friends and respectful colleagues. In 1971, exactly one month after Armstrong's death, she died onstage while performing a concert in his memory.)

As drummer Gene Krupa once noted, "No band musician, jazz, sweet, or bebop, can get through thirty-two bars without musically admitting his debt to Armstrong. Louis did it all, and he did it first."

Despite his reputation among early jazz enthusiasts and musicians, Armstrong didn't break through to the general public until his 1929 hit vocal of Fats Waller's "Ain't Misbehavin'," which Armstrong sang in an all-black Broadway revue. A follow-up vocal in the same style, "You Rascal, You," took off in both the United States and Europe and began to establish Louis Armstrong as an internationally popular musician and singer.

His voice was nothing like mainstream listeners had ever heard. It challenged—and changed—popular conceptions of "good" singing. All grit and gravel, brittle and weathered, unabashedly African-American, it was a voice of deep character, a voice you could see on the radio. Armstrong didn't sing from the diaphragm; he sang from the dirty, smoky haunts in which his music was born. His voice was not *nice* by standards of the day; it growled and snapped like an exotic beast. He hit the notes, but not necessarily the ones you'd expected; as a singer, he was improvising like an instrumentalist. And, just as important, he was *swinging*, phrasing to emphasize the rhythm of a song as well as the melody and lyrics.

Not much of this was being done at the time, though we take it all for granted now. Armstrong, whom fellow musicians often called "Pops," thus became the musical father of every singer with an idiosyncratic timbre, from Joe Williams and Ray Charles to classic-pop/rock crossover singers such as Dr. John and Buster Poindexter. And, more subtly but just as significantly, he's the patriarch of every singer with swing, from Bing Crosby and Billie Holiday to Peggy Lee, Mel Tormé, and Tony Bennett.

Armstrong has also been credited with inventing "scat" as early as 1926, when he supposedly misplaced some lyrics during a recording session and covered with nonsense syllables. (The term "scat," a short form of scatology, refers to "singing shit.") More accurately, Armstrong was one of the first jazz artists to *record* nonliteral vocal improvisation, which has antecedents in many strains of folk music, American, African, and European.

The Armstrong style delighted record and radio listeners—and particularly live audiences—in the late 1920s and early 1930s. He had so much genuine love for his music that he seemed on the verge of physically exploding onstage, popping those big, happy eyes and grinning the eighty-eight-key grin that earned him the nicknames "Dippermouth" and then "Satchelmouth." (The latter was mistakenly written as "Satchmo" by a British journalist in 1932, and the mistake somehow stuck.)

Armstrong reveled in his audience's pleasure, which he always proclaimed to be his foremost concern. He was surely an artist, but he saw himself as a professional. "I never tried to prove nothing. I just always wanted to give a good show," he explained in the late 1960s. "The music ain't worth nothin' if you can't lay it on the public. The main thing is to live for that audience, 'cause what you're there for is to please the people."

A guaranteed crowd-pleaser, Armstrong was called upon for appearances in more than a dozen movies, beginning with a piece of fluff called *Ex-Flame* in 1931. He generally portrayed an ebullient singing trumpet player and was convincing at it in such pictures as *Artists and Models* (1937), *Atlantic City* (1944), *New Orleans* (1947), *High Society* (1956), and *Hello, Dolly!* (1969). Armstrong was granted a few dramatic roles, too, most notably in *Cabin in the Sky* (1943) and an original television drama, *The Lord Don't Play Favorites* (1956), in which he starred to critical acclaim.

In the late 1940s, Armstrong's style of jazz playing came under fire from the new generation of bebop musicians such as Charlie Parker and Dizzy Gillespie, who criticized his "hot" New Orleans playing as archaic. In turn, Armstrong blasted bop, calling it "jujitsu music. It's not jazz—all them variations—it's more an exercise."

Through the 1950s and 1960s, Armstrong's last two decades of performing and recording, his playing drew increasingly on such rarefied skills as suggestion and nuance rather than sheer energy and speed. At the same time, his singing matured markedly; in middle age he was imbuing ballads such as "Little Girl Blue," "Blues in the Night," and "I Only Have Eyes for You" with an easygoing maturity, and he was handling uptempo numbers such as "Ac-cent-tchu-ate the Positive" and "Let's Do It" with a sly, wise wit.

His tastes were diverse, and so was his output in his final years. "There's room for all kinds of music," he said. "Country, jazz, pop, swing, blues, ragtime, rock 'n' roll—I dig it all." And he recorded it all, including a country-and-western vocal album and several rock songs, including John Lennon's antiwar anthem "Give Peace a Chance" (recorded for his "seventieth birthday" album in what was actually his sixty-ninth year).

Late in his life, Armstrong settled into a relatively quiet, simple life with his third wife, Lucille, in a middle-class neighborhood in Queens, New York. The kids on his block called him "Pops," and he kept candy in his pockets to give them. Now and then Armstrong would still perform on TV and in night spots such as New York's Waldorf-Astoria Hotel, where he had just wrapped up a week's run when he succumbed to a longtime kidney ailment. Louis Armstrong died in his home on July 6, 1971. The papers said he was seventy-one, although, as we now know, he is immortal.

HELEN MORGAN

*Her notoriety offered a startling contrast to
her sweet, clear voice and her soft, delicate beauty.*
—former *Metronome* editor GEORGE T. SIMON

No singer epitomized the Roaring Twenties quite the way Helen Morgan did. Or at least the prevailing image of vulnerable women lost in hopeless, unrequited love for charming but uncaring men who treated them shabbily as they ate, drank, and made merry. Seated atop the piano of a speakeasy, simply but elegantly gowned and looking forlorn, she'd pour out her heart in songs such as "The Man I Love" or "Can't Help Lovin' Dat Man." Drama critic John Mason Brown called her "the Duse of the lovelorn."

She was *the* torch singer of the era. Yet her sound never matched what later became the clichéd image of torch singers as deep-voiced thrushes who could belt out the notes of a musical lament as lustily as they could belt down bootleg gin. Nor did her sound match the robust, intense image given in the highly fictionalized (and considerably inaccurate) 1957 movie *The Helen Morgan Story*, in which rich-voiced Gogi Grant dubbed the songs for Ann Blyth to mouth as Morgan on the screen—for the real Helen Morgan had a delicate, wistful, somewhat fragile light-soprano voice. Classically trained, she phrased her lyrics elegantly and temperately, subtly underplaying the bitterness and misery the songs themselves implied. But the quiver in her lips and her nervous twisting of the handkerchief she always clutched made it clear her heart was aching. She made few recordings—less than three dozen commercially released songs over her lifetime.

Morgan credited her "discovery," at age twelve, to a *Chicago Daily News* reporter who heard her singing in the railroad yards where her father had worked in her hometown of Danville, Illinois. (Her birthdate was August 2, 1900.) The reporter convinced Morgan's mother that her daughter had genuine musical talent and that she had the connections to help get her started. A few months later, Helen had a tryout engagement in Montreal at the French Trocadero. She sang French-Canadian folk songs to the audience for several weeks, until the Gerry Society, a group battling child exploitation in show business, intervened. The Morgans returned to Chicago, where Helen enrolled in high school for a brief term and her mother found a series of menial jobs. But Morgan now knew she wanted to be a singer, and she sought out jobs in honky-tonks around Chicago. She also entered several beauty pageants—and won prizes in two of them. One of the prizes was a trip to New York to study voice with Eduardo Petri of the Metropolitian Opera School.

Morgan's studies with Petri convinced her that her small voice was not destined for greatness in opera houses. But her elegant figure landed her a job in the chorus of the 1920 Ziegfeld musical *Sally* (starring Marilyn Miller), where she caught the eye of the show's composer, Jerome Kern. Over the next few years she worked in several other Broadway musicals, but mainly she got singing jobs in New York and Chicago speakeasies, where she became a favorite of some of the underworld characters who controlled New York's nightlife in that Prohibition era. In 1924, when Billy Rose opened his first night-club, the Backstage Club, he hired Morgan as its headliner. The club, in a second-story loft above a garage on West Fifty-sixth Street, got so crowded night after night that Morgan started repeating a stunt she had first used as a child performer in Montreal—sitting on top of the grand piano so she could be better seen and heard. It became her trademark, and she even employed it for her songs in *George White's Scandals of 1925* and the 1926 Broadway revue *Americana*.

By now Morgan was specializing in lachrymose ballads about forsaken love—setting what was becoming a much copied pattern for the alcohol-tinged warbling of "The One I Love Belongs to Somebody Else" and similar tear-jerkers. Still in her midtwenties, she came to symbolize the other side of the coin from the always chipper, fun-loving 1920s flapper—the quietly chic but nervously despairing woman carrying a torch for some two-timing man. Jerome Kern, attending a performance of *Americana*, was struck by how she had changed from her *Sally* days—how her sad eyes and the soft trembling of her voice revealed not just a loss of innocence but also the real hurt and disillusionment behind the signs of outward dissipation. He knew he had found his Julie for *Show Boat*.

When it opened in 1927, the Ziegfeld-produced *Show Boat* (adapted by Oscar Hammerstein II from Edna Ferber's best-selling novel about a turn-of-the-century Mississippi show-boat family) became the most critically acclaimed musical play up to its time, establishing new standards for the blending of popular music with a serious book. And the role of Julie (a light-skinned mulatto passing for white as part of the show-boat troupe) is a pivotal one in *Show Boat*—the kind of nobly sentimental role that leaves few dry eyes in the theater. Kern gave Morgan two showstopping songs as Julie: "Can't Help Lovin' Dat Man" and "Bill." And the rest, as the saying goes, is history.

Morgan played in *Show Boat* on Broadway from 1927 to 1929, but also continued her nightclub performances most evenings after the show. By now she was such a big star that the club in which she then appeared on West Fifty-fourth Street was renamed in her honor, and she became its part owner. It turned out to be a mixed blessing. Her income was soaring, although her extravagant spending habits and her generosity to others left her with little. Moreover, every time her club got raided for violations of the Prohibition laws, it was Morgan who got arrested and *her* name that made the papers—not the underworld partners for whom she was fronting. Morgan's musical stardom seemed constantly threatened by controversy about her offstage life and gossip about her "unsavory" associates. Yet she continued to front a series of clubs named after her, even after federal agents virtually demolished several of them in their raids. The pressures and strains fed her growing dependence on brandy.

These were the years when sound was revolutionizing the movies. Broadway theater performers were suddenly in demand for talking pictures, especially those being made at Paramount's New York studios in Astoria. In 1929, Morgan filmed two of her *Show Boat* songs for a sound prologue that preceded showings of the mostly silent first film version of *Show Boat* (with Laura LaPlante and Joseph Schildkraut, and minus most of the Kern-Hammerstein score).

The same year, Paramount assigned Morgan to the lead in a talkie that young director Rouben Mamoulian was about to film in Astoria: *Applause*. It tells the story of an over-the-hill, gin-swilling burlesque queen who sacrifices her life to save her convent-raised daughter from the clutches of her no-good stepfather. The part seems almost an extension of *Show Boat*'s Julie, and Morgan brought it off to critical raves. But audiences didn't take as well to the grim, downbeat story and its squalid view of show business, and the movie was a box-office flop. Viewed today, Mamoulian's direction of *Applause* is remarkable for its taut expressionism and the fluidity of the camera movements (in relation to other pictures of 1929). But most memorable of all is Morgan's performance—one of the best in any movie of the period. Though only twenty-nine, she brings it to a touching pathos and bittersweet maturity that few more experienced dramatic actresses could have done so well. She also sings several in-character torchers, including "What Wouldn't I Do for That Man" and "I've Got a Feelin' I'm Fallin'." Morgan also filmed a cameo in 1929 in the first movie to personally involve Broadway's Florenz Ziegfeld, *Glorifying the American Girl*. Seated atop a white piano, she again sang "What Wouldn't I Do for That Man," but in a far more glamorous setting than she had in *Applause*.

In the fall of 1929, Morgan also opened in her biggest Broadway starring role—in a Kern-Hammerstein Broadway musical written especially for her, *Sweet Adeline*. Set in the Gay Nineties, it presented Morgan in a more glamorously romantic vein, although the plot gave her the chance to introduce two more tailor-made torch songs: "Why Was I Born?" and "Don't Ever Leave Me." Both songs have long since become standards, though they are usually bludgeoned by overwrought interpretations. That was not the way Morgan originally did them (as her recordings attest); she never forgot that Jerome Kern's songs required elegance above all else. *Sweet Adeline* got good reviews, as did Morgan in it. But a few weeks after the opening, the stock market crashed. Theater attendance fell off drastically, and *Sweet Adeline* ended up losing money over its seven-month run.

A year later, she went into the *Ziegfeld Follies of 1931* on Broadway. Although top-billed, she had to share its musical spotlight with another torch singer, Ruth Etting, with promising newcomer Dorothy Dell also in the cast. (Harry Richman and Jack "Baron Munchausen" Pearl were the other top-billed headliners.) There were some who believed that Ziegfeld hired Etting for the same show partly to keep Morgan's drinking habits in line and as a ready fill-in in case she couldn't go on some nights. But Morgan, as usual, proved herself a pro and made it through the show's run. The problem was the Depression, which kept attendance low. The '31 *Follies* closed after the shortest run of any *Ziegfeld Follies* produced over the previous decade. The nightclub business wasn't faring any better. Reportedly Morgan passed up some weeks' paychecks at clubs in which she appeared when she knew a club wasn't breaking even.

Morgan's career drifted quietly downhill. She went to Hollywood in 1934 for minor roles at Paramount and Fox in several long-forgotten and rarely revived movie melodramas: in *You Belong to Me* (with Lee Tracy and Helen Mack) she played a seedy beer-hall diva; in *Marie Galante* (with Spencer Tracy and Ketti Gallian) she was a Canal Zone café singer. Finally, a promising lead came along in the independently produced *Frankie and Johnny*, based loosely on the old folk legend, with Chester Morris as the man "who done her wrong." But the movie was plagued by problems. Lilyan Tashman (playing Nelly Bly) died before shooting was complete. Then there were censorship problems in that year of a nationwide morality crackdown. Release was held up for two years, until a severely cut version ended up playing on the bottom half of double-feature programs. Most reviewers dismissed the movie. The *New York Times* reviewer also dismissed Morgan's performance as "definitely maidenly."

Morgan was then signed for a Broadway-bound play, *Memory*, trying out in Hollywood. She got good notices but not the play. The producers closed the show after a week's run, claiming Morgan was drunk during two performances. An Actors' Equity hearing cleared her of the charges, but the bad publicty didn't help her win other roles. Things looked bleak until Warner Bros. offered her a seven-year contract, but with annual renewal options. In short order she played cameos in two 1935 Warner musicals: *Sweet Music* (with Rudy Vallee in a role originally intended for Russ Columbo) and *Go into Your Dance* (with Al Jolson and Ruby Keeler). Morgan was scheduled for *Gold Diggers of 1935*, in whose big Busby Berkeley finale she would introduce "The Lullaby of Broadway." But suddenly she was dropped and her contract canceled by mutual consent. At about the same time she divorced a Cleveland attorney, Maurice Maschka, Jr., whom she had married two years earlier. "Bud's a nice boy," she told reporters, "but it was all a mistake." She returned to nightclub engagements.

But then came the crowning achievement of Morgan's career, the one for which she will be remembered the longest: her definitive re-creation of the role of Julie in the 1936 film version of *Show Boat*. Her voice had darkened somewhat in the intervening years, but it still had an elegance and sweetness that make "Bill" and "Can't Help Lovin' Dat Man" two of the most unforgettable moments in a movie filled with unforgettable moments. (Incidentally, in the latter song Morgan always insisted on singing "that man" even though Hammerstein's lyrics say "dat man.") And her warmly poignant acting performance comes close to stealing the picture, even though she is in only about twenty minutes of the nearly two-hour movie.

Despite the wonderful notices she received in the '36 film version of *Show Boat*, Morgan never made another movie, and her radio engagements became fewer and fewer. She sailed for Europe in 1937 to appear in London and Dublin, saying, "I might stay there—they don't appreciate me here anymore." But she returned a year later for nightclub engagements in Hollywood, Montreal, and New York. Then, in the fall of 1939, she hit her professional bottom—joining a cast of mostly burlesque performers in a cheap touring revue, *A Night at the Moulin Rouge*. It died a few weeks after its Chicago opening to disastrous reviews and poor attendance.

Just as torch songs themselves had gone into decline, so Morgan's vulnerable, tremulous acting and singing style seemed increasingly dated as the country came out of the Depression—as a more rosy-cheeked, affirmative style settled into mainstream popular entertainment. Morgan's type of woman gone wrong seemed no longer sad but just dumb. Furthermore, her controversial offstage history and her increasingly well-known reliance on brandy made her seem a poor job risk. She continued to live in Los Angeles, hoping for a break but spending much of her time in and out of hospitals for liver and kidney ailments—with her stays mostly paid for by various actors' aid funds.

In 1940 Morgan married an L.A. automobile dealer, Lloyd Johnson, and seemed happy for the first time in many years. But just a few months later, while preparing for a Chicago engagement, she entered a hospital in Chicago and died within the week. She was forty-one and broke.

RUDY VALLEE

They tell me I'm another Rudy Vallee.
I guess that's good.
—*ELVIS PRESLEY*

It wasn't exactly a compliment at the time, but Rudy Vallee was the first major singing star to be called a "crooner." The term meant "not a singer," basically, as in one who merely croons or murmurs a song— softly, with casual inflection. A "singer," by those quaint standards, was one who produced round and vigorous tones, as the music teachers had always taught. Vallee wasn't really alone, however. While he was coming up in the Northeastern nightclub circuit, other performers had also begun to sing more conversationally, thanks to the emergence of the microphone. But it was Rudy Vallee who was the first to be widely associated with the term "crooner," and that's because the word was such an insult at the time.

Most of the critics hated him—and all the things he stood for, which included youth, irreverence, and sex. "[His] manner is that of the most cavalier stripling . . . [whose] vocal 'crooning' displays an im- putable lack of musical aptitude," chided a critic for the *New York Telegraph*. The headline of the ads for his first starring movie, *The Vagabond Lover*, said it simply: "Men hate him," and only a few dozen were music critics.

Vallee himself always admitted his shortcomings, confessing, "I've never had much of a voice." What he had, instead, were decent pitch, an Ivy League accent at a time when the collegiate style was big, and a weak, thin, nasal baritone voice. What makes his career historic is the fact that he became a singing sensation with such quirky and limited equipment. Vallee's shortcomings became his virtues, because he made them work. Defying convention, he sang the way he talked— at conversational volume, with natural inflection. And by becoming famous for it, he helped clear the way for the great singers of classic pop to come.

Rudy Vallee "cheated," of course. To amplify his voice onstage, he sang through a megaphone, which became his lifelong trademark. While other singers had tried the same gimmick before Vallee, they had adopted it for "collegiate" effect, to look like cheerleaders or rowing-team coxswains. Vallee really needed that megaphone, just to be heard above the sound of his band. He was cheating honestly.

Despite his detractors, Rudy Vallee was one of the major singing successes of the late 1920s and early 1930s. More significantly, in historical terms his success was largely extramusical, spurred almost solely by the force of infatuated girls. Vallee was a teen heartthrob, perhaps the original—the first Fabian. Lean and blue-eyed, with boy-ish good looks, fresh from the college football team (Yale, 1927), Vallee drove the girls to shriek and "swoon" at sight.

His pedigree was perfect for the Ivy League craze in the popular arts when Vallee hit the scene. Born in remote Vermont and raised in small-town Maine, Hubert Prior Vallee was as Yankee as a bean. Though his family wasn't social-registry material, they were solvent enough to put Vallee through college at a time when higher education was largely a privilege of the well-to-do. He started at the University of Maine, planning to enter his father's pharmaceutical business, and graduated from Yale with a Bachelor of Philosophy degree. Along the way, however, Hubert took up music and took on a new name, borrowed from Rudy Wiedoeft, a saxophone player Vallee liked.

Before graduation, Vallee had become adept enough at the clarinet and the saxophone to form his own band, the Yale Collegians. (He could also play a little drums and piano.) It was a somewhat novel group in construction, comprised of no brass, two strings, two saxes, and a four-player rhythm section, with Vallee at the megaphone, crooning and doing a little comedy.

As Vallee said, "The sound we had was pleasant, soothing, un-usual." Moreover, under Vallee's direction the group developed an equally unusual repertoire. Instead of merely reproducing hits of the day, like many beginning bands, Vallee sought out unknown songs from foreign countries and introduced them—singing them in French, Spanish, or Italian. In addition, Vallee had the group use a subtle ploy to try to give its shows unity and momentum. Over the course of each set, every song was played in a progressively higher key.

In a rapid-fire sequence of extraordinary strokes of fortune, Vallee and the Collegians rose from nonexistence to notoriety in less than a year. They were signed for an extended run at New York's Heigh-Ho Club in 1928 without knowing that, almost immediately and entirely coincidentally, WABC Radio would choose the Heigh-Ho Club as a location for music broadcasts. The group was a hit, and that was no coincidence. Rudy Vallee and radio were invented for each other.

Singers far more successful and seasoned than Vallee—including Jolson, the giant of the era—couldn't always adjust to it, or didn't understand it. Onstage they were playing to hundreds of listeners, and on radio, to thousands—but to *one family in one living room at a time*. Intimate and personal, radio required an entirely new type of singing. Of course, Vallee was one singer who didn't have to adjust to radio. Even if he wanted to, he couldn't sing any louder than he talked, at least not without his megaphone.

Chirping "Heigh-ho, everybody!" and singing in four languages with his band (now called the Connecticut Yankees), Vallee became so popular on radio that he was given his own national show, *The Fleischmann Hour*. In radio history the program is credited as the first network variety show ever produced, although Vallee didn't personally develop the format. For his part, he served as an amiable and affable host, beginning to show more and more of the natural flair for comedy that would later play an important part in carrying him through a long career in show business. Musically, Vallee continued to showcase little-known songs, including "As Time Goes By," which Vallee was the first to record (a full decade before the song's use in *Casablanca*), and another chestnut by the same composer, Herman Hupfeld, titled "When Yuba Plays the Rhumba on the Tuba."

And he still had the women swooning, even though they couldn't see his face on radio. In fact, *The New York Times* reported an interesting example of how strongly Vallee could affect a female. A Midwestern man, frustrated by his wife's fondness for the singer, interrupted Vallee's radio show and asked, "Why don't you get something worth listening to?" So she shot and killed him.

Behind those blue Vallee eyes, however, there always was a sharp mind. The singer wrote several of his own songs, including his original theme song, "The Vagabond Lover," in addition to negotiating writing credit on dozens of other songs to earn a share of the profits of material he popularized. Unlike other pop singers, including Elvis Presley in later years, Vallee never denied having had his name added to the credits to share in the publishing profits. "I'll admit it—and why not? A singer is entitled to a piece of the action," he wrote in one of his three books, *My Time Is Your Time* (named for another one of his theme songs).

This bold bottom-line attitude carried over to Vallee's personal life as well, where he developed a reputation as a tightwad. According to show-business gossip, which he loved to spread, Vallee wore the same suits for twenty years, never spent more than five cents on a cigar, ate in Automats and fast-food joints whenever possible, and never tipped as much as he spent on a cigar. Instead, he'd hand waiters and bellmen ballpoint pens he had produced with the printed inscription "Gratefully, Rudy Vallee."

By 1931, only three years after his arrival at the Heigh-Ho Club, Vallee was warned by one of his friends, "There'll be no more Rudy Vallee. Bing Crosby has come along, and he sings like a man." The truth was that Vallee's boyish, collegiate charm was wearing increasingly thin as he aged and the Ivy League craze fell out of crazedom. Although he remained active as a radio singer through the 1930s, his time as an important force in pop music passed quickly. Crosby and his contemporaries took the conversational idiom Vallee pioneered and added levels of intensity, energy, and rhythmic complexity that extended outside of Vallee's interests and abilities.

As an actor, however, Vallee moved on to a second career in movies and, to a lesser extent, on the stage. After a string of incidental (and mostly flop) films beginning with *The Vagabond Lover*, released in 1929 to capitalize on his early fame, Vallee developed a comedic screen personality that carried him through more than a dozen outstanding movies, including *The Palm Beach Story* (1942), *The Bachelor and the Bobby-Soxer* (1947), and *Unfaithfully Yours* (1948). By the 1960s, after a comeback on Broadway in 1962 with a costarring role in *How to Succeed in Business Without Really Trying* at age sixty-one, Vallee became a nostalgic comedic fixture on TV, appearing on such shows as *Batman, Here's Lucy,* and *Alias Smith and Jones.*

Following surgery for throat cancer in 1986, Vallee died with the words of a college boy, "You know, I love a party."

RUTH ETTING

*She lifted many a song out of mediocrity and
freed it from the clichés of the period.*
—record producer *JOHN McANDREW*

Blond, wistfully attractive Ruth Etting became one of the most famous
singers of popular songs in the late 1920s and early 1930s as much for
nonmusical reasons as for her sweet-voiced singing talents. Even after
she had retired completely from public performances (while still in
her thirties), she was remembered best for her headline-making involvement with a Chicago underworld racketeer who went to prison
for shooting the man she wanted to leave him for.

Etting's story became the basis for the 1955 hit movie *Love Me or
Leave Me*, in which Doris Day, playing Etting, had one of her best
film roles, and in which James Cagney won an Oscar nomination for
his performance as the hood. For all the movie's factual accuracy on
many key points of the story, the real-life Etting was very different
in looks, personality, and, most important of all, the sound of her
singing voice from what Doris Day projected on the screen. That is
not to detract from the genuine power of Day's acting performance;
it's just that it bore little physical resemblance to either Etting the
woman or Etting the singer. But then, that seems to be the usual case
with Hollywood biographies of singers (as *The Helen Morgan Story*
also exemplifies).

Etting had a more limpid, higher-pitched, somewhat nasal voice.
When she sobbed one of the torch songs for which she became most
famous at the peak of her popularity—such as "Mean to Me," "Out
in the Cold Again," "Body and Soul," "More Than You Know,"
"Ten Cents a Dance," or "What About Me?"—she was a master at
convincing you that her lyrics were genuinely tear-drenched, although

she usually did it more whimperingly and considerably less subtly than Helen Morgan.

A farm girl from David City, Nebraska (her birthdate was November 23, 1898), Etting didn't start out to be a singer. She went to Chicago during World War I to study art, her first love. An assignment to design a costume for a Chicago nightclub led to her being hired for the club's chorus line (providing a welcome supplement to her modest income), and then to her replacing an indisposed singer even though she had never had any formal vocal training. She caught the attention (and more) of a small-time racketeer, Martin Snyder (nicknamed "The Gimp" because of a lame leg). Those were the days when Chicago's mobsters ruled much of the city, especially its clubs and speakeasies, so Snyder lost no time opening doors for Etting. She married Snyder in 1922, and he officially became her manager. She was soon singing on pioneer radio programs (on Chicago's WGN) and making recordings, most of them of novelty tunes or light ballads.

Etting had the kind of high-pitched yet smooth and unaffected voice that came across particularly well on early crystal sets. She was also one of the first to recognize that less was more when singing into a radio microphone. Her intimate, almost cooingly soft-voiced sound (so different from the open voiced vaudeville and theatrical style of the day) quickly won her the sobriquet "Chicago's Sweetheart of the Air." Etting never hesitated to admit that she copied her style at first from Marion Harris. But to distinguish herself from Harris, she began alternating the tempo within parts of a song—singing some phrases in half-time or double-time "to create and maintain interest" (as she once put it). She also "played around" with certain notes or phrases, giving them extra little tonal variations now and then.

One of her recordings so impressed Broadway impresario Florenz Ziegfeld that he signed her to sing in his *Ziegfeld Follies of 1927*, starring Eddie Cantor. She got to introduce Irving Berlin's "Shaking the Blues Away," and it became one of the hits of the show. "I was supposed to do a tap dance after I sang the song," Etting later recalled in an interview. "I worked hard on it, but I was a lousy dancer. When I was halfway through the final rehearsal, Ziegfeld said, 'Ruth, when you get through singing, just walk off the stage.' I got the message."

The message on her singing was better. The following year Etting introduced Walter Donaldson and Gus Kahn's "Love Me or Leave Me" in another Ziegfeld-Cantor Broadway hit, *Whoopee*. Then, in 1930, in Rodgers and Hart's *Simple Simon*, Etting stopped the show night after night with the plaintive "Ten Cents a Dance." By now she was typed as a torch singer, singing what former *Metronome* editor and music historian George T. Simon has so aptly called "those mournful laments of lost loves and broken hearts." Etting became a frequent guest on top radio variety shows, and then was given her own twice-weekly, fifteen-minute program, alternating in the same time spot on CBS with Bing Crosby's three-times-a-week program.

Inevitably it was a torch song with which Etting made her movie debut, in Eddie Cantor's *Roman Scandals* (1933), sobbing Warren and Dubin's "No More Love" in the movie's famous Busby Berkeley–directed slave-market sequence (with dozens of chained chorines clothed only in long blond tresses). Since Etting was not "Hollywood pretty" in the prevailing leading-lady style of the 1930s studios, other roles were slow to follow. Another problem was that her relationship with the controversial Snyder did not open as many doors in Hollywood as it had in Chicago or New York. Still, Snyder successfully negotiated a contract for her to appear in a series of one- and two-reel musical shorts for RKO and Vitaphone. She ended up making more than thirty such featurettes between 1933 and 1936, and occasionally played singing cameos in features such as *Gift of Gab* and *Hips, Hips, Hooray*. She also continued to broadcast and to make recordings regularly.

But her personal life was coming apart. In 1936 Etting filed for a divorce from Snyder. He blamed her budding romance with pianist Myrl Alderman, whom he shot in Etting's presence. The newspapers, of course, had a field day. Alderman survived his wounds after a long hospitalization, and while Snyder's trial for attempted murder was still in process, he and Etting were married. Snyder was convicted and given a twenty-year prison term, but he won parole after serving little more than a year.

The notoriety of the whole affair led Etting to retire from show business altogether. As she told interviewers at the time, she had managed to save quite a bit from her lucrative radio earnings. "My family was German and my grandfather taught me thrift," she noted. "Even when I was making twenty-five dollars a week and working twelve hours a day, I put something away every payday, even if it was only fifty cents." Friends recalled that even in the 1920s, unlike some of her Broadway colleagues, Etting had invested wisely in California real estate instead of the stock market.

In 1947, Etting attempted a brief comeback with a local radio series for New York station WHN. She and Myrl Alderman combined songs with the type of husband-and-wife chatter popularized in those days by Ed and Pegeen Fitzgerald and Dorothy Kilgallen and Dick Kollmar. When the show failed to catch on, the Aldermans retired to a small ranch in Colorado Springs—and Etting stayed permanently retired from show biz.

Even all the publicity in 1955 surrounding MGM's biopic *Love Me or Leave Me* couldn't get her back into the limelight, except for a few newspaper and magazine interviews. The movie was daring for its time in its use of real names in dramatizing the Etting-Snyder relationship (unlike the whitewashing of Fanny Brice's with convicted gambler Nicky Arnstein for Alice Faye's earlier *Rose of Washington Square*). It also made hits again of some of the songs Etting had first popularized, although in Day's creamier, stronger-voiced versions of them. Of course, Etting's kind of unsubtle, relatively high-pitched vocalism had sharply declined as a pop-music standard during the intervening years (thanks, in part, to improvements in the fidelity and range of both microphones and radio receivers), so that somewhat lower pitches and timbres, especially in female singers, were now "in")— and Day's voice was certainly in keeping with that significant change.

Still, the continued existence of Etting's original recordings and movies enable new listeners to discover the genuine, authentic article for themselves. As Jim Bedoian writes in the liner notes for an Etting memorial LP he produced soon after her death in 1978 at age seventy-nine, "It was as a budding record collector in 1950 that I first discovered Ruth Etting. Once I had heard a dozen or so of her original 78 [rpm] records, I was hooked on the Ruth Etting sound." There will surely continue to be many more like him.

MILDRED BAILEY

*She was a genuine artist, with a heart
as big as Yankee Stadium.*
—*BING CROSBY*

As the first featured female vocalist with a major national dance orchestra, Mildred Bailey not only won herself an important place in
the annals of classic pop but also paved the way for virtually all of
the girl singers who became an essential part of the dance bands that
dominated pop music in the 1930s and 1940s. It was Paul Whiteman,
then the most popular and influential bandleader in the country, who
hired Bailey as a vocalist with his band in 1929. Her brother Al Rinker
had joined the Whiteman band three years earlier and became one
of the original Rhythm Boys vocal trio (together with Bing Crosby
and Harry Barris). Whiteman believed that a soft-voiced, ungimmicky
female vocalist would add appeal to his nationwide radio broadcasts—
and he was right. Soon other dance bands, in the copycat fashion that
has long been part of show business, were copying Whiteman on this
one, too. And just as significantly, the pattern that Whiteman and
Bailey set—an instrumental introduction and chorus, then a single
chorus by the singer, and an instrumental wrap-up—became the standard for most of the big bands.

Bailey married xylophonist Red Norvo near the end of her four-
year stay with the Whiteman band. Then, as Whiteman moved farther
away from the jazz-textured pop style he had pioneered in the 1920s,
she and Norvo left to form their own band—the first to be co-led by
a woman. Billed as "Mr. and Mrs. Swing," they toured the country
with their band, had their own CBS Radio Network show for several
years, and recorded frequently for major labels. Then, after she divorced Norvo in 1939, Bailey continued on her own until she gave it
all up in the late 1940s, convinced she was never going to be the big

star she wanted to be—or that her warm, clean, attractive sound and innate musicality would seem to have preordained she would be.

Mildred's voice was a high-pitched, sweet-sounding, rather small one—which stood in surprising contrast to her ample physical girth. Listeners seeing her for the first time were always struck by the seeming contradiction of such a wee voice coming from such a plump body. But it was an immediately appealing, warmly communicative, and remarkably flexible voice. Her instinctive sense of jazz phrasing rivaled that of Billie Holiday and created uncertainty among many listeners at first as to whether Bailey was black or white (she was the latter, although she always boasted of one of her grandparents' being part North American Indian—from the Coeur d'Alene tribe of Canada and the Washington-Idaho region.).

Record producer and jazz expert John Hammond once called Bailey "one of the three or four greatest singers in jazz." But Bailey preferred to sing ballads—usually the commercial, Tin Pan Alley–type of romantic ballads. And she was selective about the songs from Broadway shows and the movies she chose to sing, preferring those of Harold Arlen, Jimmy Van Heusen, Ralph Rainger, Hoagy Carmichael, Willard Robison, and Johnny Mercer—and the more romantic the better. She once told interviewer Margaret Winter for *Bandleader* magazine that people "like love ballads because they hit home. Love's a lovely thing that happens to most everybody once in a lifetime, and everybody likes to dream it all over again."

Except for the first years of her marriage to Norvo, Bailey herself not only was unhappy in love for much of her life, but also never realized her dream of superstardom. She lived to see singers she had clearly influenced—such as Peggy Lee and Ella Fitzgerald—achieve greater popular renown and bigger-selling record hits than she did. Bailey blamed some of this on being overweight, which she claimed was glandular in nature but which some who knew her well insisted was the result of just too great a love for eating. "She knew every good restaurant, no matter how out of the way," according to longtime friend and magazine journalist Bucklin Moon, "and she favored those where the servings were most ample. She could and did eat most men under the table."

Some others believe that Bailey's limited commercial success was more likely the result of other personality quirks. She knew she was good and was impatient with anyone she felt was not. As professional and congenial as she may have been on a bandstand or in front of a microphone, she could be difficult to work with backstage. Not only did she have a volatile temper (her tantrums were legendary among her colleagues), but her sweet-toned voice was also fluent in uttering salty profanities that few women of the era ever admitted knowing, let alone using. As former *Metronome* editor George T. Simon has written: "She seemed incapable of controlling her emotions, which alternated between towering rages (she felt special bitterness toward less musical but more successful, and especially better-looking, girl singers) and tender displays of deep affection that she showered on close friends, constant companions, and her two dachshunds."

A native of Tekoa, Washington, where she was born on February 27, 1907, Mildred Rinker (her real name) first worked as a song demonstrator in a Spokane music store, moonlighting with occasional gigs in a Spokane night spot, Charlie Dale's Cabaret. Her brother Alton, then in high school, had a six-piece band in which fellow student Bing Crosby was the drummer and a vocalist. As Bing has written, "Mildred used to get some great records from the East . . . and our band would copy them. Believe me, with such a library in those days in Spokane, we were pretty *avant*. All of this was in 1925."

Mildred left to tour with a West Coast revue and after arriving in California got a job with a radio station and another in a plush Bakersfield speakeasy known as the Swede's. Brother Al and Bing followed her to California soon thereafter. She put them up at her place and helped them get vaudeville bookings. Again the words are Bing's: "She was *mucha mujer*. She had a way of talking that was unique. Even then I can recall her describing a town that was nowhere as 'tiredsville,' or a singer who was a little zingy as 'twenty dash eight dash four.' "

After Crosby and Rinker joined Paul Whiteman's orchestra, they returned Mildred's help to them, first by leading her to jobs in Los Angeles, and then "setting things up" for Whiteman to hire her as the band's first featured female singer. Mildred joined the Whiteman band at $75 a week. A year later, after the increasingly popular Crosby had left to pursue a movie career, she demanded $1,250 a week—and Whiteman gave it to her. According to Whiteman violinist Matty Malneck, she deserved it. Although the beginning years of the Great Depression had cut bookings drastically for most orchestras, Mildred's singing on the Whiteman band's broadcasts brought so much mail that Whiteman was able to use the publicity to keep his band on top despite the loss of Crosby. One of Mildred's most requested songs during this period was Hoagy Carmichael's "Ol' Rockin' Chair"—and she was soon dubbed "The Rockin' Chair Lady," a nickname she continued to exploit when she and Norvo left Whiteman in 1934 to go on their own.

By 1938, the strain of continual traveling and one-night stands—

then the pattern for most of the swing-era bands—had worn Bailey out. Her marriage was falling apart, and she was constantly bickering with most of the musicians in the Norvo-Bailey band (just as she had in Whiteman's). She divorced Norvo, though they remained friends and continued to record together from time to time. She made New York her home base and concentrated on doing radio shows, including Benny Goodman's *Camel Caravan* series. During the 1940s she headlined shows at such New York clubs as Café Society, the Famous Door, the Onyx, and the Blue Angel, while continuing to broadcast and record regularly. There was a series of unhappy relationships with different men, until she eventually seemed to prefer being around gays, who admired her for her singing and treated her like a goddess. Bucklin Moon reports that she was also "a sucker for every new religious cult that she heard about, but she never stayed with any of them longer than it took to come by another. What was she looking for? Who knows?"

A decline in her health from a combination of diabetes, heart trouble, and hardening of the arteries forced her to retire in the late 1940s to a farm she had bought outside New York. There she lived, forgotten or neglected by most of her former friends and associates—until composer Alec Wilder got word to fellow composer Jimmy Van Heusen that she was penniless and near death in the ward of a local hospital. Wilder asked Van Heusen if he would be willing to pay to get Mildred a private room. Van Heusen said yes and then approached Bing Crosby (with whom he was working on a movie) and Frank Sinatra about splitting the tab three ways for *all* of Mildred's medical expenses, to which they agreed. Mildred recovered enough to move into a Beverly Hills apartment arranged for by singer Lee Wiley, who visited her often during this period. Then she moved back East and even made a few appearances with a band led by Ralph Burns before she died on December 12, 1951. She was forty-four and virtually penniless.

Fortunately for posterity, Mildred Bailey recorded prolifically, and transcription copies of her many broadcasts have also been preserved and transferred to disc and tape. Mildred often said she liked nothing better than singing, that it was when she felt most alive—and that radio and recordings were a way to reach more people than she could through live appearances. As she told *Bandleader* interviewer Margaret Winter, "Seems to me I've got the sort of voice that should be listened to more than looked at. People sitting at home have nothing to do but *listen*—and they do."

Yes, and they still do.

BING CROSBY

*Popular singing can quite literally be
divided into two periods: B.C. and A.C.—
Before Crosby and After Crosby.*
—singer and record producer LARRY CARR

No other popular American singer achieved such peaks of success over so many decades, nor had such wide-ranging influence in setting standards that hold with classic pop to today, as did Bing Crosby. His supremacy has been a given for so long now (despite Bing's own casual "I don't take myself seriously and you shouldn't either" attitude during his lifetime) that no one is really surprised when reminded of the following statistics: That as a recording artist, Crosby still holds the record for total sales of nonrock recordings by any individual singer. That one of those recordings, "White Christmas" (1943), has sold more copies than any other song—ever. That more songs introduced by him ended up in the Top Ten of the *Hit Parade* and other best-seller charts than those of any other single singer. That as a radio star his shows placed among the nation's Top Ten in the ratings for eighteen consecutive years. That as a movie star he long ranked among the top box-office money-makers and was the first popular singer to win an Academy Award (for *Going My Way*, 1944). There's lots more, of course—but the point is that Crosby's record is not just impressive but also monumentally unequaled.

Perhaps the most surprising thing about Bing Crosby is that he never studied music formally and could read music only in a most rudimentary way. Yet from his teen years on, he took the superb vocal equipment with which he was blessed—a light, resonant, naturally warm, mellow, and very masculine-sounding baritone—and developed an instinctive, jazz-influenced way of using it. His understated, conversational style stood out instantly as different from the then-prevalent European style of music-hall and operetta singers, with their rolled

r's and pretentious, highbrow diction. As one of Crosby's record producers, Ken Barnes, later put it, "Bing cut the silver cord to Europe,"
almost inventing by himself a whole new approach to American popular singing. Over the years Crosby's singing acquired greater polish
and he learned to shade and color his voice in more sophisticated
ways, but he never lost the intuitively easygoing, jauntily unaffected
style he pioneered from the beginning.

"I'm not a singer, I'm a phraser," Bing declared in his 1953 autobiography, *Call Me Lucky*. "I don't think of a song in term of notes.
I try to think of what it purports lyrically. That way it sounds more
natural, and anything more natural is more listenable." As for his
phrasing, that, he freely admitted, had come not from conscious study
but from a kind of osmosis through listening to recordings by black
musicians such as Louis Armstrong and working with some of the top
jazz players in both Los Angeles and New York in the late 1920s. "I
used to hang around the Dorseys and Bix [Beiderbecke] and Bunny
Berigan and Glenn Miller and Joe Venuti and Eddie Lang—all of the
musicians I admired—and I was having a helluva time," he said. "I
really had no idea I was actually *learning* anything. But I was!" And
those things would enable him, without his consciously realizing it at
the time, to set new standards for pop singing that influenced almost
every singer who came along after him.

From the beginning, however, Crosby was never a man to push
himself. A lazy student in his school days, he was renowned even after
he became an international star for hating to rehearse (and for doing
as minimal an amount of it as he could get away with). He also hated
to dress up and felt comfortable only in casual clothes. Part of that,
however, derived from the fact that he was color-blind—something
he felt he could disguise more easily with the mixed colors of sports
clothes. Perhaps the most casual thing about him was his nickname,
Bing. He was christened Harry Lillis Crosby, Jr., but after schoolmates
started calling him "Bingo from Bingsville" (because his jutting ears
reminded them of a character in a comic strip called *The Bingsville
Bugle*), he was Bing from age nine on—even to his family (except his
mother).

His perpetually casual attitude and demeanor, ironically enough,
belied the fact that Bing grew up as one of seven children in a strict,
Victorian family environment—first in Tacoma, Washington, where
he was born on May 3, 1903 (not 1904, as Bing sometimes claimed),
and then in Spokane. He attended both a rigidly Jesuit-run high school
and college (Gonzaga, in Spokane). His father, a county bookkeeper,

was descended from one of the Puritan signers of the Mayflower Compact, Edmund Brewster, but Bing often contended that what should have been his parents' traditional characteristics had gotten "twisted around"—that it was his Irish Catholic mother who was the strict disciplinarian and thriftmeister, while his father was much more easygoing. Both parents, however, loved music. Bing's father sang in amateur Gilbert and Sullivan productions, and Sunday night was "family musicale time" around the Crosby household's piano, with Mrs. Crosby's light soprano usually in the limelight, singing Irish folk songs and ballads.

Bing's musical tastes quickly moved beyond the limits of those family musicales. "When I was a kid," he later recalled to former *Metronome* editor George T. Simon, "I used to haunt Bailey's music store in Spokane. I'd spend half a day there listening to records—to Al Jolson and John McCormack and Gene Austin and, of course, all the good jazz groups. I was strictly a follower of the Memphis Five and the Mound City Blue Blowers. My ambition was to be around those guys. I never wanted anything more than that." Bing was soon dividing his nonclassroom hours between the sports at which he excelled (swimming and baseball) and singing and playing drums in a small band called the Musicaladers, which played at school dances and social functions. Bing and the band's pianist and manager, Alton Rinker (brother of singer Mildred Bailey), dropped out of college in 1925 to try to make it as a singing duo in West Coast vaudeville theaters. They drove down to California in Rinker's Model T and moved in temporarily with Rinker's sister. As Bing later wrote, "Mildred took in these two strolling players . . . [and] introduced us to a very big theatrical agent, and we were on our way—with a lot of *her* material, I might add."

A year and a half later, Crosby and Rinker were hired by Paul Whiteman, then leader of the most popular dance orchestra in the country. A cross-country tour with the Whiteman band went fairly well until it reached the Paramount Theater in Manhattan's Times Square, then one of New York's premier palaces for movies and stage shows. The manager of the Paramount took a dislike to the jazzy way the duo sang and, when he noticed the poor audience response, insisted that Whiteman not let them do any more solos. For the rest of the two-month engagement, Rinker and Crosby were relegated to playing percussion in the band and occasionally singing to lines in the lobby waiting to get into the theater. It was at this point that Whiteman, acting on a suggestion from violinist-arranger Matty Malneck, brought in singer-pianist Harry Barris to try to "fix" the duo's act. The duo became a trio, the Rhythm Boys. Working mostly with Malneck's arrangements, the Rhythm Boys developed a lightly swinging, easygoing vocal style that, over the next year, became one of the most popular elements of Whiteman's stage shows, radio programs, and recordings. Bing always credited Barris and Malneck with the Rhythm Boys' success.

Increasingly Bing, with the most distinctive voice in the trio, was given a chance to solo within the Rhythm Boys' arrangements. He started to develop a following of his own, particularly among the youngest segment of the audience. He was even assigned a key solo spot in a major production number ("Song of the Dawn") that the Whiteman band filmed in Hollywood in 1930 as part of the lavish, all-Technicolor, all-talkie revue *King of Jazz*. But the night before the number was to be filmed, Bing—who already had a reputation within the Whiteman clan as a fun-loving boozer and womanizer—was arrested for drunken driving and sentenced to thirty days in jail. Hollywood singer-actor John Boles was hastily brought in to replace Crosby for "Song of the Dawn." But for several other numbers in *King of Jazz* featuring the Rhythm Boys, Whiteman arranged to have Crosby brought to the studio under police guard and returned to jail after each day's shooting ended.

The experience had a sobering effect on young Crosby. He began taking his career more seriously, particularly with regard to the potential of musical movies. When Whiteman left Hollywood for a national tour after completing the filming of *King of Jazz*, Bing talked the Rhythm Boys into staying in Los Angeles, where they went to work as a featured act with Gus Arnheim's orchestra at the Cocoanut Grove, a nightclub popular with the movie community. Bing also began going steady with a pretty Fox Studios starlet, Dixie Lee (real name: Wilma Wyatt), whom he had met at the Grove. They were married in September 1930—to news stories that played up the angle of "rising young Fox star weds obscure crooner" (or, as Bing once put it, "Miss Big marries Mr. Little"). Dixie, who had played the ingenue lead in half a dozen Fox movies, soon gave up her career as Bing concentrated on his. He worked on improving his breath control and started singing more romantic ballads and fewer rhythmic numbers.

Slapstick-movie pioneer Mack Sennett gave Bing a big boost after he heard him at the Cocoanut Grove and liked his easygoing style. Sennett cast him in a series of shorts built around some of the songs

Bing was performing and recording with Arnheim's orchestra, such as "I Surrender, Dear" and "Just One More Chance." Working in the studios by day and at the Cocoanut Grove by night, Bing also played bit parts as a singer in two feature films (*Reaching for the Moon* and *Confessions of a Coed*) and with the Rhythm Boys dubbed an off-screen song in Amos 'n' Andy's only feature movie, *Check and Double Check*. Meanwhile, Arnheim's nightly broadcasts from the Cocoanut Grove were winning more and more fans for vocalist Crosby and his fresh, unstudied crooning style. Bing's sense of humor and quick-witted ad-libs also carried well over the airwaves, especially when he forgot some of the lyrics and would warble "boo-boo-boo-boo" in their place. Eventually he began "boo-boo-booing" phrases deliberately as a Crosby trademark. Most significantly, Crosby, more than most of his contemporaries, instinctively understood how to use the microphone—to sing caressingly to it at an intimate, conversational level instead of projecting his voice, as in a theater.

Bing's biggest boost came when William S. Paley of CBS Radio heard him and offered him a network contract. While older brother Everett (who was beginning to act as Bing's manager and held that role for the rest of his life) worked out the deal in secret, Bing left the Rhythm Boys—after a controversial walkout (over a management fine against Crosby for missing a show) that got the trio's members temporarily blacklisted by the musicians' union and permanently embittered Rinker's and Barris's relations with Crosby. (Rinker went on to become a radio producer and Barris a pianist for other acts. Although each of them occasionally worked with Crosby in later years, they did not remain particularly friendly with him.) Bing moved to New York and in September 1931 began a nightly fifteen-minute broadcast over the CBS Radio Network. As singer-pianist, author and record producer Larry Carr once so aptly put it, "After six long years of learning and honing his craft, he was an overnight success."

Crosby's zooming nationwide radio popularity brought him back to Hollywood in 1932 to play the leading role in a movie built around radio broadcasting, *The Big Broadcast*. He scored such a hit in it that Paramount signed him to a long-term contract. He soon appeared in a succession of lighthearted musical comedies especially tailored to his laid-back, down-to-earth personality—and, of course, allowing him ample opportunities to sing. But the transition to movie star was not an easy one for him at first. Paramount insisted he wear a partial hairpiece (or "thatch") to hide his receding hairline. They also used an uncomfortable glue on his large, jutting ears to keep them closer to his head—only to have the glue keep loosening under the heat of the klieg lights so that his ears would pop out in the middle of scenes. Finally, after several hit movies that quickly made Bing the studio's biggest money-maker next to Mae West, Bing said "Enough!" to the ear glue, pointing out that jutting ears didn't seem to be hampering Clark Gable's career at MGM. But the thatch stayed.

Most of the songs that Bing introduced in his early movies became nationwide hits—including "Please," "Love Thy Neighbor," "Love in Bloom," "Once in a Blue Moon," and "June in January." He also engaged in some good-natured spoofing of his own image as a crooner—first with "Learn to Croon" in *College Humor* (1933) and then with "Boo-Boo-Boo" in *Too Much Harmony* (also 1933). A strong case can be made for the fact that Bing was at his vocal and stylistic peak in this period—roughly from 1931 to 1934—and that his recordings, radio shows, and movies of this period still represent Crosby at his original best. Not that he went downhill from there, far from it, in fact. But after 1934 his style became more predictably slick and commercial, particularly with recordings. Patterns were set to which Bing stuck for most of the next decade—successfully, of course—including a preference for singing in slightly lower keys than he had originally. At Paramount he even acquired teams of top song-writers who wrote almost exclusively for him, first James Monaco and Johnny Burke and then Jimmy Van Heusen and Burke. Among their hit songs for Bing: "Moonlight Becomes You," "A Pocketful of Dreams," "Only Forever," "Meet the Sun Halfway," "My Heart Is Taking Lessons," "Sunday, Monday, and Always," "Swingin' on a Star," "Put It There, Pal," and dozens more.

Crosby now set the standard for male singers of popular music. Not only were roof-raising tenors out and mellower baritones in, but also most baritones who came along in the mid- and late 1930s—including the country's top band singers, such as Perry Como, Harry Babbitt, Bob Eberly, and even kid brother Bob Crosby—openly modeled themselves on Bing's essentially laid-back, unaffected, intimately one-to-one style. Bing's influence even extended to some of the top singers beyond our national borders—to Canada's Dick Todd, Britain's Denny Dennis, France's Jean Sablon, Germany's Eric Helgar, and others.

Successful as his movies were, it was still with radio that Bing drew his biggest audiences. Part of his radio appeal was the genuinely spontaneous "feel" of most of the shows, an inevitable offshoot of Bing's disdain for rehearsing (he preferred spending his days on the golf course or at the races) and his habit of ad-libbing around the script. Audiences loved the latter, even if some of his early sponsors did not. In the early 1930s, Chesterfield cigarettes and Woodbury soap both dropped their sponsorship of Crosby's show because Bing wouldn't stick to the script and adamantly refused to be part of the commercials. "I'm a singer," he said. "Let somebody else do that." Bing wasn't sponsorless for long. He was signed in 1935 to share the hour-long *Kraft Music Hall* with his former boss, Paul Whiteman—with Whiteman's orchestra and guests broadcasting from New York and Crosby and his guests singing with Jimmy Dorsey's orchestra from Hollywood. A year later, a still ad-libbing Crosby took over the whole program and remained with Kraft through 1946—establishing one of network broadcasting's longest-lasting partnerships. Bing didn't hog the shows for himself, either. He loved sharing the spotlight with other singers, and among his regular guests were Connee Boswell, Louis Armstrong, Ella Fitzgerald, Judy Garland, Mary Martin, and Peggy Lee.

In the late 1930s, a rising young comedian at Paramount with his own network radio show also became a frequent guest on Crosby's show—and started *out*-ad-libbing even Crosby. He was, of course, Bob Hope. From the start, Hope and Crosby ribbed each other mercilessly and hilariously, even taking swipes at each other on their own shows when the other wasn't there as a guest. It wasn't long before Paramount teamed them in a movie, *The Road to Singapore,* and one of the zaniest and most successful movie comedy series of all time was born. Over the next twenty-three years, the *Road* series would take Hope and Crosby (and costar Dorothy Lamour) to *Zanzibar, Morocco, Rio, Utopia, Bali,* and *Hong Kong*—as well as to lesser-known places overseas and in the United States during World War II as part of army and navy camp shows.

Meanwhile, Bing kept on piling up movie hits with other singing costars—particularly Mary Martin (*Birth of the Blues, Rhythm on the River*) and Fred Astaire (*Holiday Inn, Blue Skies*). But one movie in particular, 1944's *Going My Way*, brought with it a major shift in his image and reputation. Getting Bing to play its leading role of a young priest battling an old-line pastor was the idea of a longtime friend, writer-director Leo McCarey. Although a regular Roman Catholic churchgoer, Bing was reluctant at first, feeling he hadn't the right image for the priesthood. Moreover, since reaching stardom in the early 1930s, Bing (unlike some other stars) had resolutely kept both his religion and his politics a very private part of the private life he insisted on living well away from public view. (He remained throughout his life, for example, one of the few celebrities never to be photographed with a president or presidential candidate.) But McCarey finally convinced him to play the part. *Going My Way* not only was one of Bing's all-time box-office blockbusters but also won him a Best Actor Academy Award. (The picture itself, plus costar Barry Fitzgerald and one of the songs Bing introduced in it, "Swinging on a Star," won Oscars, too.) Pope Pius XII, after a Vatican screening, wrote Crosby how much he had enjoyed the way he had humanized the priesthood through the movie. A year later Crosby again played a priest in a sequel, *The Bells of St. Mary's*, in which he costarred with another Oscar-winner, Ingrid Bergman.

All of a sudden Crosby was not just a singer who ad-libbed on radio and sang romantic songs to pretty leading ladies in movie musicals. His new status as a serious actor led Paramount to delay the release of the Hope-Crosby *Road to Rio* for two years after its completion, so as not to undercut Crosby's new image too quickly with irreverent lunacy. But Crosby's radio shows continued to do some of that anyway. So the studio alternated him in lightweight musicals and more serious roles over the next decade, culminating in another Oscar nomination for his dramatic role as an aging, alcoholic singing star in 1954's *The Country Girl*. The image of fun-loving cutup was definitely disappearing. A quieter, more aloof Bing was emerging in his public persona.

Meanwhile, changing times were undercutting Bing's king-of-the-hill position. Network radio was fading with the onslaught of television, and Bing was slow to get into TV. His records, competing with a new generation of singers (such as Vic Damone, Tony Bennett, and Andy Williams) as well as with changing musical styles, were no longer the automatic hits they used to be. Although his singing voice seemed richer and more mature than ever, Bing himself was showing his advancing age on camera. He began to cut back on some of his activities. By now he was one of the richest men in Hollywood, so he could afford to spend day after day on the golf course (as he had always wanted to do anyway). He also took an increasing interest in the various projects of Crosby Enterprises and the Bing Crosby Research Foundation, which he and brother Everett had set up in the 1940s and which had helped develop magnetic audiotape and frozen orange juice, among other profit-making projects.

His personal life was thrown into turmoil, however, when his wife, Dixie, was diagnosed as having terminal cancer. She died on November 1, 1952, at age forty-one. Bing became reclusive for a while, and then kept the gossipmongers' tongues wagging as he was seen increasingly in the company of attractive young women. Then, five years after Dixie's death, Bing married actress Kathryn Grant. He was fifty-four, she twenty-four. Just as he had with Dixie and their four children, Bing then pulled a figurative "press and public keep out" window shade over his home life as he started a new family with Kathryn and, in time, their three children. He continued to make occasional movies and to tape TV shows from time to time, including an annual Christmas special.

In 1974, Bing was hospitalized with what doctors at first feared was lung cancer. It turned out to be a nonmalignant abscess, which required removal of part of his left lung. The doctors weren't sure what effect the surgery would have on his voice, but a few months later Bing was performing again—with his voice actually deeper and more resonant than ever, although he could no longer reach some of his former high notes. Between 1975 and 1977 he recorded ten new LP albums—new stereo versions of not just songs with which he had long been identified, but also of classic pop songs he regretted having missed the first time around. He even threw in a few new songs, such as "Send in the Clowns" and "The Way We Were."

In the spring of 1977, at age seventy-four, Bing undertook a major international tour, which took him back to Broadway for the first time in many decades and to London's famous Palladium. With longtime colleagues Rosemary Clooney and Joe Bushkin as part of the show, as well as wife Kathryn and their children, some wags expected that Bing would come out and do a few songs and then disappear while the others did their things. Not so. He was onstage 90 percent of the time, singing duets with Clooney and his wife as well as dozens upon dozens of solos—some with full orchestral backing and some with just Bushkin at the piano. And as we can personally attest, his pipes were in great shape throughout.

When the London engagement closed, Bing went into the recording studios to make another album, then flew to Spain to relax and play some golf. Right after finishing a game outside Madrid on October 14, 1977, he collapsed from a heart attack. He died before he reached the hospital. As Kathryn later told reporters, "I can't think of any better way for a golfer who sings for a living to finish the round."

After Bing's death, a number of hard-hitting books and articles painted a picture of him as not always such an easygoing "nice guy" as his public image—and a particularly cold and calculating businessman. Maybe so, although many colleagues were quick to rush to his defense and point out all he had done behind the scenes over the years to help professional colleagues who had fallen on bad days— including, at low points in their careers in the 1940s and 1950s, Judy Garland, Frank Sinatra, Mildred Bailey, and Louis Armstrong. As Crosby's last record producer, Ken Barnes, has written: "No question about it, there are many contradictory aspects surrounding Crosby the man and his life-style. . . . He was no saint—as he himself readily admitted—nor was he much of a sinner. Faults and all, here was a man to respect, a performer blessed with extraordinary talent. 'Legend' is not too strong a word to use in describing him."

RUSS COLUMBO

His combination of sensuous voice and good looks
created a magnetism that few women could resist.
—conductor-arranger *MARLIN SKILES*

In a few brief years in the early 1930s, Russ Columbo was the major rival to Bing Crosby's "king-of-the-hill" position among popular crooners on records, radio, and in movies. Exceptionally handsome, with a warm, mellow baritone, Columbo seemed to have everything going for him when a freak shooting accident cut short his life—at age twenty-six.

The circumstances of his death in 1934 have continued to be grist for Hollywood's ever-busy rumor mills. There are still some who suspect that Columbo's death may not have been accidental but that he was murdered—perhaps in an ex-lovers' quarrel growing out of announcements of a pending marriage to popular film star Carole Lombard. Since Columbo was an Italian-American, there were even rumors of a Mafia-linked "rubout" at a time when organized crime was becoming increasingly involved in both the movie studios and the recording business. But most film and music historians have come to accept the official police version as perhaps hard to believe but true. What happened was apparently this: Columbo was visiting one of his closest friends, photographer Lansing Brown, Jr., who kept a set of supposedly unloaded antique Civil War dueling pistols on a desk in his library as paper-weights. During his conversation with Columbo, Brown, in order to light a cigarette, struck a match on one of the pistols in such a way as to set off a long-forgotten charge still in the gun. The bullet that was discharged ricocheted off a table and struck Columbo in the head. He was rushed to Good Samaritan Hospital in Los Angeles but died a few hours later.

In the years since then, Columbo's recordings have remained in continuous circulation. At various times, movies or teleplays about Columbo's life have been announced for Tony Martin, Perry Como, Tony Curtis, and Johnny Desmond, but none has yet materialized. Meanwhile, like others cut down at an early age—such as James Dean and Buddy Holly—Columbo remains the stuff of legend, not only among nostalgia buffs who were actually around in the 1930s but also among younger fans who continue to discover his old recordings and movies and who are taken with both his good looks and his sexy singing style.

Accounts about Columbo's early life seem to have been distorted or possibly even invented by different publicists in his adult years. But there's no doubt that music played an important part from the beginning, for his father was an Italian-born theater musician. Russ, who was christened Ruggerio de Rodolfo Columbo, always claimed his birth date was January 14, 1908, but there are conflicting statements as to whether it was in San Francisco or Camden, New Jersey. In any case, Russ spent parts of his boyhood in both regions, where he began guitar and violin lessons at an early age. His teen years found the family first in the Napa Valley town of Calistoga in California, and then in Los Angeles, where Russ became a violinist in his high-school orchestra. He also got odd jobs in small combos playing "mood music" on silent-movie sets (a practice of the time to help get players in the proper mood for certain scenes, particularly love scenes). On one such set, silent-film star Pola Negri took an interest in Columbo, who reminded her of Rudolph Valentino, with whom she had been romantically linked prior to his death in 1926. Negri helped Columbo get bit parts in some late-1920s movies.

Meanwhile, Columbo began playing violin in Los Angeles hotel and theater orchestras. One night at the Hollywood Roosevelt, the band singer got sick just before a CBS Radio broadcast was set to begin, and Russ went on in his place. Not long after, he was hired by Gus Arnheim for his popular Cocoanut Grove Orchestra, officially as a violinist but also as a standby for young vocalist Bing Crosby, whose drinking habits worried Arnheim and the Grove's manager, Abe Frank. When Frank tried to impose a fine on Crosby for missing a show and Crosby walked out permanently, Columbo took over as Arnheim's featured vocalist—and quickly became popular with the Grove's movie clientele. Earlier, while working with various bands at night, Columbo (like Crosby) had played small parts in movies by day—including such major early talkies as Victor Fleming's *Wolf Song* and Cecil B. DeMille's *Dynamite*. Columbo also appeared with the Arnheim orchestra in their scenes in the 1929 RKO musical *Street Girl* (with Betty Compson and Jack Oakie).

Following an East Coast tour with the Arnheim band, Columbo returned to Los Angeles to form his own band and to open a nightclub with two of his brothers, but it didn't fare too well in those early Depression years. Things began to click for Russ about a year later, however, after he hired as his manager the aggressive Con Conrad (composer of "Ma, He's Making Eyes at Me" and later the first Oscar-winning song, "The Continental"). First, NBC signed Columbo for a late-night sustaining radio show. When Bing Crosby was signed by rival CBS, the networks' publicists lost no time in promoting a "Battle of the Baritones." Then when Crosby left RCA Victor for Brunswick Records, RCA signed Columbo—and the "battle" continued. (Crosby always insisted that it was a publicists' battle, that there was never any real rivalry between them, and that they remained personally friendly.) Meanwhile, Columbo, billed as "The Romeo of the Airwaves," bolstered his amorous image with a series of well-publicized romances—including those with singer Dorothy Dell, actress Sally Blane (Loretta Young's sister) and Hannah Williams (later married to boxer Jack Dempsey).

To distinguish himself from Crosby's fast-rising reputation as a "boo-boo-boo" crooner, Columbo told an interviewer: "I'm not a crooner—or a blues singer or a straight baritone. I've tried to make my phrasing different, and I take a lot of liberty with the music. One of the things [audiences] seem to like best is the voice obbligato on repeat choruses—very much as I used to do them on the violin."

There were other differences between the two singers. Crosby was much more jazz-influenced; even in his singing of ballads he usually expressed brighter tone colors and more rhythmic bite. Columbo, in turn, had a smoother, creamier voice that could, at times, border on the bland. He almost always sounded deadly serious, sometimes even pretentious, about the romantic lyrics he sang—in contrast to Crosby's way of distancing himself from them with a degree of self-irony and occasional kidding. Yet there is no denying the gently nonthreatening appeal of Columbo's voice and approach—and the soothing effect his voice had on millions of listeners in the depths of the Depression. It's a style that also clearly influenced the most romantic of the big-band singers of the mid-1930s, such as Art Jarrett and Jack Leonard.

Several of Columbo's first hit recordings were of songs he himself had written or cowritten: "Prisoner of Love," "You Call It Madness (But I Call It Love)," and "My Love." He once told an interviewer that he enjoyed composing almost as much as performing. "I write late at night mostly—and get some of my best ideas after I've gone to bed." (That comment must have thrilled some of his female fans.)

In 1933, Columbo was signed to sing the three songs just mentioned in a Warner Bros. musical short titled *That Goes Double*, in which he also played a dual role—as himself and as a look-alike office worker. Although Columbo's acting in this two-reeler seems more self-conscious and less "natural" than Bing Crosby's in *his* first Paramount musicals, Columbo was given the romantic lead opposite Constance Cummings in *Broadway Thru a Keyhole*, one of Darryl F. Zanuck's first features for his newly formed Twentieth Century Pictures (which would later merge with Fox Pictures to become Twentieth Century–Fox). Reviews of Columbo's acting were mixed, but one of the songs he introduced in the picture, Harry Revel and Mack Gordon's "You're My Past, Present, and Future," became a hit. Columbo also got somewhat upstaged in *Broadway Thru a Keyhole* by the appearances of Broadway's Frances Williams, vaudeville star Blossom Seeley, and the legendary Texas Guinan. The movie itself got unexpected publicity when Al Jolson publicly punched gossip columnist Walter Winchell because Jolson felt that the Winchell-based script was too close for comfort to a situation in Jolson's romance with Ruby Keeler.

For his second movie feature, Columbo was relegated to a supporting role in Zanuck's *Moulin Rouge* (starring Constance Bennett and Franchot Tone) and got no vocal solos in it. Instead, he shared Harry Warren and Al Dubin's "Coffee in the Morning and Kisses at Night" with both Bennett and the Boswell Sisters.

Just as Columbo's movie career seemed to be taking a downturn, his radio career swung sharply up again with a new NBC prime-time series, as well as with a new recording contract (again replacing Crosby, this time at Brunswick, which Crosby had left for Decca). Then, most promising of all, Columbo was picked by Universal Pictures to play the role of Gaylord Ravenal in the much-anticipated sound version of the Kern-Hammerstein *Show Boat*, opposite Irene Dunne. When production problems caused postponement of the picture, Columbo was assigned an interim lead in a low-budget "B" musical, *Wake Up and Dream* (also featuring June Knight, Wini Shaw, and Roger Pryor, and no relation to the 1929 Cole Porter Broadway musical of the same name). It was during this film's shooting that Columbo met Carole Lombard and began what critic and film historian Leonard Maltin, in his Lombard biography, has called "a serious affair." *Wake Up and Dream* was completed amid considerable hoopla in the fan magazines about the Lombard-Columbo romance and expected marriage. Then, while the studio prepared to make the most of the romance publicity for the picture's release and while Columbo prepared for a loan-out to Warner Bros. for the lead in another musical (*Sweet Music*), the gun accident took his life. "Carole wept unashamedly at his funeral," Maltin reports.

Universal released *Wake Up and Dream* a month later, to mixed reviews for both the timing of the release and the picture itself. In contrast to the "good guy" roles that marked all of Bing Crosby's work at Paramount, Columbo plays an egotistical singer in *Wake Up and Dream* who almost takes his best friend's gal away from him. If the part was designed to show a darker side of Columbo and a wider acting range than Crosby had yet demonstrated, or perhaps to pave the way for the ambivalence of the unheroic Ravenal character in *Show Boat*, all got lost in the banalities of a run-of-the-mill script.

We'll never know, of course, whether Russ Columbo would ever have become as big a star of movies, radio, and recordings as Bing Crosby. Columbo's untimely death left Crosby without a major rival for the rest of the 1930s. But just as there is a big difference between the Crosby of the early 1930s and the Crosby of the 1940s and beyond, so, too, Columbo might well have grown in ways not evident in the limited legacy of movies and recordings he left. There is no doubt, however, that his smooth, relaxed, gently direct style influenced a whole generation of band singers—and that his recordings continue to have appeal to ballad lovers for their unabashed romantic warmth.

KATE SMITH

Your Majesties, this is Kate Smith—
this is America.
—PRESIDENT FRANKLIN D. ROOSEVELT
to England's visiting king and queen, 1939

For at least five decades, Kate Smith ranked close to apple pie, base-ball, and the Statue of Liberty among America's best-loved and most instantly recognized symbols. That image hinged partly on Kate's having introduced Irving Berlin's "God Bless America" in 1939, a song she helped turn into an unofficial second national anthem. But Kate Smith's reputation as a singer of popular American music existed well before "God Bless America," and it thrived for many more years with many different types of songs.

She was a big woman in both the size of her voice and her physical girth—as well as in the direct, wholesome warmth of her usually cheerful personality. Unlike Mildred Bailey, Smith came to relatively contented terms with her ample weight early in her life. She even gave her 1938 autobiography the double-meaning title *Living in a Great Big Way*. But she didn't hestitate to express her hurt when other people joked about her size.

Although she often sang romantic ballads, she never pretended to sing them as a sex symbol. Her appeal and long-sustained popularity were more akin to that of everyone's big sister or favorite cousin—one for whom the front door is always open. And Americans gladly welcomed Kate Smith's voice into their homes, first on radio and then on television. No woman singer came near her in the number of songs she introduced or helped popularize through her daily radio shows in the 1930s and 1940s, and then after 1951 on television.

Her straight-ahead, high-alto voice had a natural brightness, tonal depth, and richness of sound that few other singers of her generation could match. She could use it to belt out full, clarionlike tones, or rein it in tenderly and intimately. Heartfelt expression was the key to the way she sang her songs; she never merely tossed off a lyric. Whatever the tempo or mood of a song, she made you believe she meant every word of every lyric with every fiber of her ample body—whether it was a ballad, a bluesy pop song, a Broadway show number, or a novelty tune.

She always insisted that her singing style and sound had come naturally—that she had never taken any formal music lessons. Once, when she was invited to join Leopold Stokowski and the Philadelphia Orchestra for a benefit concert, she stunned the maestro by revealing to him at their first rehearsal that she couldn't read music. But she assured him that once she heard a melody, her ear and her perfect sense of pitch took over, and she could then sing a song in any arrangement she and the conductor agreed on. A bemused Stokowski accommodated her by whistling parts of the song arrangements she was unsure of.

For most of her career, Kate conveyed a down-to-earth, homey, small-town image—and, indeed, her birthplace was the small town of Greenville, Virginia (the date was May 1, 1909). Raised in Washington, D.C., Kathryn Elizabeth Smith retained many of the conservative manners and attitudes of her Southern heritage all her life—and was originally billed on radio as "The Songbird of the South." She started singing in church as a child. When the United States entered World War I in 1917, eight-year-old Kate volunteered to sing at Liberty Loan rallies and even got to meet President Woodrow Wilson at one of them. From then on there was no doubt in her mind that she wanted to be a singer.

In the years following the war, she entered every amateur contest she could. Her parents were none too encouraging—not because they didn't think her voice was good enough, but because they worried that Kate's ever-increasing size as she entered her teen years would subject her to cruel taunts and make a theatrical career difficult. There was also the fact that so many of the "jazz age" singers who appealed to Kate (such as Ethel Waters and Ruth Etting) were identified with clubs and speakeasies, which ran counter to her family's straitlaced upbringing. So they convinced her to become a nurse. But Kate's heart remained in the theater. After trying out a few vaudeville song routines in Washington, and following a bitter argument with her family, sixteen-year-old Kate chucked nursing to try her luck in New York.

One night, while waiting to go on in an amateur show, Kate watched a young black man bring the house down with a Charleston dance routine. Despite her bulk, Kate was convinced she was light enough on her feet to try something like it. She worked a Charleston specialty into her closing number and, indeed, it won her an ovation. It also won her an invitation from the show's headliner, Broadway star Eddie Dowling, for a small role in a 1926 Broadway show Dowling was putting together, *Honeymoon Lane*. Kate got to sing one song, "Half a Moon," and finished it with her Charleston dance. The headline for *The New York Times* review read: "Honeymoon Lane Is Colorful & Lavish; Kate Smith, 250-Pound Blues Singer, a Hit." There was no going back to nursing after that.

Kate spent most of the next several years auditioning for and playing in several other Broadway shows. In Vincent Youmans' *Hit the Deck* (1927), Kate played a blackface mammy featured in the production number for one of that show's biggest song hits, "Hallelujah." In George White's *Flying High* (1930), Kate was cast as star Bert Lahr's mail-order fiancée. But that show was not to be one of her happier experiences, because of Lahr's continual ad-libs and relentless jibes at Kate's size. (Example: "When she sits down, it's like a dirigible coming in for a landing.") When members of her family found her in tears in her dressing room after one particularly humiliating onstage razzing by Lahr, they could not resist saying, "We told you so." They urged Kate to quit the show and return home. The stubborn Kate insisted she had a contractual obligation with the show but might indeed return home when the run ended.

When *Flying High* closed, Kate never did do another Broadway show, but she didn't return home, either. Her radio debut as a guest on Rudy Vallee's show had attracted the attention of a Columbia Records executive, Joseph Martin ("Ted") Collins. He not only signed her to a record contract but also became her personal manager—with only a handshake as their personal contract for the next thirty years. In quick succession, Collins won Kate an eleven-week engagement at the summit of the nation's vaudeville theaters, New York's Palace, *and* a CBS contract for a fifteen-minute network radio show heard at 7:00 P.M. four nights a week. Within a month of the radio show's introduction on her twenty-second birthday, May 1, 1931, Kate Smith had become a household name from coast to coast. In fact, Kate's enormous success on the new show caused NBC to move its popular *Amos 'n' Andy* comedy program to another time slot so as not to lose listeners to Kate. For the program's theme song, Collins commissioned well-known composer Harry Woods ("I'm Looking Over a Four-Leaf Clover," "Try a Little Tenderness") to adapt a poem that Kate herself had written as a teenager—and the song, "When the Moon Comes Over the Mountain," became Kate's lifelong signature, even though some wags cruelly persisted in considering the mountain a metaphor for Kate herself.

The economic depression of the early 1930s may have hurt Broadway and other aspects of show business, but not Kate Smith. Her records were selling well, and her cheerful, singsong radio greeting "*Hel*-lo, everybody!" signaled a daily reprieve from the troubles of the day. By 1933 she was making $3,000 a week—the highest of any woman in radio.

Kate made a cameo appearance in the film *The Big Broadcast*, the first in a series of musical-comedy features designed to give radio fans a chance to see what some of their favorite performers looked like (including George Burns and Gracie Allen, the Boswell Sisters, Arthur Tracy, and Donald Novis, as well as Bing Crosby in his first starring feature). Kate impressed the studio executives so much in her cameo that they decided to groom her as a homespun rival for MGM's popular 1931 Oscar winner Marie Dressler (also a woman of large proportions). For Kate's debut feature, predictably titled *Hello, Everybody!*, Paramount gave her a script adapted from a story by the then-popular Fannie Hurst (*Imitation of Life, Back Street*) about a rustic lass who saves her family's and her neighbors' farms by becoming a successful radio singer. Kate was teamed with handsome rising star Randolph Scott, but the script called for her to lose him in the romance department to Sally Blane, resigning herself (in the words of *New York Times* critic André Sennwald) to "pour out her heart in her songs and live vicariously in the happiness of others." Her songs included a new moon song (titled simply enough "Moon Song") plus five others by one of Paramount's top songwriting teams, Sam Coslow and Arthur Johnston. Kate even got to do her Charleston routine in one scene. But the movie flopped at the box office. Paramount, then on the verge of receivership from a combination of business woes, scrapped plans for further Kate Smith movies.

Kate returned to New York to concentrate on her radio and recording career, which continued to thrive. Clearly, millions of Americans preferred to *hear* Kate Smith and not necessarily *see* her playing movie roles. And in 1930s Depression America, there was something hopeful, reassuring, and even rock-solid in the sound of Kate Smith's voice and in the types of songs she sang night after night. In her programs she emphasized her optimistic belief in the future. "I'm not a great one for looking back. I much prefer to look ahead," she said.

"As a matter of fact, I live for today and hope for tomorrow." And the spunky sincerity in her voice was catching. When she sang such pop hits of the day as "When My Ship Comes In," "There I Go Dreaming Again," or "River, Stay 'Way from My Door," millions of listeners related instantly. They also related to Kate's way of expressing her three basic loves: for family, God, and country.

There were some, however, who found her just a little too square and old-fashioned. Although Kate's speaking voice on radio showed few traces of her Southern origins, some of the region's racial stereotypes crept into her early choices of material. Her 1931 recording of "That's Why Darkies Were Born" now seems blatantly racist (she wasn't alone in recording it, of course), and one of the numbers in her movie *Hello, Everybody!*, "Pickaninnies' Heaven," is so embarrassing by today's standards that the movie is rarely shown on television anymore. But such songs were never the basis for Kate's appeal. More representative over the years were "Fine and Dandy," "Carolina Moon," "Did You Ever See a Dream Walking?" "The Music Goes Round and Round," "Margie," "It's Been a Long, Long Time," "Wabash Moon," "The White Cliffs of Dover," "I'll Be Seeing You," "September Song," and "It Was So Beautiful."

As war clouds deepened over much of Europe in 1938, Irving Berlin presented Kate with an unpublished song he felt would be appropriate for her Armistice Day radio show. It was, of course, "God Bless America." Berlin had written it in 1918 for *Yip! Yip! Yaphank,* but it had been cut from that show. The song caused a sensation on Kate's first broadcast, and she had to repeat it in subsequent weeks. "Apple-pie American" Kate was indeed the right person to introduce Berlin's from-the-heart patriotic exhortation, and the song caught on like nothing since "Yankee Doodle." There was even a movement in Congress to have the song replace "The Star-Spangled Banner" as our national anthem. But Kate publicly opposed that, saying she had too much respect for the present anthem. In later years she also noted, "I never made a penny on that song." In keeping with Irving Berlin's wishes, all income from "God Bless America," including royalties from Kate's recordings of it, was donated in perpetuity to the Boy Scouts and Girl Scouts of America.

During World War II, Kate combined her radio work with visits to Army and Navy bases, war plants, shipyards, and hospitals. She once estimated she had traveled more than half a million miles entertaining servicemen and servicewomen. She also sold more than $600 million in war bonds at rallies across the nation—more than any other single entertainer. Throughout the 1940s Kate also became more outspoken in voicing some of her conservative political and social views—especially her strong anticommunism in the late 1940s. She even switched networks, charging CBS with "restrictions and censorship" on saying what she wanted to.

In 1950 Kate became one of the first major radio entertainers to move to television, as host of a daytime variety show aimed primarily at housewives. By the early 1960s, however, her popularity seemed to be waning—until Ted Collins decided it was time for Kate to give a Carnegie Hall concert in New York. Such a concert had revitalized Judy Garland's career in 1961, and it did the trick for Kate in 1963, too. She was suddenly in demand again as a guest on TV shows, and she signed a new record contract with RCA. She surprised many of her older fans—and won many new ones—by defending Elvis Presley and rock 'n' roll at a time when the rock revolution had torn asunder the long-entrenched pop-music establishment and turned most old-timers against "the new noise." "If [rock] is well done, by a voice that is neither manufactured nor has no music in it at all, and if the beat is executed correctly, there's nothing terribly wrong with that kind of music," she said. That was no lip-service comment, either. Kate added some pop-rock songs to her repertory and recast some of her older standards with a soft-rock beat.

A year after the Carnegie Hall concert, Ted Collins died. For a while, Kate seemed lost without him guiding her. She converted to Catholicism and stopped performing altogether. Then a career boost came from a completely unexpected source: the Philadelphia Flyers hockey team. Someone noticed that whenever a Flyers game was preceded by a recording of Kate singing "God Bless America," the Flyers won the game. The team made Kate their official sweetheart. As Kate later put it: "Since I became the Flyers' left hind foot of the rabbit, it's been like a rebirth of a career. The letters pour in every day." Kate was invited to guest on different TV shows (including *The Ed Sullivan Show, The Jackie Gleason Show, The Dean Martin Show,* and *The Smothers Brothers Comedy Hour*). But recurring problems with diabetes increasingly limited her schedule.

In the mid-1970s, though now in her late sixties, Kate undertook a major national tour. But after an appearance in Lincoln, Nebraska, on September 3, 1976, illness forced her to cancel the rest of the tour. She retired to Raleigh, North Carolina, to live with her sister. Kate became a virtual recluse for the next ten years, declining to give interviews. Her diabetes went out of control, putting her in a diabetic coma for four months and from which she suffered permanent brain damage, which impaired her vision, walking, and talking. In January 1986 her right leg had to be amputated, and a few months later she had to undergo surgery to remove a cancerous breast. Most Americans learned little of these agonies until after her death on June 17, 1986.

Kate Smith's place among America's great singers has been perhaps best summed up by George T. Simon, former *Metronome* editor and longtime executive director of the National Academy of Recording Arts and Sciences (NARAS): "From 1931 onward, Kate Smith did indeed seem to personify the country—idealistic, generous, home-spun, sentimental, emotional, and proud." To which many would add: And could she ever put over a song!

CONNEE BOSWELL

*When I started out, all I wanted was
to sing like Connee Boswell.*
—ELLA FITZGERALD

Connee Boswell had two careers—first as part of the Boswell Sisters trio, which revolutionized the sound of female vocal groups in the late 1920s and early 1930s, and then as a much-respected and popular solo vocalist after the sister act broke up. She also had two spellings of her first name. It was Connie when she sang with the trio, but she changed it to Connee for her solo years (reportedly because her undotted *i* when she signed autographs or business papers made it look like an *e* anyway). In either guise, this particular Boswell had a distinctive sound and musical know-how that bridged black and white musical styles like few before her.

A childhood accident when Connee was three years old in 1910 left both her legs paralyzed. She was confined to a wheelchair for most of her life and always performed sitting, her legs covered by long gowns. But her infirmity did not stop her from being the spark plug of her sisters' act, sketching most of its vocal arrangements (but never writing them out fully), or guiding the act and then her own solo career on busy professional schedules.

In the so-called jazz age of the 1920s (when the word "jazz" itself was defined fairly loosely), the Boswell Sisters got to be known as jazz singers. And indeed there were strong jazz elements in their arrangements, reflecting their New Orleans roots. But they were just as much pop singers, straddling (and sometimes blurring) the line between New Orleans and Tin Pan Alley. Later, as a soloist, Connee favored ballads most of all. In fact, Irving Berlin once called her the finest ballad singer in the business.

Her sisters' names were Martha and Helvetia (Vet), and they were all musical from early ages. Martha played the piano; Vet the violin, banjo, and guitar; and Connee the cello, saxophone, and guitar. "We weren't wealthy [growing up in New Orleans]," Connee told CBS Records producer Michael Brooks, "but we could afford help." And it was by three black members of their New Orleans household that the sisters were introduced to spirituals and blues. As Connee also recalled for former *Metronome* editor George T. Simon, "When I was a kid, my mama took me to a theater for blacks—they'd let us in only on Friday nights—and there I heard Mamie Smith. After that I tried to sing like her. She was a great blues singer—better even, I thought, than Bessie Smith. I also tried to sing like Caruso, holding on to notes the way he did. And I did, too."

The Boswell Sisters began as an instrumental trio playing classical and semiclassical selections on a local radio station in the mid-1920s, when radio programming was still in its infancy. The sisters also sang occasionally in New Orleans vaudeville houses, earning all of $1 a night each. When they were offered a two-hour radio spot five days a week, the sisters divided the show up into separate segments of instrumentals, popular vocal solos by Connee, and then songs by all three. "We'd record anything we were given," Connee told Michael Brooks, "terrible songs that no one ever heard before or since. We'd have been better off selecting our own material, but we were young and enthusiastic and thought we could do anything."

The truth was, they virtually could. There had been other girl groups before them (such as the Brox Sisters, the Ponce Sisters, the Williams Sisters, and the Keller Sisters), but the Boswells developed their own mellow, jazz-influenced blend of close harmony. "We didn't sing everything straight, the way other groups did," Connee told George T. Simon. "After the first chorus, we'd start singing the tune a little different—you know, with a beat, the way jazz musicians would." There would be sudden tempo or key changes, and variations of the rhythmic pattern. They also engaged in what some called "crossover harmony," whereby the individual sisters didn't always sustain a set position of bottom to top voices within a song, but often switched positions, sometimes on a single phrase. They were decidedly sophisticated for their time, both harmonically and rhythmically (much more so than the later Andrews Sisters).

It wasn't long before word about the Boswells got around. First Victor and then Brunswick signed them to recording contracts, and they were booked for engagements in Chicago and New York. Within a few years the Boswell Sisters were the hottest singing group in the country. "What we actually did was something that came out of the three of us instinctively," Connee later told New York broadcaster Rich Conaty. "It started as a bud, and by the time 1930 came around it had blossomed into a full-bloomed flower."

The sisters had an intuitive knack for being able to interchange each other's parts instantaneously—and with a minimum of rehearsal. As Michael Brooks has described it, "They dug to discover the pure core [of a song], slowed it down, speeded it up, worried it between their teeth, fooled around with key changes. They were alchemists who changed base metal into gold."

Between 1930 and 1936 the Boswell Sisters made more than seventy recordings, many of them with such top instrumental sidemen as Tommy and Jimmy Dorsey, Bunny Berigan, Eddie Lang, and Manny Klein. They also became regulars on Bing Crosby's top-rated radio show and had guest spots in several movies. In one, 1934's *Transatlantic Merry-Go-Round* (starring Jack Benny and Nancy Carroll), they even introduced the first rock and roll song. Well, not really (at least as we now know the term), but one of their songs in that film (by Richard Whiting and Sidney Clare) is actually titled "Rock and Roll" and deals with the rocking and rolling motions of the ocean liner on which most of the movie's action takes place.

In 1936, Martha and Vet retired in favor of married life and raising a family. Connee also got married that year—to the trio's manager, Harry Leedy. Going solo was tough at first, she later recalled to a *Look* magazine interviewer: "Producers who knew me only from radio or recordings would call and ask me to audition for a show. I'd go over and as soon as they saw me in a wheelchair they'd freeze. It hurt. Really hurt. But I said to myself, 'Connee, to get ahead, you've got to be better than the next fella. And if you've got a handicap, then you've simply got to be even better than that.' So I really started working. . . . I feel sorry for those who can't use their bodies and *won't* use their brains. They just wait for something good to grab them, instead of getting out and grabbing it themselves."

Connee continued making recordings (one of her new brothers-in-law was a Decca executive) and to sing regularly on radio (including 104 appearances on the *Good News* variety show and sixty-five on *The Kraft Music Hall* with Bing Crosby). She also toured the country for personal appearances (twice breaking records at New York's Paramount), using a specially built wheelchair that, when covered by her gown, gave the impression she was standing.

And she played cameo roles in half a dozen movies, including *Artists and Models* (1937), *Kiss the Boys Goodbye* (1941), *Syncopation* (1942), and *Swing Parade of 1946*. In the first two she introduced ballads that went on to become pop standards: "Whispers in the Dark" and "Sand in My Shoes." They are both typical of the relaxed but always lilting ballad style she favored as a soloist, although she still didn't hesitate to swing out and scat from time to time. She even started a minitrend of swinging the classics with "Martha," one of her biggest all-time hits. But some of the trends in swing and jazz displeased her. As she told *New York World-Telegram* reporter Ernie Pyle in 1938 (a few years before he became one of World War II's most famous correspondents), "Just to get up on a squawking note and keep yelling it" was not for her.

During World War II, Connee appeared in several Broadway revues and traveled throughout the country singing at army and navy training camps. She volunteered for overseas trips, but military officials denied her permission, saying her handicap posed too big a risk under war conditions. Both during and after the war, she also visited hospitals to perform for the wounded—showing by her example that a physical disability did not have to mean the end of the road. Then, as network radio and musical stage shows dwindled in the 1950s, Connee, now in her midforties, cut back on performing. After 1960 she dedicated herself almost entirely to benefits for hospitals or organizations for the handicapped.

In the early 1970s, Connee was hospitalized with stomach cancer. She underwent a series of operations, and gave her last public performance at New York's Carnegie Hall in 1975 with Benny Goodman. She was sixty-eight. A year later, she asked her doctors not to try to prolong her life and to discontinue the chemotherapy she had been receiving. "Take all those things out of my arms," she told them. "The treatment is worse than the ailment. Let me die in peace and dignity when God wants to take me." She died a few days later.

FRED ASTAIRE

He has a remarkable ear for intonation,
a great sense of rhythm, and, what is most
important, he has great style.
—BING CROSBY

You won't run into many arguments if you call Fred Astaire this century's greatest dancer. George Balanchine said so. And Mikhail Baryshnikov. Gene Kelly, too. But Astaire was every bit as great a singer, too. In contrast to his dancing, which *commanded* attention by its obvious mastery, Astaire's singing style was more laid back and less attention-grabbing, but no less masterful in reaching for and projecting the very heartbeat of a song.

The voice itself, a light baritone, was not a big one, and it was a bit reedy. But its timbre was smooth, with hardly any trace of vibrato, and his intonation was impeccable. Most important of all, he phrased naturally and clearly, in a way that was simultaneously relaxed, graceful, elegant, witty, sincere, and thoroughly engaging. As one of Astaire's movie costars, Audrey Hepburn (1957's *Funny Face*), has put it, "His dancing was sublime, out of reach. His singing somehow was more within reach, simple, to the point, but unique." More than anything else, it was the balance that Astaire sustained between the two that made him so irresistible an entertainer to several generations of moviegoers.

Astaire himself was never as confident about his singing as he was about his dancing. "I'd have been broke if I had tried to be a singer alone," he once said. Not so, argues singer Sylvia Syms, who told *New Yorker* music critic Whitney Balliett: "He invented lyric economy. He danced words. He carried the grace of his dancing over into his singing. No matter what he sang, it always had movement." Astaire's longtime dance director Hermes Pan believed that the buoyancy to his singing derived from the *way* he danced, that "a dancer has certain rhythms and phrasing which will affect his voice and his delivery."

In his movies, Astaire's songs usually served only as the introduction to a dance routine—and, inevitably, what his feet and the rest of his body did in those routines ended up overshadowing what his vocal chords had done. But when watched on its own, or listened to on his many recordings, Astaire's singing always reveals an extraordinary understanding of the lyric and exactly how it relates to the song's melodic line. It's no surprise that, as songwriter Johnny Mercer once noted, "Fred has consistently been the favorite singer of more great songwriters than any other performer."

In some ways, Astaire's singing reflected the straight-arrow unpretentiousness of his Nebraska roots. His father, an Austrian who emigrated to America in the 1890s, worked in a brewery in Omaha, Nebraska, when Fred was born in that city on May 10, 1899. He was christened Frederick Austerlitz, although his father legally changed the family name to Astaire when Fred was still a tot. Fred's mother, a native Omahan, loved music and thought it the natural thing to do when she enrolled Fred and his sister, Adele (a year older than Fred), in a local dancing school. Within a year, Adele's charm and precocity had made her the school's star performer. With kids a vaudeville staple in those early days of the century, the Astaires lost little time in trying that route. Over the next half-dozen years, Adele's act, with Fred partnering in some of the dances and playing some piano, "creeped up" (to use Fred's words) on the major vaudeville circuits.

But not everything went smoothly. The Astaires were stranded in Detroit when a vaudeville strike kept them out of work for several months. Fred's mother hocked her fur coat and engagement ring, while Fred got a job as an office boy in the Remick music publishing firm's Detroit offices. There he became friendly with songwriter Richard Whiting (composer of "Till We Meet Again," "My Ideal," and many other later hits, and father of singer Margaret Whiting). Whiting encouraged young Fred's budding interest in songwriting and influenced him considerably in acquiring an understanding of the inner workings of songwriting. "He was very kind to me," Astaire wrote in his 1959 autobiography, *Steps in Time*. "His sense of humor and the fun we had were a big help through those lean, idle months."

As a teenager, Fred developed an instinct for spotting surefire songs and working them into an act. He was particularly attracted to the catchy, jazz-influenced tunes of Irving Berlin and the long-lined ballads of Jerome Kern, which were moving Broadway shows away from

European models and toward a more distinctively American style. In 1916 Fred and Adele were among the first, for example, to sing songs by the still-obscure Cole Porter and George Gershwin. Although Porter's first Broadway show, *See America First*, had been panned by most critics and quickly closed, Fred and Adele made that shows's "I've a Shooting Box in Scotland" one of their vaudeville tour hits. Meanwhile, Fred became friendly with Gershwin, then a teenager working as a song plugger in Remick's New York office. Fred and George often talked about how they would love to work in Broadway revues. By the end of World War I, they were both doing just that.

In a series of 1920s Broadway and London shows, Fred and Adele Astaire became the most successful dance team since the phenomenally popular Vernon and Irene Castle (a team whose career had been cut short by Vernon's death in service in World War I). But there was a major difference with the Astaires: Both of them also sang. And some of their 1920s Broadway shows introduced songs written especially for them by Kern ("Every Day in Every Way" in *The Bunch and Judy*) and Gershwin ("Fascinating Rhythm" in *Lady, Be Good!;* " 'S Wonderful" and "My One and Only" in *Funny Face*). Not only were Kern and Gershwin preeminent among the composers changing the style of 1920s Broadway musicals, but Fred Astaire was also helping to change the way their songs were actually sung. In contrast to the light-operatic tenors with their oily vibratos and rolled *r*'s or the Jolson-inspired sobbers and belters with their reach-for-the-skies bravura wrap-ups, Fred sang with a more natural intimacy and ease, avoiding any kind of fancy, personal interpretation. It was a style that Astaire would not really hone until he got to Hollywood, where soundtrack microphones enabled him to sing more intimately and conversationally, without worrying about theater projection. A comparison of Astaire's mid- and late-1920s recordings of songs from Broadway's *Lady, Be Good!* and *Funny Face* with those from his Hollywood films in the mid-1930s shows how quickly and effectively he toned down and refined his style in Hollywood, softening it without any loss in his natural buoyancy. But it began for him on Broadway, at a time when the influence of the more intimate vocal styles of Rudy Vallee, Ethel Waters, and Bing Crosby (among others), working in radio and nightclubs as well as theaters, were beginning to be strongly felt. They all influenced each other, although some critics believe the biggest influence on Astaire was the London-based, Mozambique-born Al Bowlly, for many years the vocalist on Ray Noble's recordings.

Fred and Adele were also among the first Broadway stars to be tapped for "talkie" screen tests in 1927 at Paramount's Astoria studios in New York. The tests turned out badly, with Fred earning this now-famous assessment (possibly apocryphal) from a Paramount executive: "Can't act. Can't sing. Balding. Can dance a little."

More than a movie door, however, seemed to slam on Astaire in 1932. Adele, following the run of one of the team's biggest Broadway smashes, *The Band Wagon*, decided to retire from show business to marry a young English lord. Fred, who always considered Adele the real star of the act, was uncertain whether he could make it solo. For his first Adele-less effort, the Cole Porter musical *Gay Divorce*, he was teamed with a rising young blond actress-dancer, Claire Luce, who was very different in both looks and style from brunette Adele. The show got decidedly mixed reviews, but it managed a respectable run for that Depression year—thanks mainly to cut-price tickets and one of the show's songs, "Night and Day." The song quickly became a Top Ten hit nationwide in sheet-music and record sales, and it also gave Astaire his first hit record, as the vocalist with Leo Reisman's popular dance band. Ironically, Astaire wasn't sure he wanted to do the song when he first heard it, finding it very "rangey," going from very low to very high. But Porter convinced him he could handle it well. Perhaps most significantly, "Night and Day" also helped to change Astaire's *dance* image, for, unlike his outgoing, often comic brother-sister dances with Adele, his dance to "Night and Day" marked Astaire's first major romantic duet—and a slow, seductive one at that.

Meanwhile, Astaire grew fascinated by the improvements being made in sound film techniques. He also felt he needed a break from a Broadway that still identified him primarily as part of a team with Adele. It was David O. Selznick (as production chief for the RKO-Radio studios) who brought Astaire to Hollywood when he bought the rights to *Gay Divorce* and its "Night and Day." But first Selznick assigned Astaire to a secondary role in one of his favorite projects, a musical that would combine a South American background and Latin rhythms with aviation. For *Flying Down to Rio*, RKO picked rising starlet Ginger Rogers to play Astaire's wisecracking dance partner. Fred had worked briefly with Ginger in New York in 1930 when, as a favor to a producer friend, he agreed to help "doctor" a dance number that wasn't working in rehearsal for Gershwin's *Girl Crazy*—a number surrounding Ginger's singing of "Embraceable You." When *Flying Down to Rio* was released in 1933, the easygoing rapport between Fred and Ginger came across so spontaneously that they stole the picture from top-billed Dolores Del Rio and Gene Raymond, and their one dance together, "The Carioca," became a nationwide sensation. Astaire the singer also got to introduce the film's title number.

RKO quickly reteamed Astaire and Rogers in the now considerably cleaned up and retitled *The Gay Divorcee*—the latter a concession to churchmen who felt that a divorce could not be gay (in the old-fashioned sense of the word), whereas a divorcée could. Only "Night and Day" was kept from Porter's original Broadway score, but Fred's debonair singing of the song and the subtly erotic Astaire-Rogers dance that followed were the picture's high point. With it, one of the screen's most charismatic and unique partnerships took wing and soared. In quick succession, Fred and Ginger were reteamed for a series of musicals that have all become '30s classics and made them two of Hollywood's all-time biggest stars: *Top Hat, Roberta, Swing Time, Shall We Dance?, Follow the Fleet, Carefree,* and *The Story of Vernon and Irene Castle*. Most of them featured songs written especially for the films by such top songwriters as Irving Berlin, George and Ira Gershwin, and Jerome Kern and Dorothy Fields.

Significantly, with each successive picture Fred sang more and Ginger less—as Astaire's singing style grew looser and more assured in Hollywood, while Rogers' narrow vocal range limited her. Most of the songs from these pictures have become standards and are still identified with Astaire the singer through his recordings. One of them, Berlin's "Top Hat, White Tie, and Tails," became Fred's signature tune. But many others are just as instantly identifiable as Astaire songs: "Cheek to Cheek," "I Won't Dance," "The Way You Look Tonight," "Pick Yourself Up," "They All Laughed," "They Can't Take That Away from Me," "Slap That Bass," "Let's Face the Music and Dance," and "Change Partners." It's doubtful if any other singer has ever introduced and made so completely his own such an impressive list of pop classics.

In the 1940s and 1950s, Astaire went on to make other now-classic musicals, with such leading ladies as Rita Hayworth, Judy Garland, Eleanor Powell, Jane Powell, Leslie Caron, Cyd Charisse, and Audrey Hepburn. He even teamed as both singer and dancer with Bing Crosby (*Holiday Inn, Blue Skies*) and Gene Kelly (*Ziegfeld Follies; That's Entertainment, Part 2*). Many of the songs Fred introduced in these pictures, again, became pop standards. To name just a few: "Dearly Beloved," "I'm Old-Fashioned," "My Shining Hour," "One for My Baby (and One More for the Road)," "Steppin' Out with My Baby," "Something's Gotta Give," and "That's Entertainment."

Several times, Astaire announced his retirement—once in his mid-forties (an age at which most professional dancers consider cutting back) and then in his late fifties. But always he was enticed back by attractive projects, including a series of four song-and-dance television specials with Barrie Chase between 1958 and 1968, two of which won him Emmy Awards. These TV specials indicated that age had somehow taken only a minimal toll on Astaire's fleet-footedness and singing voice, and none at all on his personal charm and charisma. Although he continued to sing and dance a little on TV and in movies (*Finian's Rainbow* in 1969 and *That's Entertainment, Part 2* in 1974), after the mid-1960s Astaire turned mostly to *non*musical acting roles—acquitting himself quite deftly in more than twenty of them and winning an Oscar nomination for one: 1975's *The Towering Inferno*.

Astaire also continued to record as a singer up to the late 1970s, sometimes working with such top jazzmen as Oscar Peterson, Ray Brown, and Charlie Shavers. His last recordings show his voice becoming increasingly raspy and more restricted in range, but there is certainly no decline in its easygoing jauntiness or in his savvy phrasing and rhythmic sense. What makes some of these last albums very special, moreover, is the inclusion of many of the songs Astaire himself had written over the years. Biographer Roy Pickard quotes Astaire as saying two years before his death in 1987, "I'm a frustrated songwriter, and I would like to have written a musical-comedy score. But that's just about the only thing I didn't get done." Astaire's daughter, Ava, told English journalist Sarah Giles soon after her father's death, "The one thing that really bothered him was that he didn't write a lot of hit songs. It was the one area of his life where he was not a total success, and it really bothered him."

Actually, Astaire did have two modest hits among his own songs. Back in February 1936, the buoyant "I'm Building Up to an Awful Letdown," with lyrics by Johnny Mercer, made three weeks on radio's *Your Hit Parade*, rising as high in the listings as fourth place. And in the 1960s, the brightly lyrical "Life Is Beautiful," with lyrics by Tommy Wolf, became widely known as a theme song for television's *Tonight Show*. It has long puzzled admirers of Astaire's several dozen published songs why they never caught on, for most of them are rhythmically catchy and melodically ingratiating. Perhaps it was his sense of loyalty to the recognized giants who wrote so many wonderful songs for his movies that kept Astaire from pushing his own songs until it was too late. In recent years, however, more and more supper-club and cabaret performers, looking for fresh material in a non–rock 'n' roll vein, have been "discovering" Astaire's own recordings of such top-notch originals as "Sweet Sorrow" (lyrics by Gladys Shelley), "Not My Girl" (lyrics by Desmond Carter), and "I Love Everybody But You" (lyrics by Ava Astaire)—and are performing them. So some of these songs may yet win wider recognition, to put further luster on the song side of the century's greatest song-and-dance man.

ETHEL MERMAN

*If you write lyrics for Ethel
they better be good, for if they're bad
everybody's going to hear them anyhow.*
—*IRVING BERLIN*

Every classic-pop song was once unsung, and a lot of the best were un-unsung by Ethel Merman. "I Got Rhythm," "You're the Tops," "Anything Goes," "I Get a Kick Out of You," "There's No Business Like Show Business"—Ethel Merman sang them first, made them hits, and virtually owned them for decades as her signature songs. Of course, her musical signature was all big, bold capital letters: "I GOT RHY-THM! I GOT MU-SIC!" As Merman herself once explained, "I do one basic thing. I project. That means I belt the lyrics over the footlights like a baseball player belting fly balls to an outfield." Today, in fact, sheer volume is just about all that modern-day listeners seem to associate with Ethel Merman. Yet her strength was not merely physical; she had to have had something special, or she could never have become the Joe DiMaggio of classic-pop hits.

Needless to say, Ethel Merman didn't croon. A Broadway singer in an era when stage mikes were disdained and the ability to project was a matter of pride, Merman roared out almost every song at full voice. In this sense, she stands apart from the classic-pop vocalists from the nightclub, film, and radio tradition, who utilized the microphone to sing at conversational volume. Yet Merman was anything but a typical theatrical singer. Despite its decibel level, her singing was strikingly conversational in enunciation and phrasing. She disliked the formal and precise style of articulation she called "concert English" and sang much as the people in her audience spoke, just a lot louder.

As a matter of fact, Merman herself tended to converse privately at pretty much the same balcony-battering levels at which she sang professionally. On one occasion, which she liked to recount on TV talk shows, she supposedly tried to whisper her dissatisfaction with a restaurant meal to a dinner companion, after which her waiter rushed out from the kitchen to apologize. To her own ears, then, Ethel Merman *was* singing at conversational volume.

Her singing voice also had a tone that was entirely natural and full of color and character, in contrast to the "pure," sound-alike tone that theatrical singers were all supposed to produce in Merman's day. She sang spontaneously, retaining the head tones and the quirks of her New York accent that a typical theatrical singer would strive to expunge. All these eccentricities—technically, flaws—are what made Ethel Merman sound so "normal" and accessible; they played a great role in her popular appeal. It's no wonder that, earlier in her career, George Gershwin warned her, "Don't ever let anybody give you a singing lesson. It'll ruin you."

Although she had no formal musical education, Ethel Merman had always been exposed to music and performing at home in Queens, New York. Her father, Edward Zimmermann, an accountant, played piano and organ well enough to serve as a soloist for his Masonic lodge. It was at her father's lodge, in fact, that Ethel Agnes Zimmermann began singing semiprofessionally while still a child. (Merman's exact age has always been uncertain. She gave her year of birth as 1908 early in her career, and proceeded to nudge it up regularly. In her final years, she said she was born in 1912.)

Although she performed fairly frequently for local organizations such as the Women's Republican Club, Merman trained for a career as a secretary and worked briefly for the Boyce-Ite Company and the B. K. Vacuum Booster Brake Company—jobs she would later associate with her success in show business. "It's because I've been a secretary that I have a certain amount of poise and can handle situations," she noted pridefully in the 1950s, adding that she always wrote her stage directions and dialogue changes in shorthand. She remained lifelong best friends with another secretary from the B. K. Booster Brake Company, Josie Traeger, and always kept a working-girl quality that helped her connect with the mainstream audience. Merman could have sung, "There's no business like the booster-brake business," and she would have made everyone believe it.

Once Merman took her first singing job, moonlighting in a basement club called Little Russia in Manhattan, she would rise within the ranks of that business with shorthand speed. An agent heard her and managed to get her a movie contract with Warner Bros. But before she was cast for a film, Jimmy Durante signed her as a singer in his New

York nightclub act. This was 1929, and within a year Merman was making her Broadway debut, in George and Ira Gershwin's *Girl Crazy*.

Just as one big music video can make a singing star today, so one hit number in a Broadway show could and did turn an unknown nightclub singer into a sensation when Ethel Merman opened in *Girl Crazy*. The number was exceptional—the innovatively syncopated, vaguely suggestive "I Got Rhythm." And the singer was equally unusual in her own way. "The audience seemed to think of me as a new type of singer," Merman would later recall, "and they liked it."

As today's listeners can still hear in her earliest recordings, the style that established Ethel Merman as a star is a double-charged combination of genuine musical skill and pure personality. Her voice was much more limber than it became later in life, with a range of about four or five notes over an octave. Endowed with extraordinary lungs, she could hold a note for as long as sixteen bars (if the tempo was fast). Equally important, Merman sang with so much character. She *was* a character—indeed, almost a caricature. Big and brassy and full of pizzazz, she was the very image of the street-smart New York dame who epitomized Broadway in the early 1930s. She swaggered with her voice, sliding notes deliberately flat and clipping them short with a kick.

Merman herself often said she thought her strongest attribute as a singer was her attention to the lyrics. "I bother about making people understand the lyrics I sing," she explained. "I honestly don't think there's anyone in the business who can top me at that." She claimed to concentrate on the lyrics as she sang them, although she once admitted that she was just as likely to be mentally planning a shopping trip during a performance.

In addition, there's an exotic dual-sexuality to Merman's singing. Her words burst out with an aggressive, masculine power. Yet she sings of women's feelings in an alto range. Conductor Arturo Toscanini suggested this side of Merman in the 1940s when he described her as a *castrato*, a reference to the castrated men who sang women's roles in opera up to the nineteenth century. The description made its way to Merman, who claimed to have "loved" what she called "the double-sexed angle."

Over the course of a remarkable thirty years, Ethel Merman enjoyed one of the most successful careers in the history of the musical theater. She starred in more than fifteen major Broadway productions, including some of the best-loved musicals of all time—Cole Porter's

Anything Goes (1934), Irving Berlin's *Annie Get Your Gun* (1946) and *Call Me Madam* (1950), Jule Styne and Stephen Sondheim's *Gypsy* (1959), and Jerry Herman's *Hello, Dolly!* (1970). (Although she didn't originate the role of Dolly, two songs—"Love, Look in My Window" and "World, Take Me Back"—were added especially for her when she took over the role.) Her style changed little over the years, although her stature and her influence grew enormously. By the 1940s, composers would be writing songs especially for her brand of sassy pizzazz, including "There's No Business Like Show Business" from *Annie Get Your Gun* and "Everything's Coming Up Roses" from *Gypsy*. Moreover, Merman came to wield so much influence on a production that she could handpick a composer, at one point refusing to allow Stephen Sondheim to write both the music and the lyrics for *Gypsy*, because of what she considered his lack of composing experience at the time.

The special strengths that carried Merman so far in her stage career rarely translated well to other forms of entertainment, however. She was just too powerful a presence for the screen, and the fourteen movies she made over the years were mostly misuses of her talents. Even the Hollywood versions of her biggest Broadway successes were usually cast with "softer" actresses with proven screen appeal, such as Betty Hutton in *Annie Get Your Gun*, Rosalind Russell in *Gypsy*, and Barbra Streisand in *Hello, Dolly!* The only notable exceptions were two films by director Walter Lang, *Call Me Madam* (1953) and *There's No Business Like Show Business* (1954), both of which showcase Merman at her consummately theatrical best, although neither is especially outstanding except for the musical numbers.

In radio and recordings, Merman fared even worse, aside from broadcasts of her stage plays and original-cast recordings. As she once admitted, "I have my own specialty, and it isn't pop records. I have to play a character in a play." In the last decade of her career, however, Merman found a happy medium between the Broadway stage and recording, performing concerts with regional orchestras around the country. The high point of this stage in her career was certainly her 1982 performance at Carnegie Hall, Merman's last major public performance. Unfortunately, her last recording, the 1979 *Ethel Merman Disco Album*, was not so high an achievement. It was an embarrassing exercise in unintentional self-parody.

As tough and cocksure offstage as on, Merman went through four husbands, including actor Ernest Borgnine (to whom she was married for thirty-eight days). "When I work, I work harder than most, and when I play, I play harder than most," Merman boasted, and she lived up to the philosophy with a famous fondness for vodka, nightclubs, and sometimes a good fight. Her tastes were simple. She shopped at Lamston's, a New York five-and-dime store, and loved scouring the junk-jewelry tables at flea markets on weekends. On a certain level she always stayed an office girl from Queens, long after conquering Broadway.

In 1984, a year after surgery to remove a brain tumor, Ethel Merman died in New York, the city she was born in and starred in for thirty of the city's best years.

LEE WILEY

*On everything she does there is a marvelous
texture to her voice, something like running
your hand over a piece of fine Harris
tweed—and they both tickle.*
—DAVE GARROWAY

Like Mildred Bailey, Lee Wiley was partly of American Indian ex-
traction—in Wiley's case, Cherokee. It led to her musician friends'
later nicknaming her "Pocahontas" or "Poco," after the Indian chief's
daughter we all learned about in grade school. And, indeed, there
was always something both regal (as befitting a chief's daughter) yet
naturally simple about the style and manner of tall, slender, fair-haired
Lee. She could well have become one of America's best-known singers
if, like Pocahontas, she hadn't intervened on behalf of a man she loved
and respected. In Wiley's case, both she and the man lost their jobs.

It happened in New York in 1935. At the time Wiley, then only
twenty, had been the featured singer for two years on *Kraft Music
Hall*, one of the nation's top-rated weekly radio shows. The only other
singers who surpassed her at the time in national radio exposure were
Kate Smith and Bing Crosby. The mainstay of the Kraft show was
Paul Whiteman's orchestra, but Wiley had arranged for her numbers
to be conducted (without any on-the-air credit) by Victor Young, with
whom she had formed a close personal and professional relationship
when she first went to Chicago as a teenage job-seeker. Wiley grew
increasingly resentful of Young's not receiving credit for his work. So
when contract-renewal time came, she told NBC she wouldn't sign
unless Young started getting billing, too. NBC balked, saying that
Whiteman was the top star of the show and that his contract did not
permit crediting any other conductor of his orchestra. And so both
Wiley and Young left the show.

Her sense of personal integrity, loyalty, and disdain for some of the
ways (and deceits) of "the Establishment" would always be part of

Wiley's makeup and certainly played a role in her career ups and downs. But constitutionally the strongly independent Wiley could only do things *her* way. So she settled for singing in nightclubs and on radio and making recordings on her own terms. It was not enough to win her the superstardom she seemed headed for before 1935, but it won her a loyal, dedicated following who considered her one of the most gifted if underappreciated singers of the 1930s, 1940s, and 1950s.

Hers was a sweet, sultry-toned alto that critics delighted in referring to as sexy or erotic. There was a softly intimate, one-to-one manner in which Lee sang most songs. It was usually straightforward, mellow, and unforced. There were no big-finale flourishes like Kate Smith's or Judy Garland's for her, nor gratuitous improvisations on either the words or the melodic line. "I don't sing gut-bucket and I don't sing jazz," she once told an interviewer. "I just sing. The only vocal trick I've ever done is putting in the vibrato and taking it out. I don't believe in vocal gimmickry."

"Early on, Lee decided that less is better, and this conviction never changed," said one of her longtime friends, the late singer-pianist and record producer Larry Carr. "Her love of simplicity was evident in everything about her: her chic appearance, the way she wore her hair, and, of course, her singing." She moved with equal ease among the smart set of New York's Park Avenue and the more bohemian types of show-biz gin mills. George and Ira Gershwin's "Sweet and Low-down" could well have been written for her. It wasn't, of course, but Lee sang it often—and better than anyone before or since, with a particularly distinctive mixture of cool elegance and warm succulence. When she sang Ira's lines "Grab a cab and go down to where the band is playing . . ." or "Come on, get in it, you'll love the syncopation the minute they begin it . . ." you knew *she* had lived every word.

Her diction was once described as "an intriguing amalgam of Oklahoma, Park Avenue, and Fifty-second Street"—a reference to her birth state and the two areas of New York she got to know best in her adult years. She was born on October 9, 1915, in Fort Gibson, Oklahoma, which she described as "about as small a town as you can get." As she neared her teen years, she fell under the spell of some Ethel Waters recordings. (Later Lee admitted candidly to Larry Carr, "I loved her and I adapted her style and softened it, made it more ladylike.") Determined to be a singer, she ran away from home at fifteen—first to St. Louis and then to Chicago, where a friend of her mother's helped her get a job singing in a small nightclub. That's where she first met Victor Young, then a rising young composer-arranger-bandleader. She became his protégée and followed him to New York at just about the time Mildred Bailey was making girl singers with dance orchestras fashionable. Lee had little trouble landing jobs on radio and made a few recordings with Leo Reisman's well-known band.

Then tragedy struck. Riding one morning, she was thrown by her horse and she landed in a pile of rocks. When she came to, she couldn't see. "It's a wonder I wasn't permanently blinded from the trash those quack doctors put in my eyes," she later said. "But I never gave up hope. The piano was my salvation. I composed and sang. Finally, I got a better doctor. No operations, just treatment. A year later, my sight slowly started to come back. It was a miracle." (A highly fictionalized account of this episode in Lee's life was given in a 1970s TV drama starring Piper Laurie and titled *Something About Lee Wiley*, but it changed the time period in which it occurred and included many other factual inaccuracies and distortions.)

In 1933 Lee was signed to sing on *The Pond's Cold Cream Hour*, on which Eleanor Roosevelt gave a short weekly chat on current topics. Then came Lee's two years on Whiteman's *Kraft Music Hall*. She also began playing dramatic parts in some of the live radio dramas being broadcast from New York. As her popularity soared, Lee ended many of her nights either singing in clubs or going to see others perform—with longtime friend and record annotator Frank Driggs noting that she was seen in even more nightclubs than she sang in. All of this, particularly her heavy drinking, began to take a toll on Lee's health. Soon after her contretemps over Victor Young's billing on the Kraft show, she was diagnosed as having tuberculosis. She went to Arizona to recuperate, while Young headed to Hollywood, where he soon became one of the most successful of all film composers (*Golden Boy, For Whom the Bell Tolls, The Uninvited, The Quiet Man*, and many others).

A year later Lee felt well enough to return to New York. She was featured prominently on the 1936–37 *Saturday Night Swing Club* with Bunny Berigan as a frequent guest. At about this time, she began hanging around the Famous Door jazz club on West Fifty-second street, which was managed by her brother-in-law Jimmy Doane. She enjoyed the company of jazz musicians and could keep up with even the hardest-drinking of them over the course of an evening. Although she always insisted she was not a jazz singer, she began to work and to record with small, jazz-oriented combos, in contrast to the big bands then enjoying their heyday or the violin-heavy orchestras then standard on radio.

With jazzmen such as Eddie Condon, Joe Bushkin, Max Kaminsky, Fats Waller, Bobby Hackett, Bud Freeman, Pee Wee Russell, and Billy Butterfield (all champs at the bar, too, according to cornetist Dick Sudhalter), Lee recorded a trailblazing series of classic-pop composer albums—first Gershwin, then Rodgers and Hart, Cole Porter, and Harold Arlen. They were the first albums by a major singer spotlighting the work of individual popular-music composers—and were to be followed in later years by similar albums by Ella Fitzgerald, Bobby Short, and others. As trumpeter Max Kaminsky wrote in his autobiography, *My Life in Jazz*, "The Lee Wiley albums were years ahead of their time. Lee set the style for years to come . . . and later everyone else copied her."

The idea for the albums had come from John DeVries, a young advertising artist and music buff who much admired Wiley and resented the fact that she was being ignored by the all-powerful Big Three of the recording business (Victor, Columbia, and Decca). DeVries and Lee agreed that songwriters such as Gershwin, Porter, Arlen, and Rodgers were America's pop parallel to the concert world's Beethoven and Brahms and that the best of their songs deserved to be compiled in recorded collections by serious pop artists just as the works of classical artists were. DeVries arranged for small, independent labels to make the series and got most of the musicians to work for scale. Fats Waller took part in the Gershwin sessions but had to camouflage his appearance under the name Maurice because of his contract with Victor's Bluebird label.

Many of the arrangements were written by another Wiley admirer, Paul Weston, who was then working for Tommy Dorsey's orchestra under his original name, Paul Wetstein, and who would soon go on to fame as a top arranger-conductor. Although the instrumental backing was from men who were jazz greats in their own right, the songs were not "jazzed up" with long, improvisatory turns. There is a loose and easy-swinging feel to most of the arrangements, but Lee sings each song (including all the rarely heard verses) essentially straight— with exceptional insight into the mood of each song and the meaning of the lyrics, something one rarely got on the bland, assembly-line, beat-conscious "vocal refrains" then prevalent on most dance-band recordings.

During World War II Lee took part in weekly concerts with Eddie Condon's group in New York that were broadcast as a radio series and also transcribed for rebroadcast by the Armed Forces Radio Network. Many of those transcription discs have survived and are still available through collectors' clubs or small "pirate" record labels, though their technical quality is variable. Yet, like the composer series, they show Lee at her prime—singing the way she wanted to sing with musicians whom she liked and who liked her.

In 1944 Lee married jazz pianist Jess Stacy. When the war ended, Stacy organized a band and led it on tours throughout the country, with Lee as featured vocalist. But she hated the wear and tear of the road and quit after a year. Her marriage to Stacy lasted only a few more years. She remarried in 1966, this time to a well-to-do, retired businessman, Nat Tischenkel. She continued to perform and record only occasionally, and finally retired completely. As she put it not long before her death on December 11, 1975, "I always sang the way I wanted to sing. If I didn't like something, I just wouldn't do it. I got on a plane and went to relax in the sun."

"Lee was a complex person," said Larry Carr, "willfully indifferent toward the commercial aspects of music. She could be very snobbish with inept musicians and singers, and supportive and protective of those she liked and admired." Frank Driggs has put it even more bluntly: "The world of show business demands one be in certain places with certain people at certain times. Lee Wiley did this up to a point and then said unprintable things. . . . There were rules to be followed, and Lee Wiley, a free spirit if ever there lived one, was not all that particular about living by any set of rules."

But she made an indelible impact on classic pop anyway—by being the first to take seriously the best songs of the individual composers and lyricists of classic pop and showing how they could be turned into musical art.

BILLIE HOLIDAY

She was the angel of darkness. Billie sang
with so much beauty and so much pain.
—PEGGY LEE

The first psychological singer, Billie Holiday introduced the emotional
interior to American song. When she sang, the words and the music
were suddenly subordinated to the internal emotions her singing
seemed to suggest. Listen to her interpretation of a song such as
"Solitude," and you don't necessarily admire her range or commend
her elocution. You don't even marvel at the melody or the lyrics. You
wonder, *What was this woman going through?*

Billie Holiday's art was an inner one. She sang from the outside in,
using a song to draw the individual listener into her own personal
world, rather than trying to reach out and relate to her audience. She
was, then, an artist in the classic modern sense—a singing sister to
Marlon Brando, Miles Davis, and Thomas Pynchon, before them all.

Since her, Billie Holiday's style has been evident in every vocalist
of emotional intensity, from Judy Garland to Dinah Washington to
Peggy Lee. Holiday has been a major influence on pop singers, then,
although she herself defies categorization. Her creative sensibilities
are certainly rooted in jazz, yet she never used her voice as a strictly
improvisational instrument like other pure jazz singers such as Sarah
Vaughan and Anita O'Day. Holiday made most of her performances
and recordings with jazz instrumentation, yet she also recorded with
pop orchestras. Her repertoire was heavily oriented toward popular
songs, yet she was also comfortable with hard-core jazz and blues
material. Once again, Billie Holiday was definitely *herself*.

More than that of many other professional singers, Holiday's work
can be understood only in the context of her personal life, and even
there biographers have had great difficulty verifying the facts. Named

Eleanora Fagan when she was born in Philadelphia on April 7, 1915, Holiday was the illegitimate daughter of nineteen-year-old Sadie Fagan and seventeen-year-old Clarence Holiday. From her mother, who was the granddaughter of an Irish plantation owner and one of his African-American slaves, Holiday inherited her soft features. And through her father, a black guitarist who joined Fletcher Henderson's band in the 1920s, she was exposed to music as a young child.

She heard still more music on the radio in the red-light district where she started working as a maid at age six. As she cleaned up the prostitutes' rooms, the early "hot" jazz of Louis Armstrong and the bedrock blues of Bessie Smith left her with a deep impression, she later recalled.

After attending Baltimore's segregated schools for a few years, she moved to New York with her mother in 1928. However, her mother worked intermittently at best, and the teenager soon found herself in the line of work she had cleaned up after as a girl.

As she detailed in an interview in the 1950s, Holiday graduated from prostitute to professional singer with "more desperation than desire." She was walking through Harlem, she explained, when she saw a way out of the streets—a help-wanted sign for a dancing job at Jerry Preston's Log Cabin nightclub caught her eye. Holiday auditioned, despite the fact that she had never danced. She was turned down but was asked if she knew how to sing, instead. She gave that a shot, despite the fact that she had never sung, either. And she was hired for the very next night.

She took the name Billie Holiday, after her father and one of her favorite actresses, Billie Dove. At the Log Cabin, however, the waitresses soon pinned another name on her: "Lady." The term was meant sarcastically, to insult Holiday for her refusal to pick up tips with her labia, as other singers in the club had done. (Several years later, saxophonist Lester Young would turn the meaning of the name around by calling Holiday "Lady Day" with deep respect.)

It was at the Log Cabin that record producer John Hammond discovered Holiday, recommending her to Benny Goodman, who was then still an aspiring young bandleader. They recorded together in 1933, accompanied by Jack Teagarden, Gene Krupa, and Joe Sullivan. That first record, "Your Mother's Son-in-Law," betrayed a nervous young Billie Holiday whose stilted performance sounded more like Ethel Waters than her idol Bessie Smith.

Nevertheless, within two years Holiday would record a series of sides with Teddy Wilson and his band that would take the singer out

AL JOLSON

ETHEL WATERS

LOUIS ARMSTRONG

HELEN MORGAN

RUDY VALLEE

RUTH ETTING

MILDRED BAILEY
(Photograph courtesy of Columbia Records)

BING CROSBY

KATE SMITH

RUSS COLUMBO

LEE WILEY   ETHEL MERMAN

CONNEE BOSWELL   BILLIE HOLIDAY

FRED ASTAIRE

SHIRLEY ROSS

ELLA FITZGERALD

MABEL MERCER

of Harlem obscurity and into the midst of the mainstream music scene. In these records, including "I Wished On the Moon," "If You Were Mine," and "Miss Brown to You," Billie Holiday can be heard at the peak of her physical abilities. Her then-silky alto voice had a girlish innocence and limber vitality, although it lacked some of the tension and depth of her later singing.

After a stint with the Count Basie band in 1937 and another with Artie Shaw the following year, Holiday fully came into her own as a solo performer in a year-long engagement at Manhattan's Café Society nightclub. Here she fully developed the style she would become internationally famous for—the corsage of gardenias clipped in her hair, the head cocked confidently to the side, the fingers snapping absently a touch behind the beat. And her voice—as her recordings of the late 1930s show, Holiday still had her youthful flexibility, but her voice had gained a subtle inner tension and fragility. She had developed that almost eerie edge that makes her best work so hypnotic.

As she explained in an interview: "I do not got a legit voice, but I'm not going to change. I'm going to sing my way. You just feel it, and when you sing it other people can feel something, too. Without feeling, whatever you do amounts to nothing."

Her repertoire was almost entirely classic-pop ballads—"The Man I Love," "Summertime," "Embraceable You," "Body and Soul"—despite the title of both her autobiography and the Hollywood movie based on it, *Lady Sings the Blues*. In addition, she was now performing some original songs, including the bittersweet "God Bless the Child" and the impassioned, dramatic "Strange Fruit," written about a lynching.

Getting good, regular money and attention from both her peers and the public, Billie Holiday luxuriated in her success. It had come hardwon. And she enjoyed it just as hard—perhaps too hard. She acquired a taste for narcotics, including heroin, and the taste soon developed into a habit. By the mid-1940s, Holiday's heavy drug use was taking a toll on her singing, as most of her recordings from the period show. Her voice was becoming progressively scratchy and weak; it had lost much of its elasticity and its energy. And her personal life was becoming shattered at the same time: She scuffled through two brief marriages in succession, in addition to several rough-and-tumble unofficial unions.

Holiday trouped through her first and last feature movie, *New Orleans*, in 1946. But shortly after its release, in the culmination of a series of minor run-ins with the law over her narcotics use, she was arrested and convicted of a serious narcotics charge in 1947. She was sentenced to the Federal Women's Reformatory in Alderson, West Virginia and served a one-year term.

Ten days after her release in 1948, she immediately returned to work, performing a celebrated midnight concert in New York's Carnegie Hall. Billie Holiday was back. But her spirit was not. Continuing her use of hard narcotics through the 1950s, Holiday steadily deteriorated into a haggard shadow-image of herself. By her early forties, she sometimes looked nearly twenty years older. Sadder still, perhaps, her voice was stripped to its rawest, barest elements. She could still evoke emotion by concentrating on the lyrical content of a song, but her sense of pitch had become poor, and she often seemed to emphasize her faults by recording at excruciatingly slow tempos and resorting frequently to the same stylized mannerisms.

At age forty-four, Billie Holiday was admitted to Metropolitan Hospital in New York for congestion of the lungs. While she was asleep, a nurse said she had seen heroin powder on her nose and a tinfoil package of the drug in her fist. The patient was arrested in her bed, and the police confiscated her belongings, which included a radio, some comic books, and a box of chocolates. The drug charges were dropped when Billie Holiday died in the hospital on July 17, 1959.

At the time she had seventy cents in the bank. But $750 in $50 bills were found Scotch-taped to one of her legs. That was all Billie Holiday owned, but it isn't all she left. There will always be those few dozen songs recorded in the 1930s that showed every other vocal artist how to sing from the outside in.

SHIRLEY ROSS

Her voice was all warmth, heart, and sophistication,
and she made every song she sang the definitive version.
—composer-singer-pianist ARTHUR SIEGEL

Of all the singers who came up through Hollywood's movies in the
1930s, Shirley Ross had the creamiest, warmest, most instinctively lilting alto of them all. Alice Faye's may have been more darkly provoc-
ative, Frances Langford's more sweetly soothing, Constance Moore's
more brightly genial, Dorothy Lamour's more smokily sultry, or Wini
Shaw's more foxily sensual. But Ross's voice had a natural loveliness
and musicality like no other. And she had few equals among women
singers in the mid- to late 1930s in applying the intimate, conversational style of classic pop to roles in movie musicals. That she never
became either a major film star or a major recording artist is a regret-
table testament to the vagaries and inconsistencies of show business.

Ross is best remembered today as the other half of the duet with
Bob Hope that introduced Leo Robin and Ralph Rainger's Oscar-
winning "Thanks for the Memory" in *The Big Broadcast of 1938*—
that is, of course, among those who remember that it was originally
a duet and not just Hope's broadcast theme song (as it later became).
But 1938 was the year that major musicals died at most of the Hollywood studios—to come to life again only after the United States
entered World War II and musical escapist fare provided welcome
breaks from wartime work and duties. By then Ross had forsaken
Hollywood for Broadway, where leads in two consecutive flops didn't
make Hollywood rush to ask her back. Her own temperamental reputation also played a part in doors' being closed to her.

Ironically, Ross was never sure she wanted to be a musical star or
even a singer. Like Ginger Rogers, who at about the same time was
spurning her Astaire partnership for more dramatic movie roles, Ross

became convinced that popular-music performers would never rank as high as either straight dramatic or classical-music performers. And she had ambitions in both of those other areas. In fact, her first ambition was to become a concert pianist. While still in high school, after moving to the Los Angeles area from Omaha, Nebraska (where she was born on January 7, 1913), she gave ten piano recitals in the Los Angeles area under her real name, Bernice Gault. She also started singing in high-school theatricals and discovered that it was easier to earn money for college by singing with dance bands around town than giving piano recitals. But one engagement, as relief singer with Phil Harris's orchestra at the fashionable Cocoanut Grove, ended abruptly when the regular vocalist heard her sing and, recognizing Ross as a serious threat, saw to it that she got none of the good numbers. Ross quit in a huff.

Two years and many other interim jobs later, Ross dropped out of UCLA to join Gus Arnheim's dance band at the Beverly Wilshire Hotel as both pianist and singer. Among the room's frequent patrons were Richard Rodgers and Lorenz Hart, who had been signed by MGM and were writing the score for the projected *Hollywood Revue of 1933*. Rodgers in particular was taken with Ross's voice and asked her one night to sing some of the songs for the movie at a studio audition the next morning. She jumped at the chance. The audition went so well that Rodgers arranged a screen test for her, which, in turn, won her a part singing in a musical short with Ted Fio Rito's orchestra. She also won a small role in *Hollywood Revue of 1933*, whose production problems eventually caused most of Rodgers and Hart's score to be dropped, along with many planned sketches, before it was retitled and released in 1934 as *Hollywood Party*.

One of the songs Rodgers had asked Ross to audition was titled "Prayer," the plaintive plea of a star-struck shopgirl for divine intervention to help her become a movie star. When the song was dropped from *Hollywood Party*, Hart wrote a new set of lyrics for it to comply with a request from MGM for a song that was needed for a Harlem nightclub scene in the Clark Gable–William Powell–Myrna Loy crime thriller *Manhattan Melodrama*. Ross was given the singer's role and, wearing black body makeup and a terrible-looking black wig, sang the torchy new lyrics, "The Bad in Every Man," in a scene that is partly covered by dialogue between Loy and Powell. When MGM's music publisher refused to publish the song because he felt the lyrics weren't commercial enough, Hart went home and wrote yet another new set of lyrics (actually the fourth for the same Rodgers melody, counting one *before* "Prayer") and gave it to Ross to introduce on a radio show. In its new guise as "Blue Moon," the song ended up as one of the nation's Top Ten hits for five months in 1934. "Blue Moon" would be the only Rodgers and Hart song hit not to come from either a Broadway show or a Hollywood movie. It would also be the kind of song that perfectly showed off Ross's instinctive feeling for the long lyrical line of ballads, her caressing way with each word of the lyrics, and her unique evenness of tone. Strangely, she never made a commercial recording of "Blue Moon" (although broadcast transcriptions exist).

After small parts in *The Merry Widow* and *San Francisco*, Ross's MGM career seemed to be going nowhere until she landed the lead in a West Coast production of Cole Porter's *Anything Goes*—playing the part Ethel Merman had in the original Broadway production the previous year. The production (in which she costarred with singer-dancer George Murphy, who later became a U.S. senator from California) fared well in Los Angeles but closed after a short run in San Francisco. Ross's notices, however, were enough for Paramount to arrange to borrow her from MGM for a leading role in *The Big Broadcast of 1937*. Paramount was so pleased with Ross's performance and her singing of the movie's top ballad, Robin and Rainger's "I'm Talking Through My Heart," that when MGM dropped her option midway through the picture's shooting, Paramount promptly signed her to a contract. In quick succession she was given leading roles in *Blossoms on Broadway* (one of Frank Loesser's first attempts at a pop opera) and *Hideaway Girl* (a jewel-robbery melodrama with incidental songs that teamed Ross with Martha Raye).

Then came the big break: a costarring role with Bing Crosby in *Waikiki Wedding*, which turned out to be one of the crooner's most popular '30s musicals. Crosby's and Ross's voices blended beautifully for its Robin and Rainger score, especially on the dreamy "Blue Hawaii," which went on to six weeks on *Your Hit Parade*. The on-screen rapport between Crosby and Ross also seemed harmonious enough to suggest a reteaming, but Crosby had his eye on other Paramount actresses for his next pictures. Paramount promptly cast Ross in *This Way Please*, which would mark the return to a major Paramount musical of Buddy Rogers (the star of many early Paramount musicals) after a five-year absence. But three days into the picture's shooting, Ross stormed off the set in a fit of temperament, accusing comic actress Mary Livingstone (playing her first major movie role without husband Jack Benny) of deliberately undercutting her scenes. Ross was replaced by Betty Grable, then a Paramount contract player. Even though *This Way Please* won only lukewarm notices on its release (and didn't do much for Grable's career—or Livingstone's or Rogers', for that matter), the fallout from Ross's walkout lingered.

The studio now considered her "difficult" and gave her no new major assignments until *The Big Broadcast of 1938*, starring W. C. Fields. Even then she was listed in the credits after Martha Raye (over whom she had received top billing in two earlier pictures), but before Bob Hope (in his first Paramount feature). When the movie was released, it was Ross and Hope who got the best notices. Their duet over cocktails, "Thanks for the Memory," set a new standard for sophisticated narrative songs that conveyed intimate romantic feelings with a light but warm touch. Although the song became identified exclusively with Hope in later years, after he amended its lyrics many times as his radio theme song, its original success in *The Big Broadcast of 1938* is due as much to Ross's exceptionally touching, insightful singing of its lyrics as to Hope's own debonair yet poignant performance.

Paramount, which (like most other studios) was phasing out big-budgeted musicals in the face of a slump in industry profits, quickly reteamed Hope and Ross in a low-budget romantic comedy about young marrieds and titled it (surprise?) *Thanks for the Memory*. Frank Loesser and Hoagy Carmichael wrote them another duet, "Two Sleepy People," which quickly went on to twelve weeks on *Your Hit Parade*. But the picture fared only moderately well at the box office. A third teaming, for 1939's *Some Like It Hot* (retitled *Rhythm Romance* for TV release so as not to confuse it with the later Marilyn Monroe film of the same title), did even less well, despite a good score by Loesser, Carmichael, and Burton Lane (including still another twelve-weeker on *Your Hit Parade*, "The Lady's in Love with You"). With Paramount showing less and less interest in making musicals with anybody, Ross then finished out her contract with secondary, "other woman" roles in two tightly budgeted comedies with incidental songs, *Paris Honeymoon*, with Bing Crosby and Hungarian import Franciska Gaal, and *Café Society*, with Madeleine Carroll and Fred MacMurray. Interestingly, more than one reviewer commented that Crosby and MacMurray had both chosen the wrong character for the final fade-out kiss in each film—so much more genuine did Ross come across than the top-billed ladies.

With her Hollywood career losing momentum, Ross and her husband, actors' agent Ken Dolan (whom she had married in 1938), headed for Broadway. Rodgers and Hart grabbed her quickly for the lead in their new musical, *Higher and Higher*. Ross's introduction of such fine Rodgers and Hart ballads as "It Never Entered My Mind," "Nothing but You," and "(You Are) From Another World" won critical raves. But the show itself got mixed notices and closed after so-so attendance plagued a modest run of 104 performances. She was then signed for the Broadway-bound *Allah Be Praised*, with dour-faced movie comedian Ned Sparks, but left the show before it reached New York—where it promptly flopped. With nothing else coming her way, Ross went into a psychological slump. She told one interviewer (for the *New York World-Telegram*), "I have a kind of sweet personality that goes over in the movies, but I don't have what might be called a stylized stage personality at all." Yet she still felt she *could* be a good straight actress and hoped to prove so. But the only movie roles that came her way in the 1940s were in low-budget "B" comedies (such as *Kisses for Breakfast* at Warner Bros. and *Sailors on Leave* at Republic). Bob Hope invited her to be a guest on some of his radio shows, and she also joined him for some of his servicemen's shows throughout World War II. Then, after another Republic quickie, *A Song for Miss Julie* in 1945, she decided to give up movies altogether and, except for occasional radio appearances in which she both sang and played piano, to concentrate on raising her two young sons.

In 1950 Frank Loesser, an ardent admirer since their days of working together at Paramount, offered her the leading role of missionary Sarah Brown in his Broadway-bound production of *Guys and Dolls* (which went on to become a smash hit). "I knew it was my last real chance," she later told a UPI interviewer, "because I was no longer a kid." But she turned down the role due to the terminal illness of her husband. He died the following year. She later married California bank executive Eddie Blum, with whom she had a daughter, and gave up any further thoughts of her career—particularly after rock 'n' roll seemed to topple from the best-seller charts the kind of popular music she had specialized in.

Shirley Ross died in 1975 at age sixty-two in a Menlo Park, California, convalescent home after a long illness. Like Mildred Bailey, she never achieved the kind of stardom her exceptional musical talents seemed to ordain for her. But unlike Bailey, whose final years were marked by bitterness over her career failures and frustrations, Ross—at least publicly—tempered her disappointments and regrets with other satisfactions. As she told the UPI interviewer in 1959, "When I look at my children, I don't regret for a minute quitting show business to devote myself to them."

ELLA FITZGERALD

Man, woman, or child, Ella's the greatest.
—BING CROSBY

Sometimes it's sex appeal. Sometimes personality. Or special material or the right medium or timing. All sorts of factors figure in making a singer a star, beyond the actual art of singing. Then again, there's the story of Ella Fitzgerald.

Chunky and plain-featured, scarcely charismatic, she was never a movie idol, a TV star, or some sort of novelty or creature of a certain time and place. Ella Fitzgerald became an enduring, world-famous figure almost entirely on the basis of her singing. To do this in the age of instant and disposable celebrities, Ella Fitzgerald had to do *some* singing.

She did, and she received just about every musical honor to make it official, including twelve Grammies, the Kennedy Center Award, and seven honorary degrees from such universities as Yale and Dartmouth. Practically every singer from Sinatra to Madonna has lauded her as one of the masters of her art. And as her career entered its seventh decade in the 1990s, audiences around the world were confirming her stature with ten-minute standing ovations before she sang a note.

Her singing has always been unparalleled in both technique and style. Blessed with pinpoint pitch and a 2½-octave range, Ella Fitzgerald can hit any note an alto saxophone can. But one of her gifts is the way she will accent a lyric by subtly shading the pitch of a note. Her tone is natural and clear, with a girlish glisten, and it scarcely changes as Fitzgerald shifts from her middle register to falsetto; this, in particular, is the envy of other vocalists.

Like the best classic-pop songs, Ella Fitzgerald's singing is unpretentious and smart. She can do anything she wants with her voice, but she isn't a show-off; what she wants to do is always tasteful, no matter how complex. Her singing is often sentimental but rarely schmaltzy, and sometimes fun but almost never silly. Because of her evident sincerity and taste as well as the sheer prettiness and fun of her singing, Ella Fitzgerald has endeared herself to an exceptionally broad range of music lovers, including young listeners of the rock generation, who have tended to reject jazz vocalists for their technical detachment and Broadway singers for their razzmatazz.

She has come to be called "The First Lady of American Song," and the title hints at the heart of Ella Fitzgerald's legacy (even if it makes you wonder who "The President of American Song" is). Ella Fitzgerald's singing style is a combination of most of the major American forms of popular music developed in the twentieth century—jazz, classic pop, and blues (and, as an extension, rock 'n' roll). But she has done more than merely sing different songs in different styles; she has combined the most accessible elements of all three traditions in the form of one expressively diverse sound that's entirely hers and purely American. As she put it in an interview in the 1950s, "I steal from everything I ever heard. Even when I won the amateur contest, I was stealing from Connee Boswell."

The amateur contest at issue was Ella Fitzgerald's first public appearance as a performer, a weekly event at the Apollo Theater in Harlem that the sixteen-year-old entered in 1934. Her only prior musical experience had been songtime at New York's Riverdale Orphanage, where Fitzgerald was raised. But a presumably impressive impersonation of Connee Boswell singing "Judy" won her the $25 top prize at the Apollo—and the attention of at least one member of the audience, Chick Webb.

Within days, Webb signed Fitzgerald to his band, and she put her on-and-off plans to become a doctor on permanent "off." An immensely popular and respected bandleader in the 1930s, Webb reveled in being called the King of Swing, and went so far as to wear a crown onstage. He had a light touch that matched Fitzgerald's upbeat personality and singing style. Under his guidance she not only developed as a professional vocalist but also began cowriting songs with Webb. One, the novelty number "A-Tisket A-Tasket," became Webb's biggest hit in 1938 and made Ella Fitzgerald nationally known at age twenty (as well as the youngest member of ASCAP at the time).

Chick Webb clearly made a powerful impression on the youthfully impressionable singer, who has said, "He gave me the only advice

I've ever needed. 'Honey,' he told me, 'in this business you've always got to get there the firstest with the mostest and the newest.' "

Shortly after Webb died suddenly in 1939, Fitzgerald put her mentor's counsel to use. After a brief stint as the nominal leader of Webb's band, she launched a solo singing career that would get her to a few musical places firstest and mostest. Fitzgerald would never again become associated with a single band but would perform and record on occasion with Count Basie, Duke Ellington, and other orchestras.

Among Fitzgerald's "firstests," the best-known is probably her marriage of scat singing and bebop in the mid-1940s. Like Louis Armstrong and other jazz vocalists, including Leo Watson of the Spirits of Rhythm, Ella Fitzgerald had scatted, or improvised vocally, since her earliest days with the Chick Webb band. "When the boys would jam, I felt left out," she once explained in an interview. "So I just joined in, using my voice as an instrument." But no singer had dared try scatting in the extremely demanding, complex bebop style until Fitzgerald recorded, "How High the Moon" and "Oh, Lady Be Good," both released in 1947. To this day, the recordings are breathtaking for the harmonic sophistication and imagination of Fitzgerald's improvisations; at the same time, they're fun and accessible. This fact is one of the keys to Ella Fitzgerald's unique art: She has always used jazz to illuminate her pop work, but never to overwhelm it.

"A lot of singers think all they have to do is exercise their tonsils to get ahead," she once commented. "They refuse to look for new ideas and new outlets, so they fall by the wayside."

Over the years, Fitzgerald's interest in new ideas has brought her all over the musical map for brief excursions. Bucking her advisers' warnings, she was one of the first Americans to record calypso material, and she scored a big hit with her "Stone Cold Dead in the Market," a duet with Louis Jordan. More daringly, she enjoyed experimenting with pop-rock material in the 1960s, and said she was "a big fan" of the Beatles, the Supremes, and Marvin Gaye, in particular. In fact, in 1969 Fitzgerald recorded an entire album of rock-oriented material, including Smokey Robinson's "Ooh Baby Baby," the Temptations' "Get Ready," and George Harrison's "Savoy Truffle."

Much of this kind of musical toe-dipping was sheer playfulness, of course. As everyone who's seen Fitzgerald in concert knows, she has a fondness for teasing and surprising her audience. She's been known to take requests for songs she doesn't know at all, then proceed to improvise a whole new set of lyrics on the spot. In the 1950s she'd often pull out a harmonica and solo for a few bars. Sometimes she'll sing messages to members of the audience, working warnings to stop taking pictures or put out a cigarette into a song. In a 1990 performance at New York's Radio City Music Hall, she even did a little *rap*, to the audience's delight.

The heart of Ella Fitzgerald's work has always been classic pop, of course. Indeed, in her landmark series of *Songbook* albums recorded in the late 1950s and early 1960s, she created what many consider to be the definitive musical reference source to the work of the great composers and lyricists of the genre. In eight sets of recordings, Fitzgerald sang the work of Harold Arlen, Irving Berlin, Duke Ellington, George and Ira Gershwin, Jerome Kern, Johnny Mercer, Cole Porter, and Rodgers and Hart. As Ira Gershwin said upon hearing the collection of his songs, "I never knew how good our songs were until I heard Ella Fitzgerald sing them." Some of the *Songbooks* are better matches of composer and singer than others, however, with the Gershwin and Arlen among the strongest, and the Porter the only effort that sounds somewhat stiff. (In addition, Fitzgerald recorded another album of all Gershwin material, *Ella Sings Gershwin*, with solo piano accompaniment rather than the full orchestral arrangements of the *Songbooks*.)

Beyond her recording and concert career, Ella Fitzgerald has appeared in two movies, Abbott and Costello's *Ride 'Em Cowboy* (1942), in which she sang "A-Tisket A-Tasket," and a Jack Webb drama about early jazz, *Pete Kelly's Blues* (1955), in which she acted a little. In both films, as in her work in the recording studio and onstage, Fitzgerald stood out through her singing.

Privately, Ella Fitzgerald has long led a quiet though not quite reclusive life centered on her family. She's a grandmother through her one child, a son by jazz bassist Ray Brown, whom Fitzgerald divorced many years ago. (One earlier marriage, to Bennie Kornegay, was annulled after two years.) She has lived in suburban Los Angeles since the 1950s, when she moved from Queens, New York, for gentler weather. Ella Fitzgerald is a baseball fan.

Since the 1970s, when she developed cataracts, Fitzgerald has suffered a series of setbacks to her health. After a performance in 1986 she collapsed from congestive heart failure and had immediate open-heart surgery. In subsequent years, however, she has continued performing with some regularity—and with so much skill that she seems to defy physical laws.

Of course, Ella Fitzgerald will always be The First Lady of American Song, until she's promoted to President.

MABEL MERCER

Everything I know, I learned from Mabel Mercer.
—*FRANK SINATRA*

The Grand Lady of the Left Brain, Mabel Mercer brought an incomparable grandeur to the thinking side of classic pop. While Crosby left toes tapping and Garland left hearts swelling, Mercer left minds reeling over the *meaning* of the music. After all, one of the hallmarks of classic pop is that the best work of the great Tin Pan Alley writers *says something*, and often something uniquely sophisticated, intimate, or complex. And no singer could say it more masterfully than Mabel Mercer.

"Say" is the accurate word, too. Over the latter portion of her long career, when Mabel Mercer was best known and made most of her recordings, she abandoned conventional pop singing in favor of a form of vocalizing that verged on dramatic recitation. Her approach, called *parlando* in "musicese," is a type of talk-singing that places more emphasis on the words than on the music of a song. She would honor the underlying feeling of the melody, especially its rhythm and "line." But she scarcely suggested the notes on the sheet music, through the subtlest of shifts in her throaty, basso-profundo voice.

The words meant everything to Mercer, and that's why she could make them mean so much to her audience. "People say, 'Why, she can't sing for toffee.' I know that—I'm telling a story," she explained in a 1975 interview. As much an actress as a singer, Mercer seemed to feel every word she sang. In fact, when she was at her best, the words flowed almost spontaneously, as if they had never been written by Cole Porter or Noel Coward. Because of this rare credibility, hearing Mabel Mercer sing a song could be like hearing it for the first time. A familiar old phrase—"Can't you see I'm no good without you"—seems fresh and heartfelt. And a mouthful—"Moons and Junes and angel's hair and ice-cream castles in the air"—sounds wry and knowing in Mercer's hands.

Even so, there's a formality and a precision to Mercer's diction that can be off-putting to some listeners. Her enunciation is so refined that Mercer records have been used in diction classes at the University of California. With full, rounded vowel tones and rolling *r*'s that would humble Henry Higgins, Mercer's style sometimes seems at odds with the vernacular tone of most classic pop tunes.

Of course, classic pop is an essentially American form, and Mercer was British, born in Staffordshire, England, in 1900. From her mother, a white music-hall dancer, Mabel inherited her blue eyes, her knack for dancing, and her *veddy* proper British manner. From her father, a black musician, Mabel got her strong, handsome features and her natural musical ability. She scarcely knew her parents, though; she was raised by a maternal aunt who was also a singer, sometimes stage-named Mademoiselle DuRoche. (Some biographical sketches of Mercer state that her father died when she was an infant, or that she never met him. Both claims are false, she revealed late in life.)

A performer from early childhood, Mercer soon joined the family music-hall troupe—a "Gypsy" song-and-dance act called "The Five Romanys." Notably darker than her fellow Romanys, Mabel had to suffer some riding by both her audience and her cousins, who once tried to scrub her skin white under the tap, she recalled years later. Yet she became the best-known member of the family act by her teens, and was ready—and happy—to leave it.

Josephine Baker is credited with having discovered Mercer and put her in her first nightclub program. Dancing and singing in an elegant mezzo-soprano voice, Mercer played clubs and theater in London, and at one point appeared in a production of *Show Boat* with Paul Robeson at the Drury Lane Theatre. But it was after her move to Paris and Bricktop's renowned *boîte de nuit* that Mabel Mercer established herself as a singer, mingling and maturing among the original café society on Rue Pigalle in the early 1930s.

After seven straight years at Bricktop's, Mercer moved to the United States shortly before the war. She was free to relocate to the United States and work there indefinitely, through a marriage of convenience to a friend, musician Kelsey Pharr. She found the next-closest thing to Bricktop's—the Fifty-second Street club circuit in New York City—and soon settled into the life-style she would maintain, virtually unchanged, for the last thirty years of her life.

Although she recorded with increasingly frequency and some success, Mercer established her reputation mainly as a nightclub performer of high regard and enormous influence. At the height of her art, singing with full voice in a strong contralto, Mercer built an impassioned following as the resident attraction of such Fifty-second Street clubs as Tony's (where she played for seven years, until the building was torn down in 1947) and the Byline Room. Many of her biggest fans were fellow musicians, from jazz players working on the street to fellow singers such as Billie Holiday, Nat "King" Cole, and Frank Sinatra, who said watching Mercer at Tony's was the single greatest influence on his treatment of a lyric.

In addition to impeccable technique, Mercer brought exquisite taste to both her nightclub performances and recordings over the years. She sought out little-known songs from the most sophisticated composers and lyricists—Noel Coward's "Matelot" and Alec Wilder's "While We're Young," as well as standards by her favorites Cole Porter, Rodgers and Hart, and Johnny Mercer. Late in her career she leaned toward Sondheim and experimented with young writers outside of classic pop, such as Joni Mitchell.

As time rescinded the gift of Mercer's youthful vocal range, she adapted with a growing mastery of more subtle arts. She learned a new music—the music of meaning, a music not of sound but of spirit. She was a virtuoso of phrasing, and she could make the lyrics "sing" with nothing more than an unexpected pause, an arc of an eyebrow, or a purl of her dancer's hand.

Privately, the Mabel Mercer known by her fellow musicians and friends in rural upstate New York, where she lived part-time, had little in common with the public figure seen by her city cabaret audiences. "Behind the elegant, regal persona her audiences saw, Mabel was a lively, earthy woman with a wonderful sense of humor," her longtime accompanist Buddy Barnes told us. "She was always really a girl from the North Country, just as she had been born."

Dead at eighty-three in 1983, Mabel Mercer left the doubly rich legacy of her music as well as its deep influence on several generations of singers, from Sinatra to Peggy Lee, Tony Bennett, Lena Horne, Nat "King" Cole, Margaret Whiting, and Eileen Farrell. Mercer wasn't the only or the first singer to emphasize the lyrical content of a song, by any means. But simply because phrasing was her very lifeblood as a performer—it was all she had, for so many years—she stands as the enduring icon of the musical word.

NOT TO BE FORGOTTEN

Many other fine singers of classic pop also rose to various levels of fame and success between the two world wars. Here are miniprofiles of a few who, while perhaps not as innovative or as outstanding overall as the ones on the preceding pages, were still uncommonly distinctive and definitely memorable.

Dick Powell

Dick Powell was always frankly modest about his singing talents—and, in fact, never thought of himself as a major singer even though he introduced dozens of song hits in quite a few of the most popular movie musicals of the 1930s. He was a tenor at a time when the popular trend was to crooner baritones. But he was a tenor with a difference. Unlike the bleating tenors of Broadway revues and operettas up to the early '30s, Powell sang in a lightly casual, unaffected, laid-back manner, with an almost self-mocking twinkle in both his voice and his eyes. And his clean-cut, curly-haired good looks were as easy on the eyes as his bright, easygoing sound was on the ears. As songwriter Johnny Mercer once noted, "He was not one of those tenors who put an *h* in everything, like 'I love you in the same old w*h*ay.' "

Powell started out in his home state of Arkansas (where he was born in 1904) playing cornet in local bands, "fooling around," as he once put it, "with practically every instrument in the band." He cut his first records as a singer with the Charlie Davis orchestra in Indianapolis in 1928, and then had his own orchestra for a brief spell before a Warner Bros. talent agent brought him to Hollywood for a screen test.

In his first role, a meaty supporting one in 1932's *Blessed Event*, he played a nasty-streaked radio crooner. But Warner Bros. quickly changed his image to that of a buoyant show-biz hopeful with *42nd Street*, which became one of 1933's smash hits (and established a new, extravagant, Busby Berkeley style of movie musicals). From then on it was vacuous, goody-goody singing juveniles (which Powell hated playing) in *Footlight Parade, Dames, Broadway Gondolier*, and a dozen others, including Berkeley's popular *Gold Diggers* series (*1933, 1935*, and *1937*). "They were all the same pictures," Powell once said; "I just wore different clothes." He also usually had the same leading lady, Ruby Keeler, although he occasionally teamed with his second wife, Joan Blondell, too. Among the songs he sang in these films that became standards were "42nd Street," "You're Getting to Be a Habit with Me," "I Only Have Eyes for You," "Lulu's Back in Town," "I'll String Along with You," and "The Lullaby of Broadway."

When musicals went into decline in the late '30s, Powell let it be known he wasn't the least unhappy about it and made an easy transition into straight comedies (*Christmas in July, Model Wife*, and others). Then in 1945 he turned the tables altogether and scored a surprise hit as rugged, hard-boiled private eye Philip Marlowe in *Murder, My Sweet*. There was only one more musical after that (*Susan Slept Here*, 1954) as he established himself as a serious actor and then a director of nonmusicals in films and on radio. Powell was also one of the first Hollywood stars to get involved full-time with television in the 1950s as an actor, director, and producer—again strictly with nonmusicals. He had been married to actress June Allyson for nearly seventeen years when he died of lung cancer in 1963 at age fifty-nine.

Buddy Clark

Although Buddy Clark was one of the most active and best-liked singers from the mid-1930s to the late 1940s, he never achieved anything like the impact or influence of either Bing Crosby or Frank Sinatra in those same years. Clark was a regular from 1936 to 1938 on radio's popular *Your Hit Parade* and later starred on several other high-rated musical programs. They included three years on *The Contented Hour*—whose title in many ways summed up Clark's appeal, for he was essentially a mellow-voiced singer of romantic ballads, closer in style to Crosby than to Sinatra. By the early 1940s, that made Clark seem somewhat old-fashioned to the younger age group that was squealing and panting over Sinatra and giving Frankie record hit after record hit. But at the same time, it also strengthened Clark's attraction to the middle-of-the-road listener who favored a more straightforward style of pop singing by a baritone with a rich, clean, unaffected sound.

Clark, who was born in Dorchester, Massachusetts, in 1912, couldn't get enough of either sports or music as a kid and at first wanted to be a professional baseball player. When that didn't pan out, he started singing with local bands in the Boston area and then, at seventeen, on a Boston radio station. The station suggested he change his real name, Samuel Goldberg, to something less ethnic. He became Buddy Clark.

Within a few years he had moved to New York, as a vocalist on Benny Goodman's *Let's Dance* radio program. He also became one of the busiest pickup vocalists in the radio-transcription recording business, at a time when specially made transcription discs were a mainstay of many radio stations around the country that could not afford live musical talent for all their programs. Clark recorded with the bands of Fred Rich, Archie Bleyer, Freddy Martin, Lud Gluskin, Eddy Duchin, Goodman, and others—some of whom made these transcriptions of stock arrangements under pseudonyms (because of their commercial recording contracts). Most often, too, the vocalist was completely uncredited. Clark's reputation as a "shadow singer" became so well known in music circles that when Hollywood's Darryl F. Zanuck made *Wake Up and Live*, a 1937 movie about a radio singer known as "the Phantom Troubadour," Clark was hired to "ghost" (or dub for the sound track) the singing voice of the actor (Jack Haley) playing the character. The "inside joke" of the time was that the movie's dubber was a real "phantom crooner."

Clark remained in Hollywood to do his own radio show, *Here's to Romance*, and to play a minor role in the Lucille Ball–Victor Mature movie musical *Seven Days' Leave* (1942). After a wartime stint in the Army, Clark's career really began to take off, not only on radio but also on records, in those early postwar years when singers ruled the roost. In quick succession, Clark's recordings of "Linda," "South America, Take It Away," "If This Isn't Love," "Peg o' My Heart," "You'd Be So Nice to Come Home To," and "I'll Dance at Your Wedding" became best-sellers. He also made a promising start at a stage career with a leading role in a West Coast production of Gershwin's *Girl Crazy*. But more was not to be. Sports fan Clark and a group of friends chartered a small private plane to go to a hotly contested Stanford-Michigan football game. While Clark was rushing back to Los Angeles after the game so he could do his radio show, the plane developed engine trouble and crashed on Beverly Boulevard near downtown L.A. Clark was killed. He was thirty-seven.

Alice Faye

If Bing Crosby was the king of movie musicals into the early 1940s, then Alice Faye was their uncrowned queen. But whereas Crosby was also the king of radio and recordings, Faye's contract with 20th Century–Fox limited her radio appearances and completely forbade her to record. Studio boss Darryl F. Zanuck didn't want any other media competition for his movies, so if audiences wanted to hear Alice Faye sing, they had to come see the movies in which he featured her. The result was that Faye became a major film star, but never the superstar singer that records and radio might have made her. By the time she quit movies and decided to concentrate on radio with her second husband, bandleader Phil Harris, both she and her radio producers were content to make her singing secondary to her sitcom acting. After the program came to an end in 1954, Faye retired to her home with Harris in Palm Springs, California, and has appeared in only an occasional movie, TV show, or Broadway musical (a revival of *Good News* in 1973), remaining more interested in golf than show biz.

In her prime, Faye had a deep, distinctive alto voice and a straightforward way of singing, with emphasis always on making the lyrics convincing. Except when a movie role required it, she usually shied away from jazz effects or idiosyncratic mannerisms. Cole Porter once said, "There's something about the way Alice projects a song that spells immediate success for it." Among the songs she did just that for are "You're a Sweetheart," "Now It Can Be Told," "I'm Shooting High," "You Turned the Tables on Me," "Goodnight, My Love," "A Journey to a Star," and "You'll Never Know," all from her movie days.

Her real name is Alice Jeane Leppert, and she was born on May 5, 1915, on Manhattan's West Fifty-fourth Street, just a few blocks from its bustling theater district. By fifteen she had the figure of a more mature teenager and, with her hair bleached blond like Jean Harlow's, was able to fudge her age to get chorus-line jobs, including one in *George White's Scandals of 1931*, starring Rudy Vallee and Ethel Merman.

At a *Scandals* cast party, Vallee heard Faye sing for the first time and a few days later invited her to be a guest on his radio show. During the broadcast, she got through the song all right, but she was so consumed with stage fright that she fainted at the end. That killed the sponsor's interest in making her a regular on the show, so Vallee paid her out of his own pocket to keep her on the program until her fan mail convinced the sponsor to put her on the payroll.

Then an auto accident almost ended her career just as it seemed to be taking off. While driving with members of Vallee's orchestra in a snowstorm, she suffered serious facial bruises when their car overturned. Doctors feared she would be scarred for life. Alice underwent several plastic surgery operations, which left only minor scars that could easily be camouflaged with makeup and the reshaping of an eyebrow. Phil Harris loves to tell the story that when he first met Faye in New York right after the accident, her face was still bandaged— and that he never really got to see her face until they met again years later in Hollywood.

When Vallee went to Hollywood to film the first movie edition of *George White's Scandals* in 1934, Faye was signed for a minor role. Unexpectedly, Vallee's costar, European import Lilian Harvey, unhappy with her role, walked off the set (and, as it turned out, out of her Hollywood career). After days of haggling, the producers decided to take a chance on Faye, who had impressed them in the one production number she had already shot, "Nasty Man." A series of minor Fox musicals quickly followed, but it was not until Darryl F. Zanuck's 20th Century Pictures merged with Fox in 1935 that things really began to click for her. Faye's bleached hair was replaced with her own light brown color, and her Harlow-like image softened somewhat.

Leading roles in nearly two dozen hit musicals followed over the next decade. Among the most memorable: *Wake Up and Live* (which dealt with a radio performer who suffers from mike fright, a subject she knew something about); *On the Avenue* and *Alexander's Ragtime Band* (two Irving Berlin musicals in which, for the latter, she got top billing over her former star *Scandals* colleague Merman); *Rose of Washington Square* (a thinly disguised version of the Fanny Brice–Nicky Arnstein affair in which Faye proved she could be as torchy a torch-song singer as any of her more famous predecessors); *That Night in Rio* and *Weekend in Havana* (the best of a whole slew of '40s Latin American–angled musicals); and *The Gang's All Here* (Busby Berkeley's first color musical, in which Faye's songs were kept separate from the bigger production numbers because she was pregnant during filming). Many of the songs she introduced in these musicals became Top

Ten hits, and Faye was permitted to sing them occasionally on radio as promotions for the pictures. But recordings remained a Zanuck no-no.

It was not that edict, however, that made her walk off the Fox lot in 1945, not to return for fifteen years. Instead, it was her boredom with the same insipid kinds of musical roles she was being given year after year at what she began to call "Penitentiary-Fox." "All those films were actually the same script," she told an interviewer. "All they did was change Don Ameche over here for Tyrone Power or John Payne over there." She opted instead to spend her time with her family and to do a radio sitcom with husband Harris. The program, essentially a spin-off of Harris's role on *The Jack Benny Program*, worked two songs into each week's script: a novelty number by Harris and a song by Alice (most often one of her movie songs). She insists she has never regretted quitting when she did. As she told interviewer Michael Buckley for *Films in Review* in 1982, "I've had a wonderful life. I suppose we would all like to get a second chance at certain things. Maybe next time around."

Frances Langford

Like Alice Faye, Frances Langford owes her professional start as a singer to Rudy Vallee's popular radio shows of the 1930s. And, again like Faye, she parlayed her radio success into a movie contract in the mid-'30s. But unlike Faye, Langford never achieved major star status in Hollywood, ending up playing secondary roles or guest-singer spots in a few major movies and leading roles in a whole string of low-budget "B" musicals.

Yet there is no denying that, in her prime, Frances Langford had one of the sweetest and most luscious alto voices on radio or in the movies. There was also a classiness to her manner and to her sound—a classiness that, in a peculiarly unpretentious way, bordered on the aloof and may have been a factor in keeping her from major stardom. The '30s, after all, was an era when more down-to-earth types (such as Joan Crawford, Ginger Rogers, Ruby Keeler, and Alice Faye at the beginning of her career) generally rated higher in their appeal to Depression audiences for movie musicals. (The most sophisticated and stylish of the '30s singers, Lee Wiley, never even got to make a movie.) There were exceptions, of course, such as Irene Dunne, who could be as elegant and refined as they come but who could also kick up her heels believably in screwball comedy. Langford, in contrast, always remained the reserved, somewhat shy *lady*. It's not that Hollywood didn't cast her occasionally in everyday girl-next-door roles, but she somehow brought them off as if she were playing down or distancing herself from the roles, even when she sang. And it certainly wasn't any real stuffiness on her part or any unwillingness to "rough it," as she proved by her many tours overseas to entertain the troops during World War II. It was just that an innate refinement always remained the dominant characteristic of her singing.

And beautifully elegant singing it always was. Langford's clear, rich sound seemed to flow effortlessly, as she paid close attention to the musical line of a song, not messing around with the lyrics for individualistic emotional effect. She was, in other words, a conscientiously "straight" singer in the best sense of that term. Among the songs she introduced that have become present-day standards are "I Feel a Song Coming On," "I'm in the Mood for Love," and "I've Got You Under My Skin."

Perhaps some of Langford's classy style was a carryover from her original plans to be an opera singer when she entered Southern College in her home state of Florida (where she was born, in Lakeland, in 1914). Her soprano voice became a mainstay of the college glee club until a tonsillectomy took away not only her tonsils but also her high C. Langford emerged from the hospital a contralto, and soon thereafter decided that her new voice as well as her own temperament were better suited to popular music than to the "heavies" that operatic contraltos usually had to play. By age seventeen she was singing regularly at dances throughout the region as well as on a Tampa radio station. It was one of these broadcasts that brought her to Rudy Vallee's attention, at a time when he needed a last-minute replacement for a program he was doing from a Florida resort.

Vallee brought Langford back to New York with him and featured her on other broadcasts and in some of his nightclub performances. She won a featured role in a Broadway musical, *Here Comes the Bride*, which didn't go very far on Broadway (closing after seven performances) but got Langford to Hollywood with a Paramount contract. For her debut film, *Every Night at Eight* (with a Jimmy McHugh–Dorothy Fields score), she was billed several notches below Alice Faye but got to sing two of the film's best songs and won the leading man from Faye for the final clinch. It would be the biggest plum of Langford's movie career, yet Faye still walked off with the better notices. Paramount gave Langford the lead in another musical, *Palm Springs*, costarring her with radio crooner (and later cowboy star) Smith Ballew, but the movie did little to advance her career. Following a featured spot as a singer in MGM's extravagant *Broadway Melody of 1936* and then in *Born to Dance*, Langford was more or less relegated to low-to-modest-budget pictures at lesser studios.

Meanwhile, she continued to sing on network radio shows, becoming a regular on the popular *Hollywood Hotel* program in the late '30s with Dick Powell and gossip columnist Louella Parsons, and on Bob Hope's comedy show in the '40s. She also began recording regularly, teaming up for duets occasionally with Bing Crosby and Rudy Vallee, but mostly cutting solo discs of songs from her movies and other standards, sometimes with "name" orchestras such as Jimmy Dorsey's. Her biggest radio success came in the late '40s with a sitcom about a married couple who lived up to their name, *The Bickersons*, in which she costarred with Don Ameche. It was her most ambitious attempt to shed her "reserved lady" image, and it spawned several *Bickersons* record albums with Ameche that turned out to be as popular as any of Langford's records as a singer.

In the 1950s Langford married motorboat tycoon Ralph Evinrude and retired to operate the forty-unit Frances Langford Outrigger Resort at Jensen Beach, California. Except for a tour to Vietnam in 1966 to entertain American troops stationed there, she has limited her public singing mostly to occasional sets with the band at her resort's restaurant.

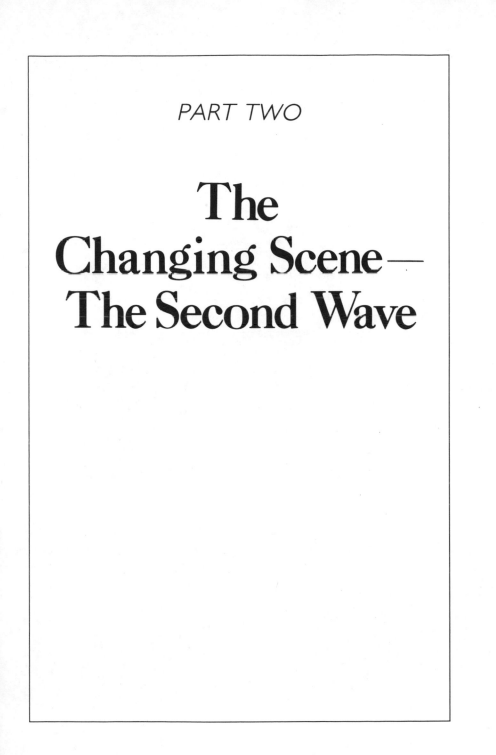

PART TWO

The Changing Scene — The Second Wave

A S the 1930s ended, all was not well behind the scenes in what seemed to be the thriving world of popular music. Just as thousands of members of the film industry (actors, writers, directors, songwriters, designers, and so on) chafed under what they considered to be the "slave contract" system of the big studios, so charges spread about the increasing control exerted over American popular music by the Hollywood studios through the American Society of Composers, Authors & Publishers (ASCAP), to which most of the important songwriters belonged.

The charges reached a boiling point in the late 1930s as the studios grew increasingly alarmed by the fact that young people were turning away more and more from the sweet bands to the newer-style swing bands (such as those led by Benny Goodman, Jimmie Lunceford, Count Basie, and Charlie Barnet). With swing bands there was less demand for standard thirty-two-bar ballads and a new emphasis on novelty tunes and up-tempo dance music, often without a vocal chorus. Some of the most popular of the big-band leaders (especially Tommy Dorsey, Jimmy Dorsey, Glenn Miller, and Artie Shaw) strived to keep a balance between sweet and swing arrangements, and to feature their vocalists in a majority of the band's numbers.

It was not the style of the music that most upset the movie-studio chieftains, however. By 1941 they were convinced that the biggest cause of their declining box-office revenues was competition from nationwide dancing to swing bands, not only at live public dances but also at private gatherings to music on records and radio. Young people, in particular, were losing the moviegoing habit. In retaliation and somewhat illogically, Hollywood decided to target radio first, and put pressure on ASCAP to double the royalties it charged for its music to be played on the air. The theory was that if the broadcasters didn't pay, there'd be less music on the radio and people would return to the movies—or if Hollywood did pay, Hollywood would then have a compensating source of revenue. When the broadcasters held firm with a unanimous "No!" ASCAP's music was banned from radio effective January 1, 1941. That accounted for virtually all the best-known songs by the best-known songwriters, not just swing tunes—and acutely restricted all the top singers.

Some of the radio companies, anticipating that trouble was brewing, had already set up their own copyright company, Broadcast Music Incorporated (BMI), and sought out non-ASCAP songwriters to provide them with songs, particularly in the "hillbilly" (later retagged country-and-western) and rhythm-and-blues styles that ASCAP had shunned. The result was that radio audiences got to hear a much broader range of music than they had previously heard—and they got to like a lot of it. Meanwhile, the movie audience wasn't getting noticeably bigger. ASCAP finally backed down and settled with the broadcasters in October 1941. But lasting damage to classic pop had been done. Few realized it then, but the nine-month ASCAP radio ban had, in effect, helped to undercut seriously the supremacy of the type of pop music that had reigned essentially unchallenged for about two decades. We certainly don't mean that *all* classic-pop tunes came from ASCAP, but the overwhelming majority up to that time indeed did.

While the ASCAP vs. BMI fires continued to burn, another historic explosion occurred, this time between the record companies and the American Federation of Musicians. Record revenues, which were low in the earliest years of the Depression, had picked up notably in the late 1930s, especially after jukeboxes became popular in restaurants, bars, and even drugstores (which, in those days, often had busy soda fountains). Records were increasingly displacing live musicians for both local and network radio programming. So the musicians' union wanted more money for its members for making records. When the record companies balked, the union called a strike on August 1, 1942, which effectively barred most of the country's professional instrumental musicians from making any records. The strike lasted more than a year, until October 1943, when the record companies gave in and settled. During that year, although the leading bands, both sweet and swing, could not make records, singers and vocal groups could.

With that, an increasing number of solo pop vocalists rose to stardom. Instead of being limited to a single chorus midway in a band arrangement of a song, these singers now had whole arrangements built around them. They moved into the solo spotlight—and, once there, many of them stayed after the strike was settled. Instead of being looked on as just "crooners" and "canaries," they were now more respectfully treated as individual "song stylists." The wartime popularity of sentimental ballads was also a singers' boon.

Ironically, it was the successful rise at this point of so many former band singers—such as Frank Sinatra, Ella Fitzgerald, Perry Como, Dick Haymes, Jo Stafford, and Peggy Lee—that speeded the demise of the big bands after World War II, especially as it became increasingly expensive to tour and present the big bands. Television, too, was now on the scene, taking audiences away from the bands as well as from movies and radio. But for singers, those first ten postwar years turned out to be "the singers' decade" for those specializing in standard Broadway, Hollywood, and Tin Pan Alley pop. Through such singers, such pop still held the greatest appeal to the mainstream American public despite the continuing post-1941 inroads of country-and-western and rhythm-and-blues.

Also contributing significantly to the supremacy of singers was the introduction of the long playing record in 1948. Instead of just recording a few sides for single 78-rpm discs, singers were now expected to record eleven or twelve selections at a time for an LP. With the trend to selections built around special themes, LP mixtures of old and new songs became common. No longer did singers record just the new hits (or would-be hits); they also delved into the best songs of past years, keeping them very much alive.

It was a golden age that was finally to be rent asunder by two factors: first, the rise to power in major record companies of A&R directors whose chief aim became reaching an ever-widening audience (and higher profits) even if it meant lowering standards and taste levels to do so; and then, partly in reaction to the insipid level to which so much new '50s pop had fallen, the explosion of rock 'n' roll in the mid-1950s and its adroit manipulation by a new breed of musical promoters.

Just as the dance music of the '20s and '30s was championed by that era's younger generation as a form of rebellion against the styles and tastes of their elders, so rock became the music of the postwar younger generation—and has remained so in one form or another ever since. But, with the passing years, the increasing emphasis by the music industry on a younger and younger target audience has led some critics, somewhat maliciously if not entirely inaccurately, to label much of the contemporary pop music since the rock revolution as "kiddie pop." And, indeed, much of today's teen-aimed music continues to be strictly that—if also extremely profitable for its practitioners.

At the same time, the earlier music that we now call classic pop, although dislodged from its many years of total supremacy, has continued to be very much a part of everyday American musical life, and it shows every indication of continuing to be so through the enduring appeal of its greatest singers. The late 1980s and early 1990s have seen a major renaissance of interest in these singers, spurred by the transfer of many of their LPs and old 78-rpm recordings to the technologically new compact discs (CDs), plus the ongoing presence of their movies on video and TV (especially cable TV), and, not least of all, a leveling-off of interest among the graying segment of the population in new rock and new contemporary pop.

As contemporary pop in particular (with exceptions, of course) seemed to reach a creative plateau in the early '90s—which some music historians relate to that experienced by Tin Pan Alley in the '50s—classic pop has achieved new esteem among young listeners and young performers, as well as keeping its hold on older listeners. And so we find not only singers such as Frank Sinatra, Tony Bennett, Margaret Whiting, Rosemary Clooney, Mel Tormé, and Vic Damone with still-active careers in the '90s, but also young newcomers such as Michael Feinstein and Harry Connick, Jr., playing to sold-out houses on Broadway as well as in clubs and theaters throughout the country. Particularly interesting has been the trend for most of these singers, old and new, to work primarily with jazz instrumentalists—in effect reviving the active links between jazz and popular music that existed in the '20s and '30 but grew apart in the '40s and '50s.

Most encouraging of all is the number of less well-known but dedicated, talented, mostly young singers who continue to make the classic-pop repertoire the bedrock of their cabaret and concert performances and recordings. Among the most oustanding are Ann Hampton Callaway, Steven Davis, Jason Graae, Jeff Harnar, Susanna McCorkle, Maureen McGovern, Rick McKay, Loria Parker, Daryl Sherman, Bob Stewart, Billy Stritch, K. T. Sullivan, Darcy Thompson, Marlene VerPlanck, Weslia Whitfield, Ronny Whyte, and Margaret Wright. Some of them, with the right breaks, may someday join the pantheon of great singers of classic pop, perhaps even forming an enduring "third wave" into the next century.

FRANK SINATRA

*There is only one guy who's
the greatest singer in the whole world.
His name is Sinatra. And nobody else.*
—*BING CROSBY*

To hell with the calendar. The day Frank Sinatra dies, the twentieth century is over.

It has often been asserted that the central theme of this century is World War II—not only the actual war, but also the early-century social shifts that foreshadowed it as well as the way the world was reshaped after the war. And in a public consciousness so strongly influenced by popular entertainment, Frank Sinatra is surely the most enduring figure of the World War II generation. He grew up amid the forces that preceded the war, a child of the Depression and a product of the rise of the ethnic underclasses. He rose to prominence during, if not because of, the war, as a home-front surrogate for the American men fighting overseas. He jetted through the postwar age as the very personification of America, the gutsy boss of the world. And as the American century winds down, Sinatra—a world-weary old lion, like his country—hangs in as a living symbol of the age he helped define.

A genuinely mythic figure, Sinatra is now the biggest star of all in the century of celebrity. Indeed, it says something powerful about classic-pop singing in general and Sinatra in particular that one of the most widely known and highly revered figures of our time is, of all things, a classic-pop singer. Sinatra has connected with literally tens of millions of people in more than eighty countries through the estimated four thousand songs he has sung over the course of some fifty years. Clearly, his songs and his singing have a special universality and timelessness. He's not merely The Voice, as he was nicknamed in his early years. He's Our Voice.

Of all the great singers of classic pop—and there are many who have been great—Sinatra is almost universally regarded as the greatest. As critic John Rockwell put it in his insightful book on Sinatra's singing, *Sinatra: An American Classic*, "Frank Sinatra is by any reasonable criterion the greatest singer in the history of American popular music." As an extension, in the words of critic Henry Pleasants, "Frank Sinatra in his prime represents a summation of all that is best and most original in American popular singing."

Like Bing Crosby before him (and Elvis Presley after him), Sinatra changed the course of popular music through the musical innovations he popularized. In fact, Crosby inspired Sinatra to become a singer, according to a story Sinatra's first wife, Nancy, used to tell. Sinatra was working at manual labor when he took Nancy on a date and happened to see a Crosby movie. As they walked out of the theater, Nancy said that Sinatra announced, out of the blue, "That's what I'm going to do." The story is certainly plausible, knowing Sinatra's now-famous decisiveness. After all, in the 1980s he quit smoking suddenly, after more than forty years of smoking several packs of nonfilter cigarettes per day. When someone noticed that he wasn't smoking anymore, he replied matter-of-factly, "Smoking's stupid."

In addition to Crosby, Russ Columbo was a strong influence on Sinatra, who says he was drawn to Columbo's early crooning style when he heard him on the radio as a young boy in the 1920s. However, until high school, when he joined the Demarest High Glee Club, Sinatra showed little interest in music. He spent his youth on the streets, becoming educated in the toughness, the resilience, and the commonsense code of honor that came to serve him as effectively as his eventual music training. Born on December 12, 1915, to Natalie "Dolly" Garavent Sinatra and Anthony Martin Sinatra, Frances Albert Sinatra grew up in a matriarchal household in the Italian section of Hoboken, New Jersey, a working-class suburb of New York City.

Like his father, who worked as a shipyard boilermaker, fireman, and prizefighter (under the name Marty O'Brien), Sinatra tried a variety of unskilled-labor jobs before taking up singing in the mid-1930s. At one point he considered becoming an engineer and briefly attended Stevens Institute in Hoboken, although he did *not* study journalism nor work as a sportswriter, as his early publicists claimed to help ingratiate Sinatra with the press.

With Crosby's success as his inspiration, Sinatra decided to enter tryouts for the popular *Major Bowes Original Amateur Hour* radio program in 1935, and he won. Since a vocal trio from Hoboken won the group competition on the same day that Sinatra won in the solo tryouts, Bowes took it upon himself to stick all the Hoboken singers together and call them the Hoboken Four. Bowes sent the quartet on a national tour in one of his many amateur touring "units" and included the group in two "soundie" musical movie shorts. However, being a professional amateur had no appeal to Sinatra, and he quit the Bowes tour after three months.

Working as a solo singer, briefly under the name Frankie Trent, Sinatra got his first regular booking at the Rustic Cabin nightclub in Englewood, New Jersey, in 1937. Performing for more than a year at the club, Sinatra developed a good reputation in neighboring New York and was signed by Harry James to join a new band he was starting. Sinatra made his first recordings with the James band, including his first version of "All or Nothing at All," but none of the records did especially well. Seizing a better opportunity, he left James after six months to join the superior Tommy Dorsey band when offered the chance in 1940.

It was with the Dorsey band that Sinatra became a star—and developed the youthful singing style that broke with the Crosby tradition. "I was a big fan of Bing's. But I never wanted to sing like him, because every kid on the block was boo-boo-booing like Crosby. I wanted to be a different kind of singer," Sinatra explained in later years.

If Crosby's bouncy phrasing was influenced by the New Orleans jazz of Louis Armstrong, Sinatra's Dorsey-period singing was equally influenced by the smooth ballroom dance-band style of the Dorsey group. Sinatra has always been quick to admit his debt to Tommy Dorsey's trombone playing, in particular. Just as Dorsey would take long, lyrical solos without pausing for breath, so Sinatra developed a manner of singing in a long, continuous line, linking phrases without pausing to breathe. He accomplished the feat through rigorous breath training, including holding his breath while he swam underwater, rehearsing his lyrics in his mind. He also tried learning the Far Eastern technique of breathing in through the nose at the same time as breathing out through the mouth. By improving his breath control, he became able to sing up to six and sometimes eight bars without a discernible breath. In contrast, most singers usually sing two to four bars before a noticeable pause. Like a trombone, too, Sinatra augmented this elegant legato phasing with a subtle use of portamento—sliding from note to note smoothly by bending the pitch of the notes.

More significantly, perhaps, Sinatra took full advantage of the microphone to bring a deep intensity and intimacy to his singing. As he wrote in a booklet titled *Tips on Popular Singing* (written with vocal coach John Quinlan), "Many singers never understood, and still don't, that a microphone is their instrument." Sinatra played the instrument masterfully, inching it close to his mouth to sing softly and effortlessly. Because he always maintained a natural, conversational tone of voice, never belting, Sinatra's singing seemed startlingly intimate.

Of course, singers from Gene Austin and Rudy Vallee to Crosby had been using microphones for years. But Sinatra was the first to seem comfortable with the *sexual* subtext of the microphone's intimacy. Crosby—buoyant and likable, with a clear tone and a bouncy sense of time—appealed to romantics of all ages in his heyday, whereas Sinatra had a sound seemingly tailored for young people, especially young women. Sinewy and blatantly sexual, boyishly brooding in down-tempo numbers, Sinatra's style seemed as radically erotic in its day as Elvis Presley's air-humping would fifteen years later. As a psychologist quoted in the 1940s put it, Sinatra was doing "a sort of melodic striptease in which he lays bare his soul."

In two years with Tommy Dorsey, Sinatra rose to become the hottest vocalist in the country and a huge jukebox star. A dozen of the eighty-three songs he recorded with Dorsey became Top Ten hits, including his first number-one record, "I'll Never Smile Again," as well as such hits as "Imagination," "Tradewinds," "Our Love Affair," "Stardust," and "This Love of Mine." Voted Outstanding Male Vocalist by both *Billboard* and *Down Beat*, Sinatra had what he wanted—enough momentum to break out successfully on his own.

No one had ever seen anything quite like the success he found. Sinatra's youthful, sexual style turned out to be perfectly matched to the social climate of the times. Lonesome at home while their boyfriends and young husbands were overseas at war, American girls, "the bobby-soxers," turned to Frank Sinatra as their collegiate surrogate love. They returned his sexual message with a sexual call of their own—"the swoon." Thinner than his microphone stand (or so said a joke of the day) and always wearing a cute, boyish bow tie, Sinatra would clutch the mike and coo one of those long, soft legato phrases, and every girl in the place would seem to buckle under at the knees. Swooning was a rite of the ritual, just as screaming through every song would later be for every girl at a Beatles concert. Setting up a home base at New York's Paramount Theater, the location of his first solo performance in 1942, Sinatra—or "Swoonatra," as the fan mags preferred—was such a sensation that literally thousands of girls would mob the streets before his performances.

His solo records, cut at Columbia under the direction of arranger Axel Stordahl, were typically soft ballads with sweet, lush orchestral backing. Stordahl liked lots of strings and woodwinds, no brass, and a nice, slow rhythm, and his light touch seemed appropriate for Sinatra's romantic early style. Among the best of the Sinatra-Stordahl sides, "Night and Day," "Lamplighter's Serenade," "The Night We Called It a Day," and "The Song Is You" still hold up nicely today.

When the boys came home from the war as men, his former bobby-soxer fans, who were also more mature, turned away from Sinatra and fulfilled his worse critics' predictions. By the late 1940s, Frank Sinatra appeared to be washed up. To help revive his recording career, Columbia's A&R chief, Mitch Miller, strong-armed Sinatra to cut more and more of the silly novelty numbers that were making the charts at the time (thanks to Miller's influence). Among these downright humiliating recordings cut under Miller, Sinatra humbled himself to sing "Bim Bam Baby," "One Finger Melody," and the now-infamous "Mama Will Bark," a 1951 collaboration with Dagmar and a dog impersonator. At the same time, Sinatra's personal life collapsed. After twelve years of marriage, he divorced his former Hoboken girlfriend Nancy, who gained custody of their three children: Nancy, Franklin ("Frank, Jr."), and Christina. Almost immediately after his divorce, Sinatra married actress Ava Gardner in November 1951. And in the same period, after starting a promising movie career at MGM, he was fired by Louis B. Mayer for making an off-color joke about one of Mayer's girlfriends.

In her adult years, his daughter Nancy Sinatra would sometimes tell interviewers a family legend about her father's birth. Following a difficult delivery, the baby Sinatra was thought to be stillborn and left on a table, not breathing. While the doctor attended to his mother, his grandmother snapped up the lifeless baby and doused him with cold water under a spigot. Sinatra came to life after he was assumed to be dead—and that wasn't the last time, as things turned out. In 1953, considered a has-been at age thirty-eight and struggling to find a way to make a comeback, he humbled himself, submitted to a screen test, and accepted a relatively paltry $8,000 (instead of his previous fee of $150,000) for a supporting dramatic role in *From Here to Eternity*. His performance as Maggio, a Pearl Harbor GI beaten to death by a sadistic sergeant, won Sinatra an Academy Award and launched him into a new phase of his career, as a mature actor and singer. As *Time* magazine reported, "Last week, still shy of forty, he was well away on a second career that promises to be, if anything, more brilliant than the first."

Though *From Here to Eternity* is generally credited with single-handedly reviving Sinatra's career, another event of the same year was also critically important. Having lost his contract with Columbia, Sinatra began recording with Capitol Records, a hip young company founded by lyricist Johnny Mercer. The antithesis of Mitch Miller, Mercer encouraged Sinatra to find his own artistic voice and helped team him with the most appropriate material and arrangers. For material, Sinatra increasingly supplanted the romantic ballads he sang almost exclusively in his Paramount days with more upbeat and thematically assertive numbers that reflected both his own maturity and the jaunty confidence of the postwar times—songs such as "I've Got the World on a String" and "Come Fly with Me." Moreover, just as Axel Stordahl had served as the ideal complement to Sinatra in his swoon phase, a new arranger, Nelson Riddle, proved to be a superb match for the singer's new hipster image. Punchy, direct, and always swingin', Riddle's arrangements were as streamlined and powerful as a V8 Caddy, and they carried the second Sinatra to a new peak with such LPs as *Swing Easy, Songs for Swingin' Lovers, A Swingin' Affair,* and *In the Wee Small Hours.*

The Capitol period, from 1953 to 1959, is unquestionably the prime of Sinatra's powers. As a result of a vocal hemorrhage, his voice had developed a new, slightly gravelly resonance; it wasn't as silky pure as The Voice of his youth, but it had more character and fit the grown-up ideas of his new work. Sinatra's range had also dropped from the light baritone (nearly a tenor) of his younger days to a cello-rich pure baritone. Through the mid- to late 1950s he still had exceptional breath control. And his diction was as impeccable as ever. (In "Night and Day," Sinatra enunciates two separate *d* sounds in the words "and" and "day.")

Most significantly, perhaps, Sinatra's interpretive abilities continued to evolve. Always profoundly concerned with the lyrical content of his songs, Sinatra in the 1950s mastered the ability to infuse not only meaning but also *motivation* into a song. Along with Billie Holiday and Mabel Mercer, whom Sinatra has always credited as his two biggest influences as an interpreter of songs, he stands as one of the most "internal" of all singers. He's a psychological artist; in the words of critic and author Gene Lees, "Sinatra was to American song what Montgomery Clift was to American acting."

Sinatra's interpretive gifts never stopping improving and actually reached their pinnacle very late in his career, past the prime of his physical abilities. In 1960, with record companies, including Capitol, feeling the pinch of the success of rock 'n' roll, Sinatra founded his own record company, Reprise Records, to maintain complete control over his work. A few of the records have untidy moments, with some out-of-character attempts to sound "contemporary" by trying such light-rock material as "Winchester Cathedral" and "Bad, Bad Leroy Brown." And Sinatra's voice is a touch shaky now and then, particularly on his comeback album, *Ol' Blue Eyes Is Back*, recorded after his two-year "retirement" in 1971 following his divorce from his third wife, Mia Farrow, and the death of his father. However, the vast majority of Sinatra's Reprise output is the work of a restless musical spirit with the highest of standards. The standouts include *I Remember Tommy*, Sinatra's tribute to Dorsey and the singer's last noble attempt at that old long, legato phrasing; *Sinatra and Basie*, with bang-up arrangements by Neal Hefti (uncredited on the album sleeve because he wanted equal billing with Basie or no billing at all); *The Concert Sinatra*, not a concert at all but a lovely studio album of mostly Richard Rodgers tunes, arranged by Nelson Riddle; *Francis Albert Sinatra & Antonio Carlos Jobim*, the startlingly perfect pairing of Sinatra with Brazilian composer Jobim; *September of My Years*, a somber album about aging, and the high-water mark of the Reprise years; *Watertown*, a vastly underrated folk-pop song-cycle; and *She Shot Me Down*, another underrated album, of sad songs of loss.

As the taste and sense of risk in Sinatra's work at his own record label demonstrate, he has always approached his music with great seriousness and ambition. The same cannot be said of his work in films. When he started his own record label, he pushed himself and sought out undervalued composers like Jobim. When he started his own film production company in the 1960s, he called up some pals and threw a party, shooting "Rat Pack" pictures such as *Sergeants 3, 4 for Texas*, and *Robin and the Seven Hoods* with Dean Martin, Sammy Davis, Jr., Joey Bishop, and Peter Lawford. He was perfectly content to let Dino and his buddies goof around on camera—but when Martin delivered a lackluster peformance in the "Rat Pack Reunion" tour of the late 1980s, Sinatra bawled him out and Martin quit the tour.

"I'm well aware of the shortcomings of some of my pictures," he told *The New York Times* in the 1960s. Still, Sinatra proved that he had the potential to be an outstanding actor when he applied himself, delivering top-class performances in such films as *The Man with the Golden Arm* (for which he was nominated for a Best Actor Oscar) and *The Manchurian Candidate* as well as *From Here to Eternity*.

In our view, Sinatra began doing some of his most expressive work in his frequent concert performances in the later years of his career, clearly invigorated by performing (and, at last, maritally content with his fourth wife, the former Barbara Marx). He uses his voice with staggeringly inventive artistry, employing all the crackles, the growls, and the shortness of breath of his weathered equipment as effectively as he ever used the range and clarity of his younger, "better" voice. As a pure artist—a master of personal expression—Sinatra has reached a new peak, drawing from everything he's learned in the course of a life that he's lived his way.

DINAH SHORE

She is many things to many people:
... to her coworkers she is a perfectionist;
to everybody she is a gracious lady;
and to musicians she is a gas.
—ANDRÈ PREVIN

Next to Kate Smith, Dinah Shore has come closest among female pop singers to becoming a national institution over the past fifty years. It hasn't been entirely for her singing, though Shore has always considered herself first and foremost a singer (with nine gold records to underscore it). She has also been one of television's most successful and longest-running variety and talk-show hostesses—first on prime time shows, then on daytime network programs, and most recently on both daytime and evening cable (with six Emmy awards to underscore that side of her career).

Along the way she also seems to have found the Fountain of Youth, as she's evolved from a genteel Tennessee belle into a radiantly attractive woman of indeterminate age. Insisting that it's her active sports life (particularly tennis and golf) that has most kept her in shape, Shore has certainly aged more gracefully than just about anyone else who's continually been in the public eye as long as she has, since the late 1930s.

She has taken her lumps over the years, however, about her terminal aura of good cheer and perkiness. "Benzedrine takes Dinah Shore to stay awake," Bob Hope once quipped. Oscar Levant was even more acerbic: "I can't watch Dinah Shore. My doctor won't let me. I'm diabetic." Shore's legendary energy, zest, and wholesome good-naturedness have always been a key part of her public persona as both a singer and a television personality. Friends and coworkers insist it's genuine.

Yet, ironically, it was as a limpid-toned singer of intimate, bluesy ballads that Shore won her first fame. It was her versions of "Blues in the Night" and "I'll Walk Alone" that helped put those songs on *Your Hit Parade* back in the early days of World War II. It wasn't until later in the 1940s that she became as well-known for easygoing novelty tunes with overly cute, often banal or syrupy lyrics, such as "Buttons and Bows," "Shoofly Pie and Apple Pan Dowdy," or "Dear Hearts and Gentle People." And although a small part of her repertory has always reflected her Tennessee origins (her hometown of Nashville is, after all, the capital of country music), she has generally concentrated on the novelty songs and romantic ballads of classic pop.

"People like Johnny Mercer and Harold Arlen have been the bedrock of the kind of music I've done throughout my career," she says, "because they wrote the blues, and Johnny's lyrics had that Southern style. But nobody was better than Lorenz Hart"—a view she has long backed up by singing many Rodgers and Hart songs on her albums and TV shows.

In the late 1930s and early 1940s, Shore openly told interviewers that she first modeled her singing on a dreamy style that Southern blacks call noodling. "It's the way Negro mammies in the South sing to their youngsters," she said, noting that as a child in Nashville she had a black nursemaid. Her name was Lillian Taylor (but "I called her Ya-Ya," Dinah says), and she took Dinah to her church to hear the congregation sing. Shore found it "electrifying" and its influences enduring. It even led to rumors later in her career (rumors that were not always intended as kindly) that Shore was partly black, because she sang the blues so instinctively.

Actually, Shore came from a Jewish family and was the victim of many anti-Semitic taunts as a schoolgirl growing up in Nashville and the smaller, nearby town of Winchester, where she was born on March 1, 1917. She had several other challenges to overcome as well in her early years: A bout with polio at age two left her with a limp in one leg for several years, which she determinedly strove to overcome and, as she has noted, "probably led to a lot of my athletic drive." Then there was her name, Frances Rose Shore, which got turned into Fanny Rose by schoolmates. "That was a very punny name," Shore recollects. "They'd say: 'Fanny Rose sat on a tack. Did Fanny rise? Shore!' I had to do something." An Ethel Waters recording of "Dinah" provided the solution, and she became Dinah Shore.

Shore had just become a cheerleader at Hume Frog High School in Nashville when her mother died. The blow hit her hard, for Dinah always felt she had inherited her mother's natural singing ability and hoped to make her proud as she developed it. Even when her father sent her to Vanderbilt University for a liberal-arts education, Dinah took voice and acting lessons on the side. A job singing over Nashville radio station WSM finally convinced her, despite her father's reservations, that she should try New York, network radio's capital. With her Bachelor of Arts degree in sociology as a fallback, she left for New York in 1938.

Jobs were scarce in New York, still not quite out of the Great Depression. Shore joined fifty other singers auditioning for a spot on a program to be headlined by Lennie Hayton's orchestra. She got the $50-a-week job, only to have the program canceled before it ever got on the air. She managed to get a nonpaying, fill-in job for a five-month stint at independent station WNEW and was even teamed on a few occasions with a young, unknown Italian-American from New Jersey named Sinatra. He nicknamed her Magnolia Blossom.

Her big break came when one of Eddie Cantor's daughters heard Shore singing on WNEW and, knowing that Cantor was looking for a new singer for his network radio show, suggested he audition her. As Shore once described that audition to interviewer Gerry Morris (for the Friars Club's *Ye Epistle*): "I was a nervous wreck. I sang and sang and sang everything I knew. And they kept saying, 'Just a little more.' Finally, this spare, beautiful little man walked out and said, 'Forgive me for making you sing so long, but I figure it's the last time I'm ever going to hear you for nothing.' That was Eddie's way of telling me I had the job."

Within weeks of her debut on Cantor's show, Shore had a CBS recording contract. Cantor put up $750 of his own money to buy the rights to the song "Yes, My Darling Daughter" for her, and it became her first hit recording. By the end of 1940, Shore was voted Outstanding New Star of the Year by six hundred radio editors polled by the *New York World-Telegram*. She also became a regular (alternating with Lena Horne and Jane Pickens) on *The Chamber Music Society of Lower Basin Street*, a fifteen-minute, tongue-in-cheek musical program that concentrated on "the three other *b*'s": barrelhouse, boogie-woogie, and the blues. She was introduced on the show by distinguished radio emcee Milton Cross as "the only singer who can start a fire by rubbing two notes together."

With hit recording after hit recording throughout the World War II years, Shore quickly became the undisputed Queen of the Juke-boxes. (Crosby and Sinatra were still fighting it out for the kingship.) She also joined Cantor and others in numerous war-bond tours and entertaining the troops at bases throughout the country. Then, in 1943, she made her movie debut in the Eddie Cantor all-star musical *Thank Your Lucky Stars*—for which Warner Bros.' cosmeticians lightened her naturally dark hair to an off-blond color, which it has remained ever since. One of the songs she introduced in that movie, "How Sweet You Are," promptly went on to *Your Hit Parade*. Samuel Goldwyn then hired Shore to costar with Danny Kaye in his 1944 debut movie, the GI comedy *Up in Arms*, in which, as an Army nurse, she introduced two new Harold Arlen winners, "Now I Know" and "Tess's Torch Song." In Hollywood she also met and married cowboy star George Montgomery.

A few other movies followed (*Belle of the Yukon, Follow the Boys, Till the Clouds Roll By, Aaron Slick from Punkin Crick*), mostly in secondary roles or in guest-star singing spots. But by and large, Shore failed to click as a box-office attraction. She says she desperately wanted to play the Helen Morgan role of Julie in the 1951 remake of *Show Boat* (as did her former *Lower Basin Street* colleague Lena Horne), but MGM finally decided on Ava Gardner (and then dubbed someone else's singing voice for Gardner's on the sound track!). Shore is typically frank and succinct: "I bombed as a movie star." But radio and recordings kept her among America's highest-paid women entertainers until television turned her into the superstar Hollywood had failed to do.

From 1951 to 1957 Shore had her own twice-weekly, fifteen-minute, songs-only telecast on NBC, immediately following the early-evening network newscast. Then in 1957 she began hosting the first in a series of enormously popular, weekly prime-time variety shows—on which she not only sang but also acted in comedy skits and took part in big production numbers. Her distinctive sign-off (blowing a kiss as she sweetly muttered something akin to "M-m-m-m-wa-a-a!") became indelibly linked with her, as well as becoming the source of numerous jibes and parodies, which she took good-naturedly. She was also unafraid to share her stage week after week with other top singers, including one now-classic teaming with Ella Fitzgerald and opera diva Joan Sutherland for some ultimate "crossover" vocalizing to Sigmund Romberg's "Lover Come Back to Me" and Gilbert and Sullivan's "Three Little Maids from School Are We." Shore's program remained at the top of the ratings nationwide well into the 1960s, after which she cut back her schedule to just a few seasonal specials and occasional guest appearances on other top shows—including another now-classic gem, as the sugar-sweet Melanie in a Carol Burnett spoof of *Gone with the Wind*.

The mid-1960s saw the breakup of Shore's eighteen-year marriage to George Montgomery (they had two children). She then wedded tennis pro Maurice Smith, but the marriage lasted less than a year. In the early 1970s she and movie star Burt Reynolds had a six-year romance that a UPI reporter once called "one of the most tastefully handled Hollywood love affairs of recent memory." Both Shore and Reynolds were nonsecretive but also discreet about their relationship, and openly remarked on talk shows that they saw no problem with the eighteen-year difference in their ages. After their breakup they remained good friends, and he even appeared occasionally on her TV shows.

In 1981, at age sixty-four, Shore embarked on a series of live stage performances for the first time in more than thirty years. As she told New York *Sunday News* reporter Mara Neville at the time, "I am basically a singer, and I found out that I was doing a lot of talking but singing only two or three times a week, which wasn't enough. If you don't sing enough, you get out of the habit, like a cook who doesn't cook. So now I'm just going to sing my tonsils to the bone." But she also admitted that she was terrified at first about "trying to remember all the new lyrics and arrangements," that she had been spoiled by all her years of singing with cue cards on TV or with a music stand in front of her in recording studios. But after a few rehearsals, her confidence came back and the shows went off without a hitch.

"I've worked hard for what I have," Shore says. "And there isn't anything I have that's been taken away from anybody else to achieve it." There aren't many in show business who can say that and mean it. Dinah Shore means it.

PERRY COMO

He is the best of the serenaders.
—*RUDY VALLEE*

If the heart of classic-pop singing lies in the laid-back, warmly intimate crooning of romantic ballads, there has been no more laid-back, warmly intimate crooner than Perry Como. He could make Bing Crosby on his laziest day look like a paragon of zip and zing. A former colleague once said that Como's so relaxed when he sings he needs someone to stand by and pinch him now and then to make sure he's actually awake. Exaggerated, of course, but stylistically not all that much off the mark.

Como himself has described his voice as "somewhere between a tenor and a light baritone." His is also an uncommonly warm and supple instrument, which he has always used in a straightforward, unaffected manner, shying away from arbitrary or idiosyncratic "interpretions." The late entertainment columnist Harriet Van Horne once commented, "When he sings, he appears to be suffering no pain at all, not even the private, exquisite pain that is peculiar to nightclub crooners."

Como also was one of the handsomest singers to reach vocal stardom in an era when clean-cut, Hollywood-style good looks counted as much in the music world as it did in the movies. But ironically, Como was not a big success when he went to Hollywood in 1943 with a seven-year contract from 20th Century–Fox. His full head of dark, wavy, always well-trimmed hair and his pleasing facial features were definitely pluses, but his height was a minus in those days (he's five-foot-seven). Even more of a hurdle was the fact that his shy, decidedly conservative personality came across on the screen as more suitable for brotherly roles than for romantic leading men. It wasn't that he was a bad actor, just a bland one. To complicate matters, 20th Century–Fox at the time also had under contract another handsome (and taller) singer, Dick Haymes—during a period when the creativity of Fox's musicals and audiences for them were in decline. After four pictures, Como asked for and got a release from his contract.

Television created no such problems for him. He just played himself, hosting an easygoing, top-rated musical program each week throughout the late 1950s and early 1960s, on which he sang and engaged in casual repartee now and then with his guests. He made audiences feel comfortably at home with him. At a time in the early days of television when a major TV criterion was whether you'd welcome so-and-so or such-and-such into your living room, Perry Como was one of the most universally welcome personalities of them all. And he remained so long after many others had worn out their welcomes.

If it weren't for the challenge of a friend, Como might still be singing only for the customers of a small-town barbershop in his hometown of Canonsburg, Pennsylvania, where he was born on May 18, 1913. He was eleven when, like the sons of many Italian-Americans of his generation, he became a barber's apprentice during after-school hours. By age fourteen he was paying the installments on his own shop. And, like many a barber before him, he liked to sing. His idol was Bing Crosby, and he's never made any bones about copying Bing right from the start. "What he would do, I would do," Como says unashamedly.

When a friend heard that Cleveland-based bandleader Freddie Carlone was looking for a vocalist, he urged nineteen-year-old Como to audition. Como got the job and traveled with the band throughout the Midwest for the next three years, building a popular regional reputation. He also married his childhood sweetheart, Roselle Beline.

Ted Weems, the leader of one of the most popular bands of the 1930s, heard Como and invited him to join his band in 1936. Como has always credited Weems with teaching him the importance of simplicity and directness in singing popular songs, without trying to embellish them with vocal tricks. "I learned to stop showing off and creating a bag of nothing," he has said.

Through the Weems band's recordings, broadcasts, and coast-to-coast tours, Como became widely known as a reliable, pleasant-sounding dance band singer—but not much more. The hotter swing bands of the late '30s were getting considerably more attention from the press and the public, and so were their singers—Jack Leonard with Tommy Dorsey, Bob Eberly with Jimmy Dorsey, Ray Eberle with Glenn Miller, Dick Haymes with Harry James, and so on. But a few of Como's recordings with Weems got frequent enough airplay to keep Como out of total obscurity. Among those recordings were "Picture Me Without You," "Goody Good-bye," "Until Today," and "Good Night, Sweet Dreams."

Then, with the entrance of the United States into World War II, Weems joined the armed forces and his orchestra disbanded. Como, tired of traveling, made plans to return to Canonsburg with Roselle and their young daughter and two sons—and open a new barber shop. He never got there. CBS offered him a radio contract, which he accepted on the condition that he could remain in one place and not have to travel. He and his family settled in a Long Island suburban town not far from New York City as he began a late-afternoon, fifteen-minute, sustaining show on CBS. The program didn't remain unsponsored for long. Frank Sinatra was riding high as the wartime bobby-sox idol, and CBS publicists painted Como as the new rival. An eight-week engagement at the popular Copacabana nightclub in New York clinched his status as the hot new romantic crooner. RCA Victor signed him to an exclusive recording contract in 1943, and soon afterward Como moved to NBC (an RCA affiliate) as the star of its 7:00 P.M. *Chesterfield Supper Club*. He appeared three nights a week to Jo Stafford's two nights, building the program over the next four years into one of the most popular early-evening, music-only shows on the air.

Meanwhile, in 1945 Como became the first pop singer to reach the two-million mark in record sales with two releases at the same time: "If I Loved You" and "Till the End of Time." Both songs are typical Como songs: pretty and unabashedly sentimental. They also exemplify the way Como always carefully balanced new songs with old on his recordings and radio broadcasts. "If I Loved You" was then a brand-new song (from Rodgers and Hammerstein's *Carousel*), whereas "Till the End of Time" was an adaptation of the long-familiar Polonaise in A-flat major by Chopin (which had been prominently featured in its original form in the 1944 Chopin movie biography *A Song to Remember*). Similarly, for every new song he sent on its way to *Your Hit Parade*—including "Long Ago and Far Away," "Hubba, Hubba, Hubba (Dig You Later)," "Don't Let the Stars Get in Your Eyes," "It's Impossible," and "Papa Loves Mambo," Como revived an older song and put it back on the charts with a new, straightforward arrangement—including 1918's "I'm Always Chasing Rainbows" (another Chopin adaptation), 1931's "Prisoner of Love," 1933's "Temptation," 1902's "Because," and 1898's "If You Were the Only

Girl in the World." This mixture of old and new helped Como's popularity to cut across the generations more solidly and successfully than that of most other singers of the '40s and '50s. Between 1944 and 1955 he was second only to Bing Crosby among male singers in the total number of hit records on the best-seller charts.

For all his relaxed, easygoing style, Perry Como's associates in both radio and television say he's always been a meticulous professional, serious about his music, well prepared at rehearsals, patient about working out difficulties on the set. He's also well known for the warmth of his feelings toward fellow musicians. One story he told former *Metronome* editor George T. Simon a few years ago illustrates how far that can go: "The guys at RCA never knew it, but I usually managed to do something [at recording sessions] that would take us into overtime, so the musicians would get something extra—you know, things like stopping to eat a sandwich, or blowing my nose a lot, or doing a few extra takes, or even going to the bathroom."

Since his weekly television show went off the air in 1963, Como has continued to do TV specials, to record new albums now and then, and to make occasional concert appearances (including a 1988 Boston Pops tribute to Bing Crosby). But he has never made a secret of the fact that he would rather play golf than sing, and that he is able to do plenty of that in Jupiter, Florida, where he and Roselle now make their home.

JUDY GARLAND

Garland audiences don't just listen, they feel.
—SPENCER TRACY

With Bing Crosby, Frank Sinatra, and Ella Fitzgerald, Judy Garland makes up the Big Four of classic pop—the ones who not only reached the pinnacle of superstar popularity but also set vocal standards that most other singers have never been hesitant about acknowledging. Of the four of them, Judy Garland still has, nearly twenty years after her death, the most hyperfanatical admirers *and* the most hyperdisdainful detractors. People either love Judy Garland or can't stand her.

For a good part of her life, she gave everybody plenty of opportunities for both reactions. There is no denying the uniquely heart-melting and musically vibrant quality of her best work in movies, and on radio, television, and recordings going back to her teen years— *nor* the sticky excesses of some of her performances and her often neurotic, self-pitying behavior (both on and off the stage), which put many people off during many of her adult years.

She was a tiny lady, just a bit over five-feet-one. But she had a big, open-throated, resonant voice that, even when she was a youngster, could fill a large theater with waves of clear sound without a microphone. The mixture of a powerful voice with an appearance of fragility and vulnerability was something no other popular singer has had in quite the same way. She sometimes called herself a belter and loved to build songs to the kind of *pow* ending that pulled audiences to their feet in enthusiastic, even screaming cheers. Yet, unlike Broadway's most famous belter, Ethel Merman, Judy Garland could also sing softly, intimately, and tenderly. Even in a quiet ballad, however, she had a light, unabrasive quaver that gave her singing a compelling quality. When these natural vocal gifts were combined with her extraordinary abilities as an actress (both comic and serious), you could come away from a Garland performance convinced that you would never again hear a particular song sung any better.

A song she later sang, "Born in a Trunk," had some elements of truth in it, for her parents had originally been bush-league vaudeville performers. When Garland entered the world as Frances Ethel Gumm on June 10, 1922, in Grand Rapids, Minnesota, her father had settled down as the manager of one of the town's two theaters. (Later she sometimes claimed she had been born in her father's hometown of Murfreesboro, Tennessee, possibly because she thought the name more picturesque or distinctive.) Frances was only two and a half when her parents let her join her two older sisters (then seven and nine) as part of their act for a Christmas show at her father's theater. The *Grand Rapids Herald-Review* reported, "The work of baby Frances was a genuine surprise. The little girl spoke and sang so as to be heard by everyone in the house." The kids were such a hit that they continued to perform on and off over the next few years, including a blackface routine in which Frances imitated Al Jolson. A bit of the Jolson style and spirit, in fact, would remain part of her throughout her life.

In 1927 the Gumms moved to Southern California, partly because they felt a change in climate would help Frances' allergies and partly because Mrs. Gumm believed the area held more promise for the Gumm Sisters' act. It wasn't long before the youngsters were signed for various vaudeville tours. Mrs. Gumm traveled with her children while their father, in declining health, remained in California. A *Variety* review of a 1931 Chicago appearance reported, "The youngest handles ballads like a veteran and gets every note and word over with personality that hits audiences. Her sisters merely form a background."

It was also in Chicago that headliner George Jessel, after getting an unexpected laugh when he introduced the Gumm Sisters, suggested they change their name—perhaps to something else beginning with the first initial of their real name, such as Garland (the name of his friend *New York World-Telegram* drama critic Robert Garland). When Jessel introduced the act for the third show as the Garland Sisters and got no laugh, the name stuck. A bit later, Frances (over her mother's objections) changed her first name to Judy, partly because she liked Hoagy Carmichael's song of that title. She was soon being billed as "Judy Garland, the little girl with the big voice."

Whenever the act played in the Los Angeles area, Mrs. Gumm

would arrange for auditions at some of the movie studios. One after another, Paramount, Universal, Fox, and Columbia turned Judy down. It was not until early 1935, after the oldest sister decided to get married and the act broke up, that writer/producer Joseph Man- kiewicz heard Judy sing at a private party and arranged an audition at MGM. This time she was signed, but only to a short-term contract at $100 a week. Just a few weeks later, her father died—personally devastating Judy, who fought continually with her mother (publicly describing her later as "the real-life Wicked Witch of the West").

Before assigning Judy to any movies, MGM arranged for her to sing on several national radio shows. On one, MGM star Wallace Beery introduced her as "twelve-year-old Judy Garland" (she was actually thirteen and a half), just the first of many studio-generated myths and distortions that were to pervade both her career and private life and to which she herself would sometimes add.

A costarring part with a then-unknown Deanna Durbin in an MGM musical featurette, *Every Sunday*, attracted little attention, as did a minor role in a college musical, *Pigskin Parade*, on a loan-out to 20th Century–Fox. What really made moviegoers take notice of Judy Gar- land was one scene in *Broadway Melody of 1938* in which she sang "You Made Me Love You" to a photograph of Clark Gable. *The New York Times* critic described it as "probably the greatest tour de force in recent screen history." Judy's option was picked up, and over the next year the studio kept her busy in a series of mostly minor and now-forgotten movies whose high points were always a Garland song or two.

Then, virtually by default, came *The Wizard of Oz*, originally in- tended for the era's top child star, Shirley Temple. As the young girl who gets blown by a Kansas tornado to the magical land of Oz, Garland permanently won the hearts of millions of moviegoers. The movie also gave Garland her lifelong theme song, Harold Arlen and Yip Harburg's "Over the Rainbow." Ironically, the song almost got cut from the film by studio executives after the first preview (they thought it slowed down the picture), but it then went on to win that year's Academy Award as Best Song. Judy Garland, too, received an Academy Award, a special junior-size statuette "for her outstanding performance as a screen juvenile" in *The Wizard of Oz*. Contrary to long-popular misconceptions, however, the movie did *not* make Gar- land an overnight star, nor did the picture itself earn back its pro- duction costs during its original release. It was not until *The Wizard of Oz* was sold to television in the late 1940s that it became a profitable and popular movie, and the classic we know it as today.

As for Garland herself, it was her subsequent 1939–1943 musicals, especially those with Mickey Rooney (*Babes in Arms*, *Babes on Broadway*, *Strike Up the Band*, and *Girl Crazy*) that really made her a major star. In most of them, the tomboyish spunkiness of her on-screen persona came to personify, as much as had her Dorothy in *The Wizard of Oz*, the "we can do it" image with which millions of young Americans of both sexes could identify in those uncertain war years. And in those pictures she proved there was no better female singer in the movies, as she turned any number of songs—including such standards as the Gershwins' "I Got Rhythm," "Bidin' My Time," "Fascinating Rhythm," and "Embraceable You"—into unforgettable Garland song vignettes. She also solidified her reputation as a singer by frequent appearances on Bing Crosby's and other top-rated radio shows.

Over the rest of the 1940s, Garland's popularity soared as her movie roles became more romantic and more adult. The best songwriters were now writing scores especially for her—Cole Porter, Irving Berlin, Harry Warren and Johnny Mercer, and Hugh Martin and Ralph Blaine. Many of the songs she introduced quickly became top jukebox hits, including "The Trolley Song" and "The Boy Next Door" from *Meet Me in St. Louis*, "On the Atchison, Topeka, and the Santa Fe" from *The Harvey Girls*, "Love of My Life" and "Be a Clown" from *The Pirate* (with Gene Kelly), and "Better Luck Next Time" and "It Only Happens When I Dance with You" from *Easter Parade* (with Fred Astaire). Her movie versions even gave new popularity to such songs as "Johnny One Note," "I Wish I Were in Love Again," and "Get Happy."

After an elopement with and brief marriage (at nineteen) to recently divorced composer and bandleader David Rose (partly, according to some sources, as a form of rebellion against both her studio bosses and her mother), Garland married her *Meet Me in St. Louis* director, Vincente Minnelli, in 1945. In addition to producing daughter Liza, they also worked together on several other major pictures plus Garland's showstopping "guest spots" in such all-star MGM musicals as *Ziegfeld Follies, Till the Clouds Roll By, and Words and Music.*

But behind the scenes, Garland's personal life was in increasing turmoil. High-strung even as a child, she developed problems coping with the pressures of her studio-imposed schedule—with its back-to-back picture-making, makeup tests and costume fittings, publicity assignments, radio broadcasts, and recording sessions. She began taking pills to help keep her going during the day and to keep her weight under control (as a youngster she'd always tended to overweight), and pills to help her come down and get to sleep at night. Not surprisingly, her nervous system got short-circuited. Minnelli tried to convince her to give up her pills, but she only seemed to grow more dependent on them and, like most addicts, found sneaky ways to get and take them. Feelings that she had no control over her life intensified, that first her mother and now the studio ran her life. Twice the studio pulled her off films she had started (*The Barkleys of Broadway, Annie Get Your Gun*) and arranged for her to enter sanitariums and hospitals for treatment and rest.

She would return to make a picture or two, but her periods of "good behavior" seemed to grow shorter and shorter. Her neurotic roller coaster began to take its toll not only on her behavior at home and at the studio, but also on her appearance (especially her fluctuating weight). Garland's voice, however, remained in great shape, as strong and vibrant as ever, as her recordings and broadcast transcriptions of the period attest. But everything else was falling apart, including her marriage to Minnelli. Finally, her absenteeism and difficulties at the studio led MGM to cancel her contract on June 17, 1950. Three days later, in an incident that made national headlines, Garland locked herself in her bathroom and tried to commit suicide. She was saved just in time. She had celebrated her twenty-eighth birthday only ten days before.

Not only had Garland been fired by the studio that had made her a star, but it also turned out she was broke, except for a paid-up $100,000 insurance policy and some small income from one investment left over from her childhood. No other studio seemed willing to touch her, and only Bing Crosby continued to offer her occasional radio guest spots. As Garland later told an interviewer, "All I wanted to do was eat and hide. I lost all my confidence."

Within the next year, Garland met Sid Luft, a former B-movie producer. Soon after his divorce from actress Lynn Bari, Luft married Garland and began managing her career. He arranged singing engagements for her, first at the London Palladium and then at Broadway's Palace Theater. Both were sensational successes. A now plumper Garland seemed to thrive on singing directly to audiences, and her audiences thrived on being in the Garland presence.

In 1953 Luft convinced Jack Warner, head of the Warner Bros. studio, that the success of Garland's stage appearances meant she still had tremendous box-office appeal. She returned to Hollywood to make a musical version of *A Star Is Born*, a 1937 movie about Hollywood behind the scenes that Garland had loved ever since she did a radio adaptation of it in 1942. Personal friends Harold Arlen and Ira Gershwin were signed for the score, arguably the best ever written for Garland and out of which she got her greatest adult hit, "The Man That Got Away." Not only was her singing voice on the sound track fuller, richer, and more obviously mature than ever before, but so, too, was her acting performance (in both the comedy scenes and the tragic ones). However, the movie itself was plagued by cost overruns (some of them blamed directly on Garland) and by production problems (including a decision after shooting was under way to redo everything in the then-new CinemaScope wide-screen process). Then, after complaints from exhibitors following the movie's premiere that its three-hour length was too long, the studio cut nearly a half hour out of it, over the objections of Garland, Luft, and director George Cukor. Despite exceptionally good critical reviews and an Academy Award nomination for Garland, *A Star Is Born* could not recoup its excessive costs. Judy Garland would never again star in a major Hollywood-made musical.

Over the next decade, Garland concentrated on the thing she loved best: singing. She did a number of TV specials (including one with Frank Sinatra) and played Las Vegas as well as various theaters, clubs, and resorts in the United States and Britain. Most significantly, she made a series of outstanding albums for Capitol Records, mostly with Nelson Riddle or Gordon Jenkins in charge of the arrangements— albums of classic-pop standards that still stand as her finest vocal achievements and, arguably, among the finest albums any American singer has ever made. Gone was the innocence of her younger sound, to be replaced by a more openly heartthrobbing and self-revealing musical pathos. Her versions of "Come Rain and Come Shine," "Last Night When We Were Young," "I Concentrate on You," "This Is It," "The Red Balloon," and many others became the standards by which all other versions had to be judged.

However, this period, too, was plagued with fluctuations in both her emotional and physical health, including a hospitalization for hepatitis, after which she couldn't work for seven months. Her weight would balloon up, then plummet. There were temper tantrums and canceled engagements, audience ovations for some performances and boos for others in which her voice cracked or in which she seemed drugged or drunk or both. Her marriage to Luft (during which they had two children, Lorna and Joey) became increasingly marked by public arguments and charges that he was compounding her financial difficulties. They divorced in 1962. Yet, from the depths of wretchedly uneven performances, Garland could pull herself together, sometimes in a matter of weeks, for spectacular evenings of great singing.

The peak came with Garland's one-night Carnegie Hall concert in New York on April 23, 1961—one of those legendary nights that left most of the audience hoarse from cheering and the critics scrambling for words to describe the impact of her singing. Its success, and that of the best-selling live recording of that concert made by Capitol, led CBS to offer Garland a weekly Sunday-night television series. It ran for nearly seven months in 1963–64 to only modest ratings (more Americans were interested in watching the hit Western-drama series *Bonanza* on NBC). But that TV series, and its preservation on video, not only provides us today with a splendid representation of Garland singing songs with which she will be forever identified, but also shows her in once-in-a-lifetime duets with such other great classic-pop singers as Lena Horne, Barbra Streisand, Ethel Merman, Jack Jones, Vic Damone, and daughter Liza Minnelli. Classic pop has rarely known such a *musical* bonanza from prime-time television.

After the TV series, Garland resumed the up-and-down life of personal-appearance touring. There were good months and bad months, flush times and broke times. There were romances with actor Glenn Ford, publicist Tom Green, and songwriter Johnny Meyer, and marriages in 1965 to actor Mark Herron (eighteen years her junior) and in 1969 to nightclub manager Mickey Deans (eleven years her junior). A few months after her honeymoon with Deans, Garland arrived in London for a nightclub engagement, looking tired and haggard. Then, on the morning of June 21, 1969, she was found dead in her London apartment. Daughter Liza later told an interviewer, "She did *not* kill herself. She didn't die of an overdose or any of that crap. Her body just gave out on her. She just passed away, joined the choir, however you want to put it. She died with dignity, when she was still able to work. She would have hated not being able to work. And I miss her terribly." One American reporter wrote at the time, "Suicide? Accident? No, she just wore out." She was forty-seven.

PEGGY LEE

If I'm Duke, man, Peggy Lee is Queen.
—DUKE ELLINGTON

Chatting and laughing, clanging cocktail glasses, the audience was louder than the band, as Peggy Lee tells the story. It was 1941, at a swanky club in Palm Springs called the Doll House. Lee was booming out her songs, but nobody seemed to care much about hearing her. Then she got a thought. For the next tune, whose title she doesn't recall, she lowered her voice to a hush, quieter than the crowd, and the audience started settling down and listening. Apocryphal or not, the story nicely dramatizes the inverted emotional physics at work in Peggy Lee's singing. By reducing how much she gives her listeners, she increases how much they get.

Few people seem to know about it, because it's been fifty years since she's let anybody hear it, but Peggy Lee's natural voice is quite full and strong (or was until the late 1980s, when her health declined severely). When she sings with that alluring purr of a voice, she's revealing a bare hint of everything she's got, like most alluring women. Of course, many of the best classic-pop vocalists sing at conversational volume. But Peggy Lee never tries to dominate the conversation. As F. Scott Fitzgerald described Daisy Buchanan, she brings others close to her with the softness of her voice.

Once she's pulled you in, Peggy Lee is able to communicate much more intimately and subtly than singers who belt out tunes in the big, broad theatrical style. There she is, nose-to-nose with you. She can't very well start mugging like a stage ham, when a half-smile or a wink would make her feelings clear. All Peggy Lee needs to do is pause a half-beat on a lyric or bend a note a quarter-tone, and she has you intrigued. One of the most hypnotic of all pop singers, she knows the power of suggestion.

Lee has been entrancing concert audiences, record buyers, and moviegoers for half a century now, still maintaining an active schedule of recording, performing, and songwriting as she passed her seventieth year in 1990. She's more than a survivor; she's also a victor. Through several life-threatening illnesses, four troubled marriages, and rock 'n' roll, Lee has prevailed as the only woman to have Top Ten hits in the 1940s, the 1950s, and the 1960s. Beyond her singing, too, Lee is the only major female singer in the classic-pop style to emerge as an important songwriter of songs not only for herself but also for other major singers. And, as a sideline, she's acted well enough to be nominated for an Academy Award.

"People wonder how you can survive in show business," she mused in her later years. "My strength came from the training I got as a girl, working as a hired hand on a farm. I shucked grain. I pitched hay. I drove the water wagon for a threshing ring." Raised in Jamestown, North Dakota, where folks know what a threshing ring is, Norma Deloris Egstrom was the seventh of eight children born to a Norwegian railroad worker and his Swedish wife, who died when Norma was four years old. Before her adolescence, Lee had started working at grown-up jobs, first with her father for a small railroad company, then on the local farms, and, by the time she was fourteen, singing on the Jamestown radio station. "My teachers told me I had a good voice, so I put it to work," she later explained. "It beat shucking grain, although I still did some waitressing in between my spots on the radio."

From her earliest days as a singer, Lee showed the potent combination of independent spirit, appetite for work, and natural talent that would fuel her for some fifty years. Renamed Peggy Lee by a program director at a radio station in Fargo, North Dakota, she bolted for Hollywood after high-school graduation with her accumulated savings of $18. She landed a job—waitressing—and even managed to do a little singing at the Jade Club before heading back north to Minneapolis, where she sang with Sev Olson's regional big band for a while. From the Olson group, Lee soon moved up to her first glimmer of the big time with Will Osborne's orchestra. It was around this period that she played that date at the Doll House in Palm Springs, which would prove to be only slightly more important in the making of Peggy Lee than a subsequent gig in Chicago in 1941. That's when

Benny Goodman heard Lee at the Ambassador Hotel and brought her all the way into the very big time, signing her to replace Helen Forrest.

"I learned more about music from the bands I worked with than I learned anywhere else," she says. From performing dance music with swing bands, she developed an especially acute sense of time. Her singing always swings, ever so softly sometimes. Even on ballads and contemporary material, Peggy Lee sings with a light, rhythmic lilt that's rooted in her dance-band days. As she puts it, "I really have no sense of time except swing time."

Because of both her sense of rhythm and her understated phrasing—to say she understates is an overstatement—Peggy Lee is often associated with Billie Holiday. While an admirer of Holiday, Lee credits Maxine Sullivan as her strongest influence. "I wasn't drawn to any particular singer until I heard Maxine Sullivan. I like the simplicity and the economy of her work," she explains. "She communicates so well that you really get the point of her songs right away."

There is more to Peggy Lee's singing than simplicity and economy, or she would be the Hyundai of pop singing instead of the Jaguar. She is, of course, one of the sexiest of pop singers, and not only because of her exquisite Nordic looks. There's a creamy warmth to the tone of her voice that gives it a sensually conspiratorial quality. Most of her hits have been songs that play on this sexiness, including the lusty 1943 release with the Goodman band that first launched Peggy Lee to national prominence, "Why Don't You Do Right?" (which had been released far less successfully by Lil Green four years earlier). With "Lover" (1952) she transformed what composer Richard Rodgers called "my little waltz" into a driving sexual assault. And then there's "Fever" (1958), a song that separates sex from love altogether and set a standard for pop eroticism that has yet to be surpassed, no matter how explicit and raunchy contemporary pop songs get.

While the public that makes million-selling records may always associate Peggy Lee with her sexiest hits, she would prefer to be thought of as a respected composer of pop standards and film scores. The only major female pop singer to achieve note as a songwriter, Lee has been crafting songs from the mid-1940s to the present day. Her songs, for which she usually writes lyrics in collaboration with composers, are generally as straightforward as her singing, if not quite as sophisticated and rich in subtext. She has recorded most of her songs herself, and scored hits with several, including "Mañana" and "I Don't Know Enough About You," both written with her first husband, Dave Barbour. Her specialty has been adapting songs from movie themes, such as "Johnny Guitar" and "About Mrs. Leslie," both written with Victor Young; "The Heart Is a Lonely Hunter," written with Dave Grusin; "The Shining Sea," the theme for *The Russians Are Coming, The Russians Are Coming,* written with Johnny Mandell; and the entire score for the Disney cartoon feature *Lady and the Tramp,* written with Sonny Burke. (In mid-1990 Peggy Lee released a newly recorded compilation of original songs she had written over the course of her career, titled *The Peggy Lee Songbook.*)

As she's felt fit, Lee has dabbled in acting from time to time as well. She's good at dabbling—she's done some sculpting and some painting, with a fondness for rendering the hands of famous men such as Albert Schweitzer; she's written some verse, compiled in a book that sounds as if it's about her singing, called *Softly, with Feeling.* As an avocational actress, she made her debut with a brief appearance with Bing Crosby in *Mr. Music* (1950). A little later she took on a featured role opposite Danny Thomas in the 1953 version of *The Jazz Singer.* She's done a bit of dramatic TV, including parts in *The Girl from U.N.C.L.E.* (1967) and *Owen Marshall, Counsellor-at-Law* (1972). Yet she clearly had the potential to become a successful actress, had she wanted, as her performance in the 1955 drama *Pete Kelly's Blues* demonstrates. She was nominated for an Oscar for Best Supporting Actress for her finely shaded portrayal of an alcoholic blues singer in the early days of jazz.

Peggy Lee's life has not been charmed, however. For all her hits, she's had her share of misses—most notably her one and only appearance on Broadway, in 1983, in an original autobiographical musical, *Peg.* A painfully honest piece of personal expression (and we mean painfully), the show featured numbers such as a song about Lee's childhood, "One Beating a Day, Maybe More." It didn't leave 'em laughing, and *Peg* closed in one night.

Her love life hasn't been all fun, either. Lee has married four times: Dave Barbour in '43, Brad Dexter in '55, Dewey Martin in '56, and Jack Del Rio in '64. In addition, she's long suffered from a variety of health problems, including diabetes, various lung ailments, and a failing heart, for which she underwent double bypass surgery in the 1980s. Since breaking her pelvis in a fall on a slippery Las Vegas stage in the 1980s she has rarely been able to walk on her own and relies on a wheelchair. Moreover, respiratory problems have made her dependent on a transportable oxygen apparatus that she travels with and uses in her dressing room during breaks in live performances.

Wheelchair and portable oxygen tent and all, Peggy Lee was writing songs, recording, and performing regularly as she began her second half-century in music in the early 1990s. "I don't like time. I think of everything as now," she says simply. Then again, she was never one to overstate her point.

LENA HORNE

*Let us resign ourselves to the fact that Lena cannot be
easily defined or categorized. We can, however, be properly
grateful to the deity of our choice that we are here, on
her planet, in her time.*
—author-producer *NAT SHAPIRO*

As famous as show business is for its beautiful women, there have
been few more beautiful than Lena Horne. For many years she was
considered the copper-skinned Hedy Lamarr, almost too ideally beautiful to be true. Ironically, her looks and sex appeal have sometimes
tended to overshadow the fact that she is also one of her generation's
finest singers, with a sultry, sensual voice of considerable range, flexibility, and focused power.

With that combination of attributes, it's no wonder Hollywood wanted
her. But then when it got her, it didn't know what to do with her. In
a succession of glossy musicals, she became little more than a sepia
Barbie Doll, singing as a sort of featured guest star but taking no part
in the rest of the films' action around her. For in the 1940s, when she
rose to fame, even though she came closer than any previous black
performer to the then-prevalent white ideal of feminine beauty, Lena
Horne ran head-on into the racial barriers that had bedeviled and
limited the careers of Ethel Waters, Billie Holiday, and other talented
black singers before her. At first Horne fought back quietly, politely,
and generally ineffectually—uncertain what she could do about it. But
as the civil-rights movement gained momentum in the 1950s and 1960s,
Horne became a more committed, sometimes angry activist, earning
praise from some and criticism from others, including blacks who
accused her of being a Johnny-come-lately to the movement.

Horne traces her ancestry to the former French West African colony
of Senegal, as well as to American Blackfoot Indians and white slave-
owners. She has never been shy about pointing out the accomplish-
ments of her proudly middle-class family before her. Her maternal
grandfather, for example, was the first black member of the Brooklyn

Board of Education, and her paternal grandmother was a prominent early member of both the National Urban League and the National Association for the Advancement of Colored People (NAACP). An uncle, Dr. Frank Smith Horne, was a government administrator who served as an adviser to President Franklin D. Roosevelt on race relations.

Her actress-mother, Edna Scottron, was a member of the touring Lafayette Players, a black stock company that presented plays in major East Coast cities. After Helena Calhoun Horne was born in Brooklyn on June 30, 1917, her mother continued to tour, leaving the child with various relatives for long periods. "I never let myself love anybody," Horne once reminisced to a *People* magazine reporter, "because I knew I couldn't stay around much." Later, when her mother fell ill and could no longer work, a family friend helped Helena, already shapely and vivacious at sixteen, get a job in the chorus of the famous Cotton Club in Harlem. It wasn't long before she graduated to feature spots in Cotton Club shows. Now billed as Lena Horne, she also landed a small role in a Broadway play, *Dance with Your Gods*, but it lasted only nine performances.

Enter Noble Sissle, the bandleader-composer who had teamed with Eubie Blake in creating Broadway's first all-black revue, *Shuffle Along*. He had heard Horne at the Cotton Club and hired her as the singer with his band. Still using the name Helena Horne, she toured for two years with Sissle's band throughout the East and Midwest, until she could take no more of the one-night stands and third-class accommodations blacks had to endure along the way. To get away from show business altogether, she married a friend of her father's who was active in Pittsburgh politics, Louis J. Jones. Over the next three years she and Jones had two children. But she couldn't give up singing completely, and began performing at private parties. When a small, independent film company offered her a leading role as a singer in a low-budget, all-black movie titled *The Duke Is Tops*, she jumped at the chance. Although the film played only in theaters in black neighborhoods, it won her another Broadway chance, in Lew Leslie's 1939 edition of his earlier megahit revue *Blackbirds*. Like her earlier Broadway bid, this one also lasted only nine performances. But Horne was determined to keep trying, despite her husband's objections. (They separated in 1940 and were divorced in 1944.)

In 1940, on returning to New York, she became the vocalist with Charlie Barnet's orchestra, one of the swing era's most jazz-oriented dance bands. Independently wealthy and a natural rebel, Barnet was in a better position than most of his colleagues to buck the commercial strictures of the era. That meant not only being able to stick more faithfully to the adventurous kind of jazz-influenced arrangements he favored, but also being one of the first (beginning in 1937) to hire black musicians to play side by side with whites. Benny Goodman and Artie Shaw, of course, had both hired Billie Holiday to record with their orchestras before Barnet hired Horne, but it was still a bold move in 1940. Horne, however, lasted only four or five months with Barnet, during which time one of the four songs she recorded with his band became a popular hit, "Good-for-Nothin' Joe."

What took Horne away from the Barnet orchestra was an offer from New York nightclub impresario Barney Josephson to solo at his Café Society Downtown, where the house band was led by her friend Teddy Wilson (of the original Benny Goodman Trio fame). What was intended as a three-or-four-week engagement ended up as a seven-month stint as word spread about the sensational young singer at the club. Mostly she sang ballads, the same romantic ones that the leading white singers also sang. But she sang them with a distinctively bluesy tinge, making them seem less innocent and less superficial. Because he had to turn away so many customers night after night, Josephson sponsored a concert for Horne at Carnegie Hall. Billie Holiday was at the concert and reportedly became upset when Horne sang a number of songs previously identified with Holiday. When Horne learned this, she went to the club where Holiday was appearing, assured Holiday of how much she idolized her, and asked permission to continue singing some of the songs, which was granted.

Soon after the concert, RCA Victor signed Horne to a recording contract, and she also began to appear on network radio shows, including the celebrated tongue-in-cheek *Chamber Music Society of Lower Basin Street* program, on which Dinah Shore had helped build her national reputation. A recording of Harold Arlen and Ted Koehler's 1932 "I Gotta Right to Sing the Blues" got a good critical reception, and two ballads, "Love Me a Little Little" and "Don't Take Your Love from Me," both with Artie Shaw's orchestra (also under contract to RCA Victor), became modest hits. But further recording plans were cut short by both the ASCAP and musicians' union strikes.

When Horne opened a singing engagement at the Little Troc nightclub in Hollywood in 1942, Roger Edens, a staff composer and arranger at MGM, arranged a screen test for her, and MGM promptly offered Horne a contract. At first she was uncertain whether to accept. She knew how demeaningly other blacks had been treated by the major studios—especially Ethel Waters, who was relegated to playing

Jeanette MacDonald's maid in the movie *Cairo*, then being filmed at MGM. But Count Basie and Walter White, the NAACP's executive secretary, urged Horne to sign, arguing that her youth, looks, and talent might help pave the way for better roles for a new generation of black artists. When MGM promised her one of the leads alongside Ethel Waters in the film version of the all-black Broadway musical fable *Cabin in the Sky*, Horne signed. But she insisted her contract include a clause that she would never have to play maids or prostitutes.

Things did not start off auspiciously. For Horne's first MGM film, *Panama Hattie* (1942), the studio tried to pass her off as a Latin American, costumed ridiculously in what looked like a Carmen Miranda reject as she sang a Latin-tempoed version of Cole Porter's "Just One of Those Things" in a production number directed by Vincente Minnelli. Her single sequence, moreover, was designed so it could easily be cut out (without damage to the plot) in Southern theaters unwilling to present racially mixed entertainment.

But then MGM kept its promise about *Cabin in the Sky* (1943). It was not an enormous hit, but it did well enough to establish Vincente Minnelli (directing his first complete film) as a major director and Horne as a major movie name. To supplement Vernon Duke's original Broadway score, Harold Arlen and Yip Harburg wrote a showstopping duet ("Life's Full o' Consequence") for Horne and male star Eddie Anderson, and also a solo for Horne ("Ain't It de Truth"), which got cut (but was later used in an MGM short). As temptress Georgia Brown, Horne sings well, but from today's perspective, her mannered acting is not as memorable as how beautifully she photographs.

There was even more emphasis on looking and singing pretty in her next movie, another all-black musical, *Stormy Weather* (1943). This time, on a loan-out to 20th Century–Fox for its not-very-accurate biography of dancer Bill Robinson, Horne got top billing among a cast of such musical greats as Robinson himself, Fats Waller, Cab Calloway, Ada Brown, Dooley Wilson, the Nicholas Brothers, and the Katherine Dunham Dancers. And, indeed, she stole the show from all of them in the film's big finale with her plaintive singing of the Harold Arlen–Ted Koehler song from which the movie took its title. From then on, "Stormy Weather" would be primarily linked in the public's mind with Lena Horne, not with Ethel Waters as before.

But after *Cabin in the Sky* and *Stormy Weather*, MGM could (or would) find nothing for Horne other than more interpolated numbers in major musicals. Usually the sequences turned out to be a highlight of each of these films—with Horne giving unforgettably sensuous accounts of such standards as "Honeysuckle Rose" (in *Thousands Cheer*), "Somebody Loves Me" (in *Broadway Rhythm*), "Paper Doll" (in *Two Girls and a Sailor*), "Love" (in *Ziegfeld Follies*), and "The Lady Is a Tramp" (in *Words and Music*). She was photographed so often leaning provocatively against a pillar or a wall that she herself once said, "I became a butterfly pinned to a column, singing away." She also acquired a reputation for being cold and aloof on-screen. "The image I chose to give," she has said in response, "is of a woman the audience can't reach and therefore can't hurt."

She desperately wanted to play the mulatto Julie in MGM's remake of *Show Boat*, and thought she was the front-runner for the role after she played it in a series of extended excerpts filmed as part of MGM's 1946 Jerome Kern "bio-pic" *Till the Clouds Roll By*. But the studio picked Ava Gardner, ironically one of Horne's closest personal friends on the MGM lot. There were some who believed that at least part of the decision stemmed from the studio brass's irritation over Horne's activism in the Screen Actors' Guild on behalf of black performers, as well as her biracial marriage to Lennie Hayton, an MGM music director, in 1947. When Hayton's contract was not renewed the following year, he and Lena decided to leave Hollywood. She was still a top nightclub attraction, earning one of the highest fees then paid anyone in Las Vegas, $12,500 a week.

The Haytons' plans to settle in New York ran into problems. When they tried to find an apartment in Manhattan, they found three snags: She was black, he was Jewish, and they were married. What particularly outraged Horne was being turned down by the building on Central Park West that was then owned by C. M. "Daddy" Grace, the black religious leader whose million-dollar income had come largely from blacks. The Haytons finally settled in Brooklyn.

But still more problems were lurking. At the height of the McCarthy era's witch-hunts, Horne found herself unable to get radio or television work because her name was listed in *Red Channels*, the book that purported to expose celebrities with pro-Communist sympathies or membership in "suspect organizations." Horne flatly denied any Communist links and said that in her civil-rights work she "belonged to all the same outfits that Mrs. Roosevelt did." Eventually Horne was cleared, and by 1957 invitations were coming in again from Ed Sullivan, Perry Como, Steve Allen, and *The Bell Telephone Hour* for her to appear on their shows.

Meanwhile, Horne finally achieved her dream of a hit Broadway show when she opened in Harold Arlen and Yip Harburg's *Jamaica* in 1957. Although it produced no hit songs to rival the popularity of the earlier Arlen songs with which she is still identified, it ran for 555 performances.

With the coming of the politically activist 1960s, Horne became more openly engaged in the civil-rights movement, singing at rallies and fund-raising benefits. She cut half a dozen new albums, mostly for smaller labels, in which she mixed old standards with contemporary songs by the Beatles, Bob Dylan, and others. Most of her arrangements (by husband Hayton and others) were now gutsier and more expressive, with Horne seeming less afraid than ever to stretch the limits of her voice. She also returned briefly to Hollywood for a dramatic role as Richard Widmark's love interest in the 1969 Western *Death of a Gunfighter*. It turned out to be only a so-so movie, but she felt she was at least helping to bury some old Hollywood casting taboos.

Then tragedy seemed to hit with a vengeance. Within a year, her father, her son, and her husband died. At first Horne said she'd never work again. But Tony Bennett finally convinced her to do a three-week Broadway concert with him, titled *Tony and Lena*. She later did a similar show, this time as a TV special, with Harry Belafonte. She also agreed to play Glinda the Good Witch in the movie version of the all-black Broadway musical *The Wiz* (based on *The Wizard of Oz*).

Finally, in 1981, at age sixty-four but still looking more beautiful than many half her age, came Horne's professional peak: her one-woman Broadway show *The Lady and Her Music*. Originally scheduled for six weeks, it ended up running for forty-two sold-out weeks before being taped for television and home video and then moving to London for an extended run. In the show, Horne sang many of the songs with which she had been identified over the years and talked candidly about the ups and downs of her career. She sang "Stormy Weather" twice—once to close Act One, singing it in the sultry, "pretty" manner she said Hollywood had forced on her, and then toward the end of Act Two in the more earthy, protest-song manner she really felt. "Not only have we heard a great singer top what we thought to be her best work," wrote *New York Times* critic Frank Rich, "but we've witnessed an honest-to-God *coup de théâtre*." Horne won a special citation from the New York Drama Critics' Circle, and the "original cast" album won two Grammys. And there was little doubt after each two-hour performance that the cheers were as much for Horne-the-knockout-of-a-singer as for the spunky lady herself.

DORIS DAY

I knew Doris Day before she was a virgin.
—OSCAR LEVANT

Before she became a virgin—the eternally innocent symbol of sexless love in all those light movie comedies—Doris Day was a pop singer and her image was anything but virginal. As a matter of fact, Doris Day's singing style was as warm and creamy as her screen persona was cool and tough-surfaced. The movies cleaned her up, just as they would Elvis Presley a decade after Day entered films. Unfortunately, to audiences of the past couple of generations whose conception of Day (and of most other performers) has been framed by TV, she is known almost exclusively for her thirty-nine movies and for the sitcom she did in the late 1960s and early 1970s. Since she all but retired from nightclub and theater performances in the early 1950s and stopped recording regularly before the start of the 1960s, her early work as a singer is virtually forgotten today.

Forgotten, perhaps, but not forgettable. Doris Day, the singer, deserves to be rediscovered, particularly by contemporary listeners who know only the actress. Of course, there was always a touch of dramatic skill in her singing, before she learned to speak a line of dialogue. As she explained to jazz critic Ralph Gleason, who rated her among the all-time best band singers, "I really sing the lyrics rather than the music. I try to sing the words the way you speak them." Yet not even Doris Day spoke the way she sang. There was a girlish sensuality in her tone and a teasing, almost nasty bite to her phrasing that combined to give her singing voice a seductive energy that her acting rarely matched.

Because of her strengths in both music and movies, Doris Day is the only female singer of her generation to become a major star on records and on-screen. In fact, the only other artists of either sex to accomplish the same feat were Bing Crosby, Frank Sinatra, and Judy Garland, until the rock era. Doris Day would probably have been successful *dancing*, too, if her childhood success as a dancer hadn't been abruptly cut short at the age fourteen. Performing in the dance team of Doris and Jerry at age eleven, she and her partner won the grand prize at a Cincinnati amateur contest in 1935. When she was fourteen, however, a locomotive hit a car in which she was a passenger and seriously injured her legs.

While recovering, bedridden, she listened to the radio enough to convince her mother, Alma von Kappelhoff, to switch her daughter from dance to voice lessons. Doris von Kappelhoff began studying with a local Cincinnati music teacher, who made such an impression on her that she was still praising her by name forty years later. "Grace Raine taught me to make the lyrics mean what they say," she noted in the 1970s. "She told me to sing to one person, and each listener will think it's him."

For some time after she became famous, Day told reporters that her father, William von Kappelhoff, was a music professor and had instructed her in music. In 1961, however, a UPI story revealed that he was a longtime proprietor of a tavern. Soon after, Day began opening up about her deep problems with her father, whom she, at age ten, had discovered sleeping with her mother's best friend.

Named Doris after Doris Kenyon, an actress her mother liked, Day was given her stage surname by her first boss, bandleader Barney Rapp, who hired her at age sixteen after hearing her do some amateur singing on a Cincinnati radio station. Her big number was "Day After Day," although she says she never cared much for the song—nor for the name she got from it. "I never liked it. Still don't. I think it's a phony name," she says. (Good thing her big number wasn't "Chattanooga Choo-Choo.") As a result, her closest friends have made an inside joke out of calling her even phonier names. Some use "Do-Do," she has said. Rock Hudson preferred "Eunice."

Looking back on her career, Day boasted in her 1975 autobiography *Doris Day: Her Own Story*, "I must emphasize that I have never had any doubts about my ability in anything I have ever undertaken." The attitude is understandable, considering her extraordinarily rapid rise to national prominence. Within months of her debut with the Barney Rapp orchestra, Bob Crosby heard her and signed her to sing with his band, and Doris Day was in New York City and the big time at age sixteen. Under pressure from a radio sponsor who disliked Day or her voice for reasons unknown, Crosby had to let her go shortly after hiring her. But she was snatched up immediately by the band that would bring her her first big hits and many of her finest moments in music, Les Brown and his orchestra.

Altogether, Day sang with Brown for six years and recorded all of her classic big-band sides with him, including the hits "My Dreams Are Getting Better All the Time" and "Sentimental Journey," which made number one in 1944. Early in her tenure with the band, however, she abruptly decided to retire. At age seventeen, she quit singing to marry Al Jorden, a trombonist with Barney Rapp's band, and moved back to Cincinnati to raise their son, Terry (named after Terry and the Pirates, a favorite newspaper comic strip of Day's). But the retirement was short-lived, and Day returned to New York to sing with Les Brown again within a year. (In the 1960s, Day's grown son would become a rock songwriter, impresario, and producer of records by such groups as the Byrds and Paul Revere and the Raiders. He was tangentially associated with the Charles Manson case, as the previous owner of the house in which the Manson murders were committed.)

Like every other singer we know who's ever worked with a big band, Doris Day has always extolled the experience. "The great thing about singing with a band is that it gets you out before hundreds and hundreds of people every night," she says. "I wish all the new singers could have the same opportunity I had to sing with a big band."

Opening up at least one job for a new singer, Day left Les Brown in 1946 and pursued an audience of millions and millions of people every night, in the movies. When Betty Hutton got pregnant and couldn't shoot *Romance on the High Seas* (1948), director Michael Curtiz screen-tested Day and gave her the starring role, despite the fact that she had no previous acting experience. She certainly fit the All-American-girl mode of movie star prevalent right after the war— cute, slim, and blond, with a slightly smirky smile and bright, sharp eyes. Years later, James Garner would say she had "the best ass in Hollywood." Plus, in a bonus that other stars in the same mode (such as Betty Grable) proved wasn't really necessary, Doris Day could act. Although most of her early roles required her to sing, she was strong enough in her first straight drama, *Storm Warning* (1951), for Alfred Hitchcock to cast her in his 1956 remake of *The Man Who Knew Too Much* with James Stewart. Hitchcock said he had never heard her sing, and had seen her only in *Storm Warning*. Even so, her role was rewritten as a former singer, and Day was called on to sing "Que

Sera, Sera," which became her biggest hit since "Sentimental Journey," and won that year's Oscar as Best Song.

Enormously popular as an actress, Day was twice named the number-one audience attraction nationwide in the annual polls of film exhibitors in 1960 and 1962. In fact, she was only the fourth actress in movie history to be voted the top box-office draw, along with Shirley Temple, Marie Dressler, and Betty Grable. All told, Day made thirty-nine movies from 1948 to 1968, when she retired from films after *With Six You Get Eggroll*, understandably.

Today, Day's best-remembered films may be the string of frothy bedroom farces she made with Rock Hudson, Cary Grant, and Clark Gable in the late 1950s and early 1960s, in which she cemented her reputation as the movies' perennial virgin. A married mother at seventeen, divorced twice by the age of twenty-four, and famous as a thirty-five-year-old virgin, Doris Day was clearly a damn good actress, and earned an Oscar nomination in 1959 for her performance in the best of these farces, *Pillow Talk*. Her all-time most impressive performance, however, was probably her portrayal of Ruth Etting in the 1955 bio picture *Love Me or Leave Me*, despite the fact that she bore little resemblance to Etting, physically or musically.

As TV came into its own in the 1950s, Day chose to steer clear of the medium. "I just don't like it," she explained at the time. "I'm scared of it, I guess. I'm like Perry Como is with the movies—tried it, don't like it, won't do it anymore." The difference between Perry Como and Doris Day, however, is that Day married Marty Melcher, her third husband. (Day husband number two had been Les Brown's saxophonist George Weidler, '46–'49.) Melcher was afraid of neither TV nor his wife—nor the law, evidently. He used his power of attorney over Day to sign her to star in her own network TV sitcom, without mentioning this to her. When he died of a heart attack in 1968, shortly after arranging the deal, Day found the TV commitment to be a blessing in disguise. She discovered that she needed the work because Melcher had embezzled her entire life savings of $20 million and lost it. After working in the top ranks of show business for nearly thirty years, Doris Day was broke. It took six years for her to recoup the losses, through a lawsuit against her husband's business partner that resulted in an unprecedented award of more than $22 million in damages. Her TV show did less damage to her career—it was a harmless trifle that cast Day as, essentially, a forty-five-year-old virgin.

After five years in her sitcom and five in another marriage (to restaurateur Barry Comden, '76–'81), Doris Day unofficially retired, retreating to an estate in rustic Carmel, California, where she dedicates most of her time to the dogs, cats, and other animals that have become the great loves of her later life. "All my life, I have never felt lonely with a dog I loved at my side," she explains. "I love people and animals, though not necessarily in that order."

In the mid-1980s, speculation about a singing comeback started circulating after *The Hollywood Reporter* noted that Day had begun rehearsing with a vocal coach. She came back, all right, but as the host of a short-lived TV series about animals called *Doris Day's Best Friends*. She sang, but mostly the praises of pets.

Que sera, sera.

DICK HAYMES

*His need and urgency to sing was
present in every song.*
—songwriter ALEC WILDER

For a few years in the 1940s, it looked as if the male singer who might eventually beat out Frank Sinatra and Perry Como in dethroning Bing Crosby as the nation's favorite crooner was Dick Haymes. Boyishly handsome and considerably taller than Sinatra, Como, or Crosby (though not the six feet that Hollywood publicity claimed for him), Haymes was blessed with a rich, warm, smoothly textured baritone voice that brought him fame and fortune on records, in nightclubs, and in Hollywood movies. But it would be an unhappily short-lived fame and fortune—not because of a tragic accident, as in the case of Russ Columbo or Buddy Clark, but rather because of his fondness for wine and women over song.

As Haymes once candidly admitted to an interviewer, "My swinging days got so involved with my own ego that I blew it. . . . When you live at the rate I lived—fast cars, luxury homes, and women who want money spent on them—you soon get rid of your dollars." Although he reportedly earned at least $4 million as a singer during his heyday in the 1940s, Haymes spent most of the 1950s, 1960s, and 1970s in headline-making legal entanglements over unpaid taxes and alimony to his ex-wives, and equally headline-making bouts with alcoholism that eventually took their toll on his voice, gave him a reputation as an undependable singer, and undercut several attempts at a comeback.

But in the 1940s there was no more dependable, glorious-voiced singer than Dick Haymes, particularly of intimate, romantic ballads. After his first hit record in 1944, a revival of the 1920s song "I'll Get By," he went on to achieve some forty major hits and nine gold records before the end of the decade, with such songs as "You'll Never Know,"

"Little White Lies," "It Might As Well Be Spring," "Till the End of Time," and "Mam'selle."

Haymes's approach to all these songs was straightforward and un-gimmicky. His tone was smooth and flawlessly controlled, his inter-pretations sensitive and expressive without overdoing it. That was if the song was a ballad. He was less successful with novelty tunes or jazz rhythms. Like Como and unlike Crosby and Sinatra, Haymes didn't always swing very well. And he wasn't all that comfortable with Latin rhythms, even though he was Argentinian by birth.

Actually, Haymes's father, a Briton of Scottish and Irish ancestry, had become a cattle rancher outside Buenos Aires a few years before son Richard was born there on September 13, 1918. Three years later, when the ranch was destroyed by locusts, Dick and his parents moved first to New York and then to Paris for about ten years, returning to New York in the early 1930s. It was at about this time that Dick—who always said his mother (a well-known vocal coach and author of a book on vocal production) had been his only voice coach—began singing at school dances and entering amateur theatricals at New Jer-sey shore resorts. Johnny Johnson, who led the band at a Spring Lake hotel, heard Haymes in one of these productions and signed him up as a vocalist with the band for $25 a week.

At eighteen Haymes decided to head for Hollywood on his own. He managed to get a few low-paying jobs singing at night in what he called "dives," and playing bit parts in "B" Westerns by day at so-called Poverty Row studios. He even tried organizing his own combo, called the Katzenjammers (after a popular 1930s comic strip), but it folded when it couldn't make enough money to meet operating ex-penses in those late-Depression days. His first marriage, to singer Edythe Harper, also failed at this time.

Haymes returned to New York in 1939, hoping to have better professional luck as a songwriter. When he heard that Harry James, who had recently left Benny Goodman's band to form an orchestra of his own, was looking for new material, Haymes arranged to audition some of his tunes for James (some reports say he crashed a rehearsal of James's band). When he finished several songs, James said to him, "Your songs, no. But you, yes." And so Dick Haymes joined Harry James's orchestra as its male vocalist, replacing a still relatively un-known Frank Sinatra, who had just been hired away by Tommy Dor-sey after only six months with James. Haymes stayed longer (about two years), polishing his style and learning to phrase ballads in a way that met James's rigid requirement that all arrangements be easy to dance to.

"Harry taught me to sing every single song with all my heart," Haymes once told an interviewer. After that, Haymes would never sing a song he himself didn't like or believe in. He made a dozen or more recordings with James, most of them for small, independent labels, after James's contract with Columbia was not renewed when his first recordings didn't sell too well.

Haymes left James to sing briefly with Benny Goodman's orchestra and then joined Tommy Dorsey's orchestra in 1943, once again replacing a singer named Sinatra. By now Sinatra was well known, having had quite a few major recording hits with Dorsey's orchestra. But any hopes Haymes might have had of repeating Sinatra's recording successes with Dorsey were quashed by the musicians' union's ban on recording. However, Haymes did get to go to Hollywood with the Dorsey band to appear in the MGM movie version of Cole Porter's Broadway musical *DuBarry Was a Lady*. Within the year, Haymes had followed Sinatra in going out on his own, first in New York nightclubs and then in movies.

Meanwhile, he had married again—this time to New York model and actress Joanne Dru. When Haymes was offered a contract with 20th Century–Fox, it was back to wartime Hollywood, where leading men were in short supply because of service enlistments and the draft. As a citizen of Argentina, Haymes won an exemption from the U.S. draft—making his movie career possible, but at the cost of forfeiting any chance of later becoming an American citizen. (He later insisted he had asked for the exemption because of a family crisis involving his wife, and that he had tried to enlist later, only to be rejected because of a heart irregularity.) Ironically, his first Fox movie role cast him as a GI in *Four Jills and a Jeep*.

Over the next three years, Haymes played in a number of major Fox musicals, including the leading role of composer Ernest Ball in *Irish Eyes Are Smiling* (opposite up-and-comer June Haver); one of five principal roles in Rodgers and Hammerstein's first original film, *State Fair*; and then leading man to the reigning queen of the Fox lot, Betty Grable, in *Diamond Horseshoe*. The pictures were hits, and several of the songs Haymes sang in them went on to *Your Hit Parade* ("That's for Me" from *State Fair* and "The More I See You" and "I Wish I Knew" from *Diamond Horseshoe)*.

But while he came across on-screen as a nice, clean-cut guy, the studio bosses finally concluded that Haymes did not have the makings of a major star. He would be teamed once more with Grable (then ex-boss Harry James's wife) for *The Shocking Miss Pilgrim* and with James himself (plus Maureen O'Hara) in *Do You Love Me?* but when neither scored that well at the box office his contract was not renewed. He moved over to Universal for two Broadway adaptations that he hoped in vain would buoy his sagging movie career: *Up in Central Park* with Deanna Durbin and *One Touch of Venus* with Ava Gardner. Thereafter, the roles got smaller in smaller pictures. At the same time, his recording career suffered from the fact that he was under contract to Decca, which gave preference for most potential hits to its still number-one star, Bing Crosby.

Haymes returned to nightclub work, but more and more the headlines involved his stormy private life. His divorce from Joanne Dru ended in messy alimony battles over child support for their three children. His successive marriages to and divorces from actresses Nora Eddington and Rita Hayworth (after the latter's divorce from Prince Aly Khan) were also marked by public fights. One of his worst moments came when the U.S. government instigated proceedings to deport him in 1963, because he had violated the law that specified that aliens who had claimed draft exemption and then left the Untied States without permission could be denied readmission. Haymes had left the country without such permission to join Hayworth, who was filming in Hawaii (then still a territory, not a state). After a year-long court battle, Haymes won the right to remain. But the adverse publicity didn't help him when he tried to resume his nightclub career (mainly in Las Vegas). Neither did increasing reports about his drinking and the toll it was taking on his voice. Aside from occasional joint appearances with his sixth wife, singer Fran Jeffries, he pretty much disappeared from public performances in the early 1960s. He bought a home in Dublin and became an Irish citizen in 1965. In 1968 he married his seventh wife, English model Wendy Jones, with whom he had two more children.

Haymes attempted an American comeback in the 1970s, asserting that his drinking days were behind him. He cut a few new albums to show that his voice was still in decent shape, even if the bloom of earlier years was missing. But neither the club managers nor the public seemed to be buying. Once again he slipped out of public view. The end came in Los Angeles in March 1980, from a combination of lung cancer and liver disease. He was sixty-one.

JO STAFFORD

*She's fantastic—one of the great women
singers for technique. She can hold notes
for sixteen bars if she wants to.*
—FRANK SINATRA

Jo Stafford has had *several* notable careers as a singer, and then some. First she was the crystal-clear-toned lead singer of the Pied Pipers, one of the most popular vocal groups attached to any dance band in the early 1940s. After she left the group to go out on her own, she quickly skyrocketed into one of the most popular and most distinctive-sounding singers on records, radio, and TV, becoming the first female singer to "go platinum" for a disc selling more than two million copies. Along the way she also won separate fame—and no little notoriety— by moonlighting as a couple of other singers of much more dubious vocal merit: Cinderella G. Stump and Darlene Edwards.

Anyone who knows Jo Stafford's voice, with its smooth, vibrato-free purity of tone and its sensuously cool sound, usually has trouble at first recognizing that Cinderella G., Darlene, and Jo are one and the same. In fact, in 1947, when Stafford secretly cut Cinderella G.'s first record—"Timtayshun," a rollicking, strident, hillbilly send-up of the 1933 hit "Temptation"—Capitol Records sent it to disc jockeys around the country saying only that Cinderella G. Stump was really a well-known singer having some fun. Everyone was encouraged to guess who it was, but practically no one guessed it was Stafford. After "Timtayshun" reached the million-seller mark as a best-selling novelty hit, Capitol finally gave in and publicly revealed the singer's true identity. Many people still refused to believe it was Stafford until she re-created the song live before a studio audience on a coast-to-coast broadcast. What had helped make the vocal characterization so convincing was the fact that, although Stafford herself was a native Californian (born in Coalinga in 1919), her family was originally from

Tennessee, so she had more than a passing acquaintance with the style and accent.

Stafford carried her wicked sense of musical camp even farther when she and husband Paul Weston went public with Jonathan and Darlene Edwards in the early 1950s. They had created the couple as a lark at friends' parties, as a send-up of all the ill-equipped lounge singers and pianists they had heard in their travels around the country. At the piano, Jonathan blithely missed notes, fumbled for others, and completely misplaced still others, usually while completely garbling the beat. Darlene, meanwhile, kept madly up with him in all respects, continually sliding into notes or wandering blithely off-key (usually exactly a quarter-tone off), holding on to notes or jumping ahead of Jonathan unpredictably, always demonstrating more gusto than musical accuracy. When Columbia Records issued the first Edwards album in 1952, the only clue to its being a put-on was the photograph on the cover: a close-up of two hands side by side on a keyboard, two *left* hands. The album became such a party-record hit that the Westons—pardon, we mean the Edwardses—ended up making four more albums.

The marvel to many has always been that Jo Stafford, so known for her perfect pitch and impeccable musicianship, could actually sing so deliberately wrongly—and pull it off so hilariously. But then those who have known her throughout her career always comment on her wonderful sense of humor behind the scenes. In front of the microphones with the Pied Pipers, however, and then as a solo singer specializing in romantic ballads, Stafford always came across first and foremost as a serious, always tasteful young musician. Yet she never took herself all that seriously. "I must admit I didn't look like much of a comer when I started out," she confessed to a magazine reporter in the 1950s. "I had a nice, sweet-as-syrup voice and too much avoirdupois."

While no rival to either Kate Smith or Mildred Bailey in the ampleness of her frame, the tall (five-foot-ten) Stafford was decidedly on the plump side when she became one of the Pied Pipers as a teenager in 1939. The group was an octet at first, but when Tommy Dorsey hired them to sing with his band, he wanted only four. Onstage the group was usually arranged to camouflage Stafford's heft. But there was no camouflaging her sound, which quickly made the Pied Pipers a popular part of the Dorsey ensemble.

When she worked with Dorsey's orchestra, Stafford's phrasing increasingly took on the straightforward smoothness of Tommy's trombone playing. More and more he began to feature her in his arrangements, even teaming her occasionally with his fast-rising young male vocalist Frank Sinatra. For the two and a half years that Sinatra, Stafford, and the Pied Pipers were with Tommy Dorsey, his orchestra—which also included now-legendary trumpeters Bunny Berigan and Ziggy Elman, pianist Joe Bushkin, drummer Buddy Rich, and arrangers Sy Oliver and Paul Weston—was arguably the best dance band in the country. Those years were certainly Tommy Dorsey's peak years. "Tommy always expected the best from you and was surprised when he didn't get it," Stafford has said about Dorsey's reputation as a strict disciplinarian and perfectionist.

Stafford left Dorsey soon after Sinatra went out on his own. (The Pied Pipers replaced her with June Hutton and continued as a recording group for several more successful years.) Johnny Mercer lost no time in signing Stafford for his NBC radio show and then to a recording contract for his newly formed Capitol Records. She slimmed down considerably and lightened her hair color. She also began working almost exclusively with conductor-arranger Weston, whom she eventually married in 1952.

Before the end of World War II, Stafford became Dinah Shore's major rival as the most popular female singer in the country, especially among GIs. After the war, the Voice of America hired Stafford to do a weekly half-hour musical show, which was beamed to both Europe and the Far East. Her VOA audience was estimated at two hundred million. Meanwhile, she continued turning out hit records for Capitol and alternating with Perry Como on the popular 7:00 P.M. *Chesterfield Supper Club* radio program on NBC.

As television began to supplant network radio, Stafford guested now and then on major musical shows, including one now-classic edition of Dave Garroway's nighttime program (fortunately preserved on video) on which she teamed with Ella Fitzgerald for a scatting duet that left even Ella open-mouthed in admiration for Stafford at its end. Not so incidentally, the combo backing them for that duet (and other duets that night) comprised Benny Goodman, Harry James, Lionel Hampton, Teddy Wilson, and Buddy Rich, jazz giants all.

Stafford limited her TV work, however—not because she didn't photograph well but because of her eyesight. She admits candidly that she's as blind as a bat without her glasses. "Idiot cards don't exist for people with eyesight like mine," she says ruefully. The combination of having to memorize everything for television and the irritation of working under the bright lights required for early television kept her from accepting much of the television work offered her.

When Stafford and Weston switched from Capitol to Columbia Records in the early 1950s, her hits kept coming for a while (including "You Belong to Me" and "Make Love to Me"), but she grew less and less interested in the new material being offered to her by the ruling A&R men. She turned instead to recording more and more older standards, Broadway show tunes, and an album titled *Jo + Jazz*, which teamed her with such Duke Ellington colleagues as Johnny Hodges, Ben Webster, and Ray Nance. Most of the critics liked these albums, but sales were only so-so (some partly blame "unenthusiastic" promotion by Columbia). Stafford was not one to sulk. By now she and Weston had two children (a son, Tim, and a daughter, Amy Anne), and Jo was content to stay home and concentrate on her family. Then, with the onslaught of rock 'n' roll, she saw the writing on the wall for her kind of music and decided to retire altogether from performing. Weston left Columbia at about the same time to become the music director of several major television shows in Hollywood, including *The Danny Kaye Show*.

Although Jo Stafford quietly shut the door on her career in the 1960s, she came out of retirement briefly in the late 1970s to do one more stint as Darlene Edwards, for an album of Fats Waller and Duke Ellington songs. When compact discs came along in the late 1980s, both Jo Stafford discs and Darlene Edwards discs began reappearing in plentiful supply. No other singer—nor the classic-pop listening public—has ever enjoyed such a rich and felicitous case of professional schizophrenia.

NAT "KING" COLE

*Rock 'n' roll has been good to me.
But I really always wanted to be
Nat "King" Cole. There was a singer.*
—CHUCK BERRY

Scientists at Duke University say they're close to coming up with what they call an "electrochemical snapshot" of the emotion we call love. We bet it turns out to be a microscopic picture of Nat "King" Cole. He's virtually the essence of lovability, one of the few figures in popular music regarded with affection by virtually every group of listeners—classic pop fans, jazz buffs, rockers, blacks, whites, Americans, whatever. Nat "King" Cole may well be the single most broadly beloved pop singer of his time.

His voice is surely one of the most pleasing sounds in classic pop. "Mo-na Li-sa . . ." You can hear him smiling as he sings, and you can't help smiling back. Effortless and unadorned, with that deep, throaty resonance, Nat "King" Cole's singing has a masculine warmth that makes it inspire trust, like the calm comfort of a big brother. There's also something about his impeccably crisp, almost exaggerated articulation that strikes a nice emotional chord—it's the way grade-school teachers tend to speak to children.

Onstage or on camera, he looked just the way he sounded. Straight-backed and graceful, he had a noble bearing. When he accompanied himself on piano, he would sit sidesaddle on the stool, never watching the keys, so he could face the audience straight-on. Standing at a mike, he would tend to slip into a slow, hypnotic, rocking motion. He smiled a lot, but it was not an empty smile; he genuinely seemed to love what he was doing.

His public loved him back enough to make him one of the top-selling recording artists of the 1950s and early 1960s. In addition to making more than a dozen million-selling records, Cole starred in his own musical TV series (the first ever by an African-American), appeared in fifteen movies, and made hundreds of sold-out appearances in nightclubs and concerts around the world. Some critics chided him in his day for abandoning the pure jazz of his early years. Some also accused him of Uncle Tomism for seeming to pander to the tastes of the white mainstream. But looking at Cole and his work in perspective, it becomes clear that these issues weren't so cut-and-dry.

Nat "King" Cole was always more of a professional than an aesthete. He started in jazz, having grown up with jazz. Born Nathaniel Adams Coles in Montgomery, Alabama, in 1919, he moved north at age four when his father, Edward Coles, a Baptist minister, was transferred to Chicago. Nat Cole learned to play the piano by age five, with the help of his mother, Perlina, a soprano in the church choir, and took over as the church organist by the time he was twelve. Coming of age in the 1930s, the young musician was molded by the sounds of King Oliver, Louis Armstrong, and the Chicago school of jazz on local radio. While still in high school, he put together his first group, a fourteen-piece band in the Oliver mode that played dances for $1.50 per night. Cole led the orchestra and played piano, singing only in church.

After high school, he took a job leading the pit band for a touring company revival of the all-black song-and-dance revue *Shuffle Along* and landed in California at the point when a member of the company disappeared with all the tour's money. Cole turned to the West Coast nightclub circuit for a living, putting together a quartet. However, on the night of the group's first gig, the drummer never showed up. Nat Cole had a trio, and a bit of jazz history was made.

At the time, trios were generally considered appropriate for cocktail music but not for nightclub performances. The King Cole Trio was different, because it sounded bigger than many quartets. The secret was Cole's piano style, which drew on the stride tradition of Earl Hines to lay down a solid rhythmic foundation. At the same time, moreover, Cole complemented his own rhythm with unusually gentle, lyrical counterpoint. The sound was both "hot" and pretty, Chicago jazz played by the church organist. By 1943 the group was recording for Capitol Records—its first release, an original Nat Cole composition, "Straighten Up and Fly Right"—and soon emerged as one of the first trios in jazz to become commercially successful. Indeed, if Nat Cole had never taken up singing, he would still be historic as one of the seminal jazz pianists, the stylistic link between Teddy Wilson and Bud Powell.

Like all good professionals, Cole seemed to have an instinct for capitalizing on his opportunities, no matter how they came his way. And some came roughly, as usual for black performers in Cole's time. His now-famous nickname, for one, was given to him by a teasing patron, who made a tinsel crown out of a nightclub decoration and plopped it on Cole's head, according to backstage legend. Cole removed the crown but kept the nickname, recognizing a good thing— that is, a thing that could be good at helping make him more successful.

His singing career started much the same way, as another Cole legend has it. The trio was performing "Sweet Lorraine," the theme song of New Orleans–born clarinetist Jimmie Noone at the time, when a drunken nightclub patron insisted that Cole sing the words. Under threat, he acquiesced and purred the tune in his now-renowned baritone. Cole must have recognized a good thing in the audience's response, because he kept singing from that point on.

For Nat "King" Cole, singing wasn't entirely an act of compromise or marketing strategy, however. It was, at least in part, an act of generosity. He was giving the people what they wanted. As jazz pianist Mary Lou Williams described Cole late in her career, "He would give anybody anything they wanted. Nat wouldn't have had a penny if it wasn't for his wife." (Williams was referring to Cole's second wife, Maria, whom he married in 1948. He had previously married and divorced one of the dancers from *Shuffle Along*.)

Cole didn't give away any of his talent as a musical interpreter when he took up pop singing in the early 1950s. Like Jackie Robinson switching from football to baseball, Cole simply changed the ways in which he used his gifts. In all his early vocal hits—"Nature Boy," "Walking My Baby Back Home," "For Sentimental Reasons," "It's Only a Paper Moon"—his strong rhythmic sense is carried over to his singing, adding a subtle lilt to the melodic lines. And the sunny delicacy of his instrumental work is echoed in his light, easy-flowing vocal phrasing.

As he became more popular in the late 1950s and early 1960s, the orchestrations used by the producers of his records veered to the sweet side. Yet even on his most sentimental material—"Too Young," "Mona Lisa," "Unforgettable"—Cole's voice comes through as natural and unpretentious. Of course, like most pop singers, he recorded his share of fluff, such as "Lazy, Hazy, Crazy Days of Summer," although his fluff seemed to sell better than most other singers'. He found no fault in this phenomenon, having five children to support (including Natalie Cole, who would become a pop-rock singer in the 1970s).

When asked about his critics, he made his priorities clear. "Critics don't buy records. They get them free," he pointed out.

The tens of millions of people who paid for Nat "King" Cole's records bought tickets to see him in more than a dozen movies, including *Here Comes Elmer* (1943), *Swing in the Saddle* (1944), *See My Lawyer* (1945), *Kiss Me Deadly* (1955), *Istanbul* (1957), and *The Night of the Quarter Moon* (1959). Although most of his appearances were brief roles performing musical numbers, he did a credible job in one starring role, portraying the famous popularizer of the blues W. C. Handy in the Hollywood-veneered bio picture *St. Louis Blues* (1958). In the mid-1950s, as TV emerged, Cole was featured in his own national musical series, and enough of his fans tuned in to have made the program a hit, if not for the fact that not one national sponsor was willing to advertise on a program starring a black performer. Despite its good ratings and network support for sixty-five weeks, the program never earned a penny and was canceled.

Nat "King" Cole never made a public issue out of the racism that cut short his TV series, just as he continued a tour of the Deep South in the 1950s after five white men stormed the stage at a performance in Birmingham, Alabama, and roughed him up. He was silent, too, after he bought an estate in the exclusive Hancock Park section of Los Angeles and found signs posted on his lawn scrawled, "Get Out" and "Nigger Heaven." He preferred to speak through the eloquence of his own behavior. "I'm a performer, not a professional agitator. I'm not for talking, criticizing, blasting," he explained in an interview in the late 1950s. "I'm interested in doing something positive." Cole saw his music as a bridge between the races, and saw himself as bridge-builder, not one to march across triumphantly.

"Some of the worst bigots in the country have my records," he pointed out. "One of the biggest problems is that we have white and colored in the same world, and they don't even know each other. By listening to the same singer and enjoying him together, by having a good time, people forget about their prejudice, if just for a minute."

A heavy smoker, Cole was admitted to Santa Monica Hospital with lung cancer shortly after filming his last movie appearance, in *Cat Ballou*. He died at age forty-five in February 1965. There were forty-eight honorary pallbearers, including Robert F. Kennedy, Frank Sinatra, Jack Benny, Sammy Davis, Jr., Jimmy Durante, Count Basie, and Ricardo Montalban, marching across that bridge he built.

MARGARET WHITING

*Margaret sings with more musicality, warmth,
and downright understanding of her material
than just about anyone you can think of.*
—MEL TORMÉ

Of all the singers who reached the top in classic pop's "second wave,"
Margaret Whiting had much more than a splendid set of pipes going
for her. As the daughter of Richard Whiting, one of the great songwriters of the 1920s and 1930s, she inherited an instinctive feeling for
and an understanding of what makes a song *good*.

At home, from her earliest years, Margaret was exposed on a close-
up basis to some of the top musical talent with whom her father worked
on Broadway and in Hollywood, mainly through the Saturday-evening
parties the Whitings were famous for in their Beverly Hills home. The
guests often included Harold Arlen, Jerome Kern, Jule Styne, Harry
Warren, Frank Loesser, and Margaret's godmother, Sophie Tucker.
They all took turns around the Whiting piano. Then, to top that off,
Margaret honed and refined her own natural talent under the guidance
of another great songwriter, Johnny Mercer, her longtime mentor and
surrogate father after her dad died just as she was about to enter her
teens.

Even with that kind of a head start, Margaret Whiting would never
have become the household name she became in her own right without
the rich, full-bodied, distinctively warm, and supple alto voice she has
and the warmly direct, no-phoniness personality behind it. First on
records and radio, then in nightclub acts, theater appearances, concerts, and TV work, she's always made it unmistakable that this is a
lady who *loves* singing—and gets as much joy out of it as her audiences.
She says the great influence in that respect was jazz pianist Art Tatum.
As she told jazz critic John S. Wilson a few years ago, "Growing up
in Hollywood, I got to be his friend. I was impressed by his musicality,

his rhythm, his chord structures, and his happy approach to how to do it. I learned *enjoying* to sing from him. Some people freeze up when they sing. It's labored. Art Tatum taught me what singing should be: You open your mouth and out it comes.''

And out it has come in an almost steady stream since her radio debut as a teenager in the early days of World War II. It was Johnny Mercer who first put her in front of a microphone, as part of an anniversary tribute to her father on an NBC show he did at that time. She sang a duet with Mercer to one of the last songs he had written with her father, "Too Marvelous for Words." Everyone liked it so much that she was invited to become a regular on the show. Those were the days when a number of other very young singers had won popularity on radio and in the movies (such as Rose Marie, Deanna Durbin, Judy Garland, and Gloria Jean), so Margaret's tender years didn't seem all that unusual. As Margaret says about the Hollywood environment in which she grew up, "Children were *supposed* to perform."

What was especially unique in Margaret's case was that her voice matured quite early. "Even at fifteen, I sounded like a woman, not some kid," she writes in her lively, witty, and candid 1987 autobiography *It Might As Well Be Spring*. By sixteen, while still in high school, she had an NBC contract and was singing on musical shows from NBC's Hollywood studios virtually every night.

Then came what Margaret thought would be her big break. She was sent to New York with a four-week test contract to sing on *Your Hit Parade*, the era's top popular-music program. But after the second week, orders to fire her came directly from George Washington Hill, the imperious head of Lucky Strike Tobacco, the program's sponsor. His complaint: Margaret phrased too much and didn't always sing on the beat. Since Hill loved to dance to the program with his secretary in his office above the broadcast studio and assumed millions of listeners also danced to the program each week, a firm, consistent beat was a must. But Margaret had never been a dance-band singer and so had no discipline in that area. She bent the notes where she thought the lyrics justified it. She liked to hold on to certain tones. To Hill, she was falling behind the beat and dragging the tempo. Margaret may have been humbled by being fired, but she was not out by any means. She returned to California and worked on her technique.

Almost simultaneously, styles in pop music were slowly but surely changing *away* from singing on the beat. On hit recordings by the likes of Frank Sinatra, Dinah Shore, and Perry Como, the role of the solo singer was increasingly taking precedence over the performance of the dance band; no longer was it just a "vocal refrain" sandwiched between the band's instrumental opening and closing. Just as significantly, these singers were beginning to exercise more freedom in the way they phrased their songs, romantic ballads in particular. They were now meant to be listened to as well as danced to. And Margaret Whiting would become one of the most successful practitioners of the new style with her first recordings in 1943 for a new company that old pal Johnny Mercer helped found and guided on its way to becoming one of the most prosperous in American music history: Capitol Records.

For her first Capitol recording, Mercer asked Margaret to sing her father's "My Ideal." But before it was released, he called her back into the studio to be coached by himself and composer Harold Arlen in a new song they had just written for the wartime movie musical *Star-Spangled Rhythm.* The song: "That Old Black Magic." Ella Mae Morse had been scheduled to record it, but she was pregnant and canceled. So Mercer decided to take a chance on teenager Whiting— "The Kid," as he had always called her, going back to the days when he worked with her father. Margaret's "That Old Black Magic" was rushed into release and quickly became a nationwide hit. The release of "My Ideal" followed, and Margaret Whiting was suddenly a recording star. She got $75 a side and no royalties for those first two Capitol recordings.

In quick succession over the next year, Margaret had more hits to her credit, including her first two-million-seller, "Moonlight in Vermont." She also became a frequent guest on the popular radio shows of Bob Hope and Eddie Cantor. With the country in the midst of World War II, she joined Hope, Cantor, Jack Benny, Bing Crosby, Al Jolson, Red Skelton, and big bands and small combos in dozens of volunteer performances at Army camps, air bases, and Navy bases, as well as weekly stints singing and waiting on tables at the famous Hollywood Canteen. "I became a vocal pinup," she writes in her *It Might As Well Be Spring.* "Jo Stafford, Peggy Lee, and I were the recording equivalents of [Betty] Grable and [Rita] Hayworth. Their pictures were stuck on barracks walls. Our records were spun on beat-up phonographs all over the world. We were that sound of home. I wasn't The Kid anymore."

When the war ended, the popularity of these three top "vocal pinups" continued to soar. Margaret Whiting also had the satisfaction of knowing that she was now introducing many of the hit songs that turned up week after week on radio's *Your Hit Parade*, the same *Hit Parade* from which she'd been fired just a few years earlier. The list of Whiting hits from that period includes many that have since become classic-pop standards, such as "It Might As Well Be Spring," "A Tree in the Meadow," "Come Rain or Come Shine," "Guilty," "Faraway Places," and "(I'm in Love with) A Wonderful Guy." With her stardom in the music world secure, there wasn't even any sibling rivalry when Margaret's kid sister Barbara (six years her junior) scored a hit in the popular radio sitcom *Junior Miss* and went on to make several movies—although at one point, when Barbara was taking singing lessons, Margaret cracked to a reporter, "If she gets much better, I'll have to get rid of her."

In some ways, Margaret Whiting's singing in the mid- and late 1940s reflected the postwar world around her at that time. There was an innocent optimism and a pertinacious brightness to her sound. Almost everything she sang was slick and polished and soothing, with no jarring elements. For all its commercial success (or, perhaps, what made it a commercial success), her singing (like Jo Stafford's) put its emphasis on the smooth beauty of the musical line. Not that Whiting didn't pay attention to the lyrics and the meanings behind the words; she was much less bland, in fact, than most of the band singers who were beginning to strike out on their own. But she never overemoted, sticking instead to a straightforward, unaffected delivery that only probed just so far beneath the surface. People had been through enough hard times with the war, and now most of them wanted the rainbow they had been promised at its end. This was the period of the silkily lush, easy-listening pop arrangements of Paul Weston, Frank DeVol, Percy Faith, and Axel Stordahl. Margaret Whiting's vocal style fit in well with all that.

She also felt it was time to try to fit in with what then seemed expected of every young woman in her twenties: settling down and raising a family. "The war was over, and I guess I believed all those lyrics I sang," she would later write. "Dream houses, dream weddings, followed by dream marriages, dream children, everything happily ever after, with nothing but blue skies." She had previously had a brief marriage to CBS executive Hubbell Robinson (for a year in which they rarely saw each other because of their conflicting professional schedules) and romantic involvements with composer Jimmy Van Heusen and actors John Garfield and Hal March. But in 1950, Margaret decided to settle down in married life with pianist-conductor Lou Busch, best known to many for his ragtime recordings under the name Joe "Fingers" Carr. Their Beverly Hills home and daughter Debbie held center stage for three years, until Margaret realized she wanted, and needed, more than well-heeled suburban home life could offer. She divorced Busch but remained good friends with him until his death many years later.

When television began supplanting radio, Margaret was among the first singers to be tapped for regular guest appearances on the top variety shows. Then, in 1955, two of the writers of *I Love Lucy* (the highest-rated show in all television at that time) approached Margaret and sister Barbara about a sitcom series that would be *Lucy*'s summer replacement. *Those Whiting Girls*, about two sisters in show business living in Beverly Hills, never reached the megahit status of *Lucy*, but it lasted two seasons—and Margaret got to sing at least one song on each program.

Meanwhile, the recording industry was in the throes of the rock 'n' roll revolution. Margaret is frank in saying that, from the start, she liked its energy and, yes, its beat. "But I flubbed my only try at it miserably," she notes. "I could rock but I couldn't roll." She did better when, at Capitol's urging, she tried cutting some country sides, several as duets with country star Jimmy Wakeley. They sold well, but her other recordings weren't doing well at all. She knew that the heyday of the intimate romantic ballad, the kind of music she sang best and *felt* instinctively, was over. Yet she was also confident that it would survive, perhaps not in the form of new hit singles on the weekly best-seller charts but in the form of albums spotlighting the best standards in good arrangements that sold respectably enough.

After seventeen exclusive years at Capitol and thirteen gold records, Whiting left that label in 1960 to record for other companies, including a series of composer albums (Jerome Kern, Johnny Mercer, Richard Whiting), as well as albums that mixed old standards and the new ballads she kept seeking out. She continued to play supper clubs throughout the country in the 1960s, 1970s, and 1980s. She also took on lead roles in such touring productions as *Call Me Madam, Anything Goes, Girl Crazy,* and *Gypsy,* and costarred for five years with Rosemary Clooney, Rose Marie, and Helen O'Connell in the cross-country run of the revue *4 Girls 4.* She has also, as she puts it, "sung for Catholic Charities, Jewish charities, the City of Hope, AIDS, Meals on Wheels, arthritis, muscular dystrophy, you name it. If I haven't had it, I've sung for it."

Meanwhile, a brief third marriage, to cinematographer and PanaVision executive John Richard Moore, also ended in divorce.

Then, during a two-year affair with songwriter-novelist John Meyer in the early 1970s, Meyer pushed Margaret to "let go" more in her singing—not to be afraid to probe deeper into a song's emotions, especially to seek out something unexpected and to bring together both her acting and singing experience. "I wasn't sure I could do that," she writes in *It Might As Well Be Spring*. "I had been trained by my father to respect the songwriter. I knew how carefully all these songs had been crafted and put together." She also knew how much most composers hate the idiosyncratic "interpretations" some singers give their works. But Margaret did begin to let go, extending herself from a controlled, straightforward "surfacer" into a more openly expressive singer. In the process, Margaret found her voice growing stronger. Even if the overall extent of its range was no longer what it had been in her twenties and thirties, she was singing more engagingly and convincingly than ever—with the distinctive richness and suppleness of her voice very much intact. And that's the Margaret Whiting who is still singing today, nearly five decades after she started.

Never one with the all-out drive to be a superstar, Margaret seems content with all she's achieved, but makes it clear that she's not the sort to live in the past or linger on it, that there's always something new and fresh to be explored somewhere. "I've had a successful life," she acknowledged unboastfully to a *New York Times* interviewer a few years ago. "I've never been a Judy Garland or a Paul Newman, but I've gone everywhere and seen everything. And I'm always learning new things. Charles Laughton once told Bette Davis, 'Never be afraid to hang yourself.' I keep that in my wallet."

For the past thirteen years Margaret Whiting has made her home in New York with writer and former adult-movie star Jack Wrangler, some twenty years her junior. "We love one another very much and are one another's best friend, critic, and support. It's turned out to be the best relationship I ever had," she told us with her customary directness. Wrangler now writes most of her concerts and club acts, which continue to emphasize the classic-pop songs that have always been such a natural part of Margaret Whiting. She says Wrangler has "opened up the final doors" to expressiveness in her singing and "enabled me to expose myself more completely on a one-to-one basis in nightclubs."

Her performances almost always also include songs by young new songwriters she feels have something to say beyond present "kiddie pop" trends or styles. She has also been active in recent years in helping young singers through the O'Neill Foundation in Waterford, Connecticut, passing on to them what she learned from her father and Johnny Mercer and others along her own way to the top—most of all, respect for the songwriter's craft and the joy of communicating their songs to others on a person-to-person basis. There are few who understand and *feel* that more naturally than Margaret Whiting.

MEL TORMÉ

*He has mesmerized me since I used to catch him
in the Chicago clubs. He makes you listen.*
—*ELLA FITZGERALD*

Some singers are at home in classic pop, others just work there. It's where Mel Tormé grew up.

To audiences who know him primarily through his later work, Tormé is a standard-bearer of the classic-pop style and repertoire. He's on classy PBS specials and new video cassettes. He's featured in concerts with big bands and symphonic orchestras around the country. And as long as reruns of *Night Court* are playing somewhere, Judge Harry Stone is exalting Mel Tormé every night. Silver-haired and grandfather-chubby, Tormé has become the great ol' bear of American song, crooning the classics in the unmistakable reedy baritone that early on earned him his nickname, "The Velvet Fog." But there have been many, many Mel Tormés over the six decades since he first sang onstage. Contemporary audiences may not realize how much Tormé has changed, how far he's come, and all that he's done over the years to become the Tormé of today.

He certainly got an early start, making his first singing appearance at age four in 1929, when drummer Carleton Coon propped him on his knee and let the kid sing "You're Driving Me Crazy." The scene must have been a little like the cartoon short that Tormé once contributed his voice to, in which Daffy Duck decides to sing in a nightclub—after a spritz of "Eau de Tormé," Mel Tormé's singing voice suddenly purls out of Daffy Duck's beak. The four-year-old onstage was already singing with that distinctive foggy tone, as Tormé describes the event. The Tormé sound came about when a partial growth of tonsils reappeared following a tonsillectomy.

Like many singers, Tormé turned to acting after frequent engagements on Carleton Coon's knee, and began performing in Chicago-
area radio programs at age eight. He was, if not quite pushed, certainly
encouraged by his parents to pursue show business. Sophie and William Torme (whose Russian name had been Torma before Ellis Island;
Mel added the accent as a teenager) were such movie freaks that they
named their son after Melvyn Douglas and their daughter after Myrna
Loy. They raised their family in what Tormé calls "a poor but musical
Jewish household" on the South Side of Chicago, selling eggs and
butter from a wagon till sunset and passing the nights together with
sing-along tunes such as "Till We Meet Again."

By age fourteen, Mel Tormé had taken to writing his own songs.
(Who wouldn't, after fourteen years of "Till We Meet Again"?) Remarkably for a teenager in the 1940s, he sold one of his songs, "Lament
of Love," to Harry James, and it became a jukebox hit. Ever since,
Tormé has continued writing songs, amassing a catalog of some 250
compositions, including "Born to Be Blue," an orchestral piece titled
"California Suite," and the classic "The Christmas Song" (as he calls
it, "my annuity").

At fourteen, Tormé hadn't really started yet, and neither had the
big problems that his early career would bring him. At sixteen, he
landed a spot in the Chico Marx orchestra playing drums as well as
singing and arranging rhythm vocals. At eighteen, he put together his
own singing group, the Mel-Tones, and within two years they were
recording with Artie Shaw. By the time he was twenty-one, Tormé
had become a full-fledged bobby-soxer idol, with lines of teenage girls
twenty feet deep waiting to see him at the Paramount Theater in New
York. Sinatra's lines were only eight feet deep, Tormé points out
today.

Although they were not quite as much a mark of honor as the size
of one's line at the Paramount, Tormé was labeled with more goofy
nicknames than Sinatra, too. The disk jockeys and columnists dubbed
him "Mr. Butterscotch"; "The Kid with the Gauze in His Jaws"; and
the one that stuck, "The Velvet Fog," first used by New York City
deejay Fred Robbins in 1946. Tormé hated the nickname, and claimed
for many years to prohibit its use by contract. Perhaps he really hated
the way the phrase was sometimes twisted around as "The Velvet
Frog." In any case, Tormé finally came to take the name with a sense
of humor late in life, and referred to it in the title of his 1988 autobiography *It Wasn't All Velvet.*

While his extraordinary early success helped Tormé grow as a performer, it took failure to help him grow *up*. He stumbled first in the movies, playing parts in a string of flimsy musicals in the mid-1940s that capitalized on his bobby-soxer appeal. Hopping from studios literally every year (or sooner), he did *Higher and Higher* (1943) for RKO, *Pardon My Rhythm* (1944) for Universal, *Let's Go Steady* (1945) for Columbia, and *Good News* (1947) for MGM. The critics were not warm to him, but their tepid acknowledgment of Tormé's still-undeveloped talent would seem like an Oscar compared to what he would endure in 1947.

Booked at the Copa in New York, Tormé did a performance that would prove to be an epiphany for the twenty-two-year-old singer. Accustomed to singing for swooning, goo-goo-eyed teenagers, Tormé had no experience with an audience of relatively sophisticated and critical (and partly drunk) adults. He was literally booed off the stage, and the critics seemed to take advantage of the event to release some of the sentiment that had been mounting against Tormé. Behind the scenes over the past few years, he had been building a reputation for arrogance and insensitivity. As Dorothy Kilgallen wrote, "Mel Tormé is nothing more than an egotistical, untalented little amateur whose only claims to fame are his dates with Ava Gardner."

In Tormé's own interpretation, "The boy-genius routine has no appeal to most people." Unfortunately, it was the only routine the American public had seen Tormé do. So he went looking for a new public. Tormé virtually disappeared from the American entertainment scene and took refuge in Europe, living and working in England for several years. As a matter of fact, he became a fairly big star in England by the time he was ready to return to America in the 1950s. He came with a new routine he calls his "serious phase."

The new Tormé was a dramatic actor and—something new—novelist and dramatic writer. Very grown-up things. Instead of *Let's Go Steady*, he appeared in the critically acclaimed *Playhouse 90* drama "The Comedian" (1957), which starred fellow former teen star Mickey Rooney. Nominated for an Emmy for his sympathetic portrayal of an alcoholic comedian's agent, Tormé parlayed his newfound esteem as an actor into roles in such dramas as *The Fearmakers* (1958), *The Big Operator* (1959), and *The Private Lives of Adam and Eve* (1960).

While he was in this serious phase, Tormé wrote a novel, a Western adventure titled *Dollarhide* that he adapted into a teleplay for the *Virginian* series in the 1960s (and guest-starred in). From the '60s on, in fact, Tormé gave increasing attention to writing, and produced some work of note, including episodes of other '60s TV dramas such as *Run for Your Life* (which he also guest-starred in). The high point of his career as an author is certainly his 1970 book *The Other Side of the Rainbow*, an incisive memoir of the nine months Tormé spent working behind the scenes of Judy Garland's TV variety series in the early '60s. *The New York Times Book Review* positively gushed about the book, calling it "a knowledgeable and lucid tribute to its subject in the spirit if not the scope of genius of Sigmund Freud's tribute to Leonardo da Vinci." His follow-up efforts—a semiautobiographical novel called *Wynner* and a seminovelistic autobiography called *It Wasn't All Velvet*—failed to fulfill the high promise of *The Other Side of the Rainbow*. Tormé has been working on a rewrite of *Wynner*, he says, but has pushed the project back to concentrate on a book whose subject may bring out the kind of intimate and knowing writing that distinguished Tormé's Garland book—a biography of his longtime friend Buddy Rich. Tormé says Rich asked him to write his life story, "warts and all," as his deathbed request.

As a singer, Tormé didn't fully came of age until the mid-1970s, when he was nearly fifty years old. His fog thinned out, and his voice sounded reedier and more "normal." Because of both this reediness of tone and the jaunty swing of his phrasing, Tormé's later singing sometimes brings Fred Astaire to mind. Tormé cites Harry Mills and Patti Andrews as his greatest influences, and the precision of a group singer still underlies his phrasing—he'll rarely veer far from the beat, as jazz singers will. But he likes to impress, and usually finds a way to work some scat into his shows. His scat singing is clever and fast, with fine intonation, although it sometimes sounds a bit too much like the labor of a singer trying to impress rather than express free-flowing musical ideas.

A frequent performer in clubs and concert halls around the country, Tormé doesn't do much studio recording. He's primarily a performer, not a recording artist, and always has been. In fact, he's never had a hit as a singer; the closest he ever came was reaching number thirty-six in 1962 with a Ray Charles–influenced rhythm number called "Comin' Home, Baby." He satisfies his artist's impulse to do new work by changing his live shows from night to night. Tormé claims to know five thousand songs.

He is a compulsive collector not only of songs but also of almost anything in which he has any interest. He has a collection of antique guns, with more than five hundred pieces. He collects model trains and items related to historic aircraft. He used to collect antique cars. He's had four wives.

"The biggie," he says, is his collection of show-business memorabilia. Amassed over the course of his entire career, the collection includes more than ten thousand items, including posters, lobby cards, programs, props, music scores, and scripts—everything Mel Tormé grew up with.

ROSEMARY CLOONEY

My favorite songstress.
—BING CROSBY

Show business is full of battlefield metaphors: "He slayed 'em"; "She killed 'em"; "The show died." Sometimes, however, the victims aren't merely metaphorical.

Forced to record second-rate material, abandoned by Hollywood, and eventually all but unemployed, Rosemary Clooney found herself institutionalized in the 1960s, close to becoming one of show business's literal casualties. However, Clooney emerged as one of the great survivors of her generation, a singer who just began to hit her stride as an artist in the late 1970s and who has gotten better and better ever since.

There are singers—Wayne Newton, Kenny Rogers—who are more gifted at the *music business* than they are at *music*; they're business-people whose business happens to be singing. Others—Bing Crosby, Barbra Streisand—have been equally adept at both art and commerce. Rosemary Clooney's gifts have always been purely musical. She can sing the dickens out of anything she's given. But for years she would indeed sing anything she was given by Mitch Miller, the artist-and-repertory chief at Columbia Records in the 1950s. Under Miller, Clooney became known for singing disposable novelty numbers such as "Come On-a My House" (composed by the creator of Alvin and the Chipmunks), "Botch-a-Me," and "Mambo Italiano." This stuff, which first established Clooney as a jukebox star, linked her name with the era of silly Top Ten pop that sped the decline of classic pop and the rise of rock 'n' roll. However, Rosemary Clooney has always been a far more deftly skilled singer than her early hits suggest, and her reputation deserves to be extricated from the junk heap of prerock schlock.

She actually had more than ten years' experience before recording "Come On-a My House" in 1951. Born May 23, 1928, in Maysville, Kentucky, to Frances and Andrew Clooney, Rosemary Clooney first sang publicly as a youngster, performing with her younger sister, Betty. The girls performed at political rallies for their paternal grandfather, the mayor of Maysville, with whom they lived after their parents' separation. Switching over to their maternal grandparents, the girls moved to Cincinnati and made their professional debut singing on radio station WLW during the summer of 1941. The Clooney Sisters were a hit, Rosemary later recalled, although they had to quit the program when school started, because it aired past the girls' bedtime.

Tony Pastor passed through Cincinnati in 1945, when the Clooney girls—Rosemary, seventeen; Betty, fifteen—were old enough to stay up late and audition for a spot as featured singers with Pastor's orchestra. They were signed and took off immediately for a national tour, accompanied by their maternal uncle and chaperon George Guilfoyle. The pace was uncommonly demanding, even by tour standards, as Clooney has described her band days. Since Pastor played one-night stands almost exclusively, the girls would perform and then sleep on the bus until they reached the next town to perform again. After three years of this in place of school and friends and family, Betty quit the Pastor band. Rosemary endured the grind for another year before moving to New York to try starting a solo recording career.

She had done one solo recording three years earlier, in 1946. But the now-forgotten record, "I'm Sorry I Didn't Say I'm Sorry When I Made You Cry," was scarcely a showcase of Clooney's talent. As a matter of fact, it sounds nothing like Clooney at all. The voice on the disc is practically a whisper, an effect that Clooney attributes to "sheer terror."

Trained to project in the dance halls and college gyms where the Pastor band performed, Clooney developed a strong, limber alto voice with a light, warm tone (marked by a noticeably short-breathed manner of phrasing). Her sense of time shows band experience, too—she hangs back from the beat just far enough to give her phrasing drive, but she rarely toys with time so much that dancers can't sway to the rhythm of her voice. Unfortunately, few of these attributes are apparent in Clooney's early hits. Following her first national exposure on the *Songs for Sale* TV music series in 1950, the twenty-three-year-old Clooney cut a series of soft, sentimental tunes for Columbia Records, including "You're Just in Love," a duet with Guy Mitchell; and "Beautiful Brown Eyes," which hit the number-eleven spot on the charts.

Hoping to capitalize on Clooney's light, bouncy voice and youthful amiability, Mitch Miller instructed her to cut "Come On-a My House," an adaptation of an Armenian folk tune written by the offbeat team of William Saroyan, the Pulitzer Prize–winning playwright of *The Time of Your Life*, and his cousin Ross Bagdasarian (who later changed his name to David Seville). Clooney refused to sing the song at first but found that her contract gave her little choice. A million-seller and number-one hit for six weeks, "Come On-a My House" encouraged Miller to have Clooney cut a variety of other novelty numbers, including "Botch-a-Me," "Mangos," "This Ole House," and a duet with Marlene Dietrich, "Too Old to Cut the Mustard." Fortunately, Clooney got her chance to try some superior material as well, and showcased her sensuous side with "Tenderly," "Pet Me, Poppa" from *Guys and Dolls*, and "Hey There" from *Pajama Game*, which made number one on the charts.

"I always wanted to sing sad ballads, but I didn't get many opportunities," she explains. "At the same time, you can't quarrel with success. If it hadn't been for 'Come On-a My House,' I probably wouldn't have gotten anywhere."

Launched by her hit records, Clooney began what promised to become a second career in movies, costarring in such musical programmers as *The Stars Are Singing, Here Come the Girls* (both 1953), and *Red Garters* (1954) as well as her only enduring picture, *White Christmas* (1954). Plain-featured and straight-framed, with a smile that has a habit of drifting into a mischievous smirk, Clooney's cool, sisterly screen appearance never matched the warm sensuality of her singing. She looks mannered on film, because, as she has always admitted, she never learned to overcome her fear of the camera.

If nothing else, Clooney's movie experience brought her together with two of the central men in her life—Bing Crosby, her *White Christmas* costar, longtime friend, and booster; and her only husband, José Ferrer, with whom she appeared in her fifth and final movie, the Sigmund Romberg bio picture *Deep in My Heart* (1954). The relationship with Crosby proved to be deeper and longer-lasting. In fact, if Rosemary Clooney's career is one of the Cinderella stories of pop music, Crosby is her prince. (By extension, this would make Mitch

Miller the taskmaster stepmother who kept her from her dreams.) It was Crosby at Clooney's side at the peak of her popularity, and it was Crosby who later helped rescue her from decline.

As her prospects for a movie career faded and rock 'n' roll took over the pop charts, Clooney's nerves buckled under the strain, and she turned to pills and alcohol. "My emotions couldn't handle the overload. It caused a short circuit," she later said. Over the course of the 1960s, her state steadily deteriorated until she lost all self-control. Her nightclub performances were erratic; she rambled incoherently onstage and drifted in and out of extreme moods. By 1968, at one performance in Reno, she finally stepped over the edge, lashing out at her audience in a drug-induced tirade before storming offstage in a fury.

A medical team waiting in the wings clamped her in restraints and flew her to a Los Angeles hospital, where she was strapped in a straitjacket and locked up in the psychopathic ward. It was four weeks before Clooney was released, to begin the long process of recovery from a decade of decay. "I learned to cook and put in a vegetable garden in the yard of my home. I went through analysis and group therapy. I was lucky I survived," she recalls.

"Bing helped me so much. He gave me a job every time he worked during the last year and a half of his life," including his much-acclaimed early-1970s engagements on Broadway and at the London Palladium. Encouraged by Crosby, Clooney slowly regained both her confidence and her singing skills in an astounding recovery documented in a 1977 autobiography, *This for Remembrance*, which was dramatized for TV as *Escape from Madness* in 1978.

But the most dramatic demonstration of Clooney's newfound strength is surely her musical work since the late 1970s. Not only has her singing never been better, it also was never even close to being as emotive as it has become in recent years. Her tone is still light and warm, but it has a newfound womanly depth. She's taking on only the material she likes, and she has sterling taste, with a series of recent albums in jazz settings dedicated to the songs of such composers as Harold Arlen, Irving Berlin, Jimmy Van Heusen, Duke Ellington, and Ira Gershwin.

Of course, she still sings "Come On-a My House" in her regular nightclub and concert appearances around the country. "Maybe I'm getting sentimental," she says, "but I'm actually fond of the song now."

FRANK SINATRA

DINAH SHORE   PERRY COMO

JUDY GARLAND

PEGGY LEE

LENA HORNE

DORIS DAY

DICK HAYMES   JO STAFFORD

NAT "KING" COLE

MARGARET WHITING   MEL TORMÉ
(Photograph by Charlie Mihn;
courtesy of Margaret Whiting)

ROSEMARY CLOONEY   VIC DAMONE

DINAH WASHINGTON
(Photograph by Herman Leonard)

TONY BENNETT
(Photograph by Annie Leibovitz)

SYLVIA SYMS
(Photograph by Marc Raboy)

BARBARA LEA

BARBRA STREISAND
(Photograph by Ellbar Productions)

LIZA MINNELLI

VIC DAMONE

The best pipes in the business.
—FRANK SINATRA

We call them singers, but we tend to expect pop-singing stars to do much more than sing, and the most successful singers generally do so. They act, they dance, they tell jokes. They're sex symbols or role models and, these days, usually instrumentalists and songwriters. It is a rare artist indeed who can succeed as a singer with the ability to do nothing else particularly well, and nobody can do nothing else as well as Vic Damone. Not only can't he act or dance or tell jokes with any special flair, the guy also has a sleepy personality, spotty taste, and a habit of attracting very bad luck. By all rights, he should have gotten nowhere. Instead, Vic Damone has survived more than forty years in show business on the virtue of the one thing he can do, which is sing in a voice that's practically perfect.

Perhaps, had he been blessed with something extra—a powerful personality like Sinatra or a theatrical aura like Judy Garland—Vic Damone might have been able to parlay his top-class voice into a career in the top class of pop-singing stars. After all, neither Sinatra, Garland, nor most other classic-pop giants were gifted with raw vocal equipment as sterling as Vic Damone's. Most unusually, his voice is both consummately naturalistic and exceptionally powerful. Like Peggy Lee and Perry Como, he seems to sing effortlessly—there's almost never a hint of affectation or "singerly" labor in Damone's voice. But he isn't a whisperer. Damone's singing has a controlled power, a casual masculinity that rarely oversteps into macho. His tone, moreover, is clear and warm; like a fresh bath, it has a pleasant, relaxing quality.

To some present-day listeners unfamiliar with his best work, Damone is sometimes mistakenly associated with Robert Goulet, Englebert Humperdinck, and other schlocksters who happen to appear at the same nightclubs and play on the same radio stations. Yet Damone has an almost underground following of fans aware of his excellence, and they have filled enough nightclub tables and bought enough records (mostly by mail order, late in his career) to keep Damone working steadily through his sixtieth year. Some of his biggest fans don't buy concert tickets, however. They're other singers such as Ella Fitzgerald, Tony Bennett, and Frank Sinatra, who personally anointed Damone with his often-quoted line about having "the best pipes in the business."

To Damone's detractors, the Sinatra comment has sometimes been interpreted as a backhanded compliment—suggesting, since it mentions only his "pipes," that the way in which Damone uses them might not be so great. Over the years, Damone has often been criticized as an unemotional interpreter and an unimaginative stylist, although we feel these views are shortsighted. They stem, typically, from a comparison of Damone to Sinatra and Tony Bennett, his colleagues in the Italian school of emotive male pop singers who emerged as solo singing stars as the big-band era declined. Vic Damone has never completely fit in, though. Neither especially emotional nor creative, certainly, Damone stands out for the precision of his vocal readings and his respect for the songwriters' intent. He doesn't change the words to fit his attitude, and he doesn't vamp on the melody to show off those pipes. Vic Damone sings the songs meticulously, and lets the music and the meaning of the material inspire his listeners to do the emoting. His art is one of understatement, a concept for which there is no word in the Italian language.

He has, nevertheless, certainly invited the inevitable comparisons to Sinatra, who clearly inspired Damone's naturalistic delivery and conversational phrasing (as well as many of his career choices). There is more Sinatra in Vic Damone than there is in Frank Sinatra, Jr. In fact, it was Sinatra who originally inspired Damone to become a professional singer, when Damone was still Vito Farinoli and working as an usher at New York's Paramount Theater.

The kid could already sing. By age seventeen in 1945, Vito had had several years of informal vocal training with his mother, Mamie, who played piano when the family sang popular Italian tunes together. Vito's father, Rocco, strummed the guitar a little when he wasn't working late at his job as an electrician in the Farinolis' Brooklyn neighborhood. Rocco encouraged his son to become an electrician, too, and the kid put in some time at Alexander Hamilton Vocational High School. Preferring the encouragement of his mother (whose maiden name he later adopted), Vito gave singing a shot, entered Arthur Godfrey's *Talent Scouts* program, and won first place (in a tie with comic Sid Raymond). Impressed after hearing the teenage singer from backstage, Milton Berle set up his first nightclub engagement, at La Martinique in Manhattan. In one day's time, before his eighteenth birthday, Vito Farinoli went from would-be electrician to professional singer.

Looking back at Damone's early career, it seems he got a whole life's worth of good luck jammed into his first few years. Shortly after his professional debut, he was signed to Mercury Records by Mitch Miller. Vito had some cosmetic surgery done to his nose and his name, and in 1947 released his first record, a mushy Neapolitan ballad called "I Have but One Heart" with which Frank Sinatra had already flopped. Damone's version—actually more strongly sung than Sinatra's—became a Top Ten hit.

Neither a band singer nor a Broadway star nor an established nightclub attraction, Vic Damone was one of the first singers to become a success through the star-production machinery of the record business, which fully came into its own after the Second World War. For the next forty years (until the rise of music videos, which changed the system again), the Damone model would serve as the standard formula for alchemizing green kids into gold-record makers. Damone had the right raw materials—he was still a teenager, pillow-book handsome (with his little new nose), Italian (the ethnicity of choice for boy singers of the day), and he could sing whatever the producers put in front of him, beautifully. For its part, Mercury Records shipped Damone off on a round of national tours to sing the songs he recorded, and a string of them became hits.

Lushly produced by Mitch Miller, most of Damone's early records were sentimental ballads with melodies rooted in Italian music, including "Again," "Vagabond Shoes," "Longing for You," and Damone's number-one hit from 1949, "You're Breaking My Heart" (based on "Mattinata"). These snappy songs and their syrupy arrangements don't hold up very well today—neither do most of the Miller-produced recordings of Bennett and Sinatra—but Damone's gifts manage to come through. Indeed, his voice sounds far more controlled and mature than Bennett's was at the time.

In the mid-1950s, after Miller changed record labels, he brought Damone over to Columbia, where the singer had slightly less popular success but made better records. His material was certainly more varied, including such hits as "Gigi," "An Affair to Remember," and "On the Street Where You Live" (which hit the Top Ten). Unfortunately, Miller's production remained as flowery as ever.

Outside of recording, Damone started to stumble in the early 1950s and took more than two decades to recover his footing. Signed by MGM after an engagement at Hollywood's Mocambo nightclub, he played featured roles in half a dozen pictures, from his debut with Jane Powell in the fluffy *Rich, Young, and Pretty* (1951) to Vincente Minnelli's overproduced *Kismet* (1955) to his attempt at xeroxing Frank Sinatra's movie breakthrough, in a World War II movie called, shamelessly, *Hell to Eternity*. The camera didn't love him; in fact, it didn't even seem to know him. Damone was simply not gifted with a screen presence to match the power of his singing voice, and his failure to click in films began a twenty-year streak of poor fortune.

An admitted "lousy money manager," Damone misspent twenty years of earnings before ten years had passed. He owed on both sides of the moral fence—to the IRS, as much as $112,000 at one point; and to various casinos, gambling tabs as high as $30,000. The mob offered to bail him out many times, and at least once, he has said, he didn't refuse. According to insiders, in fact, it was Damone and his admitted debt to the Mafia, not Frank Sinatra and his supposed mob ties, that were dramatized in *The Godfather*. As a matter of fact, director Francis Coppola offered Damone the part of his own alter ego, Johnny Fontaine (played by Al Martino in the film). Although he said he wanted the role to help his flagging career, Damone declined—ironically, because he was still in such bad financial shape that he couldn't afford to work for the $700 per week that Coppola was paying.

In an effort to end his nagging financial problems, Damone began several businesses over the years. The most ambitious one patented a device designed to be incorporated into cigarette vending machines; put the money in, and before you pull the lever to choose a brand, a slip of paper with a message like "Why not try a pack of Larks?" pops out. Damone lost the patent when he finally declared bankruptcy in 1970, after two partners from another of his operations took out a loan in Damone's name and moved to Beirut.

As his fortunes began declining in the 1950s, Damone developed a fondness for both hard liquor and the pharmaceutical stimulants that increase the body's ability to consume more hard liquor. "I drank and popped pills all the time," he later recalled. He fell into (or attracted) a crowd of heavy drinkers and pill freaks in Las Vegas. (Two of his four wives died of overdoses after their separation from Damone.) His own salvation came in the offbeat form of an ancient Persian religion called Baha'i, which forbids consumption of alcohol and drugs. He threw himself into the religion eagerly and talked it up all the time in the 1960s, including an occasion that must be one of the most surreal moments in pop-culture history—on *The Tonight Show*, when Damone and guest host Woody Allen chatted animatedly about the divine precepts of Baha'i.

Damone himself was the host of one of the great forgotten TV oddities of the 1960s, a 1962 summer-replacement variety show called *The Lively Ones*. A jazz answer to *Hootenanny*, a successful folk-music variety show at the time, *The Lively Ones* showcased "far-out and different music," in Damone's words, including Dizzy Gillespie, Dave Brubeck, and Ella Fitzgerald. Most of the guests did live duets with Damone, some of which rank among the hippest performances of his career.

His all-around *best* performances are unquestionably his work today, however. After floundering through the 1970s and early 1980s, doing good journeyman work in Las Vegas and releasing occasional mood music albums on his own record label, Damone shifted gears around the time of his sixtieth birthday in 1988. Or maybe the transition was his marriage to singer-actress Diahann Carroll in 1987; there's no knowing. But Damone started singing with a new depth. He now seems more concerned with the story of a song, and he phrases more interpretively than ever. He's not only singing, he's also listening. He's still got those pipes, not at all rusted with the years, and he appears to know more about what to do with them.

DINAH WASHINGTON

*Dinah is many things—a unique interpreter
of pop songs, a great blues singer, and a
performer with complete savoir faire.*
—*LEONARD FEATHER*

Gospel, blues, jazz, classic pop—in almost every genre of popular music, connoisseurs claim Dinah Washington as their own. In fact, if they remembered that she sang tunes by Hank Snow and appeared in movies such as *Harlem Rock 'n' Roll*, country-and-western buffs and rock fans would probably want their own pieces of her, too. Washington did indeed sing gospel, blues, and jazz as well as pop and other music. But she was no vocal quick-change artist like Bobby Darin, who moved into different areas of music by adopting different singing styles. Dinah Washington's assimilation of a variety of styles was "horizontal" rather than "vertical." She drew from many traditions all at the same time, instead of progressing from one to another over the years.

Her singing has the passion of gospel, the depth of the blues, the spontaneity of jazz, and the elegance and the intelligence of classic pop, all of which are held together by Washington's extraordinarily powerful will. Some other singers who have tried crossing over or combining diverse music genres have tended to sound uncertain or strained. Dinah Washington has never been known for uncertainty or straining herself. If hecklers harassed her, she would find them after the show and personally beat them up. If she weren't paid her agreed-upon fee, she would demonstrate her dissatisfaction by pulling out a pistol. In recording sessions, she would submit to singing one and only one take of a song, with rare exceptions. She went through something like *nine* husbands. (No one knows for sure how many of her many unions were legal.) And her singing sounds very much like the work of a woman with these attributes.

Powerfully individualistic, Dinah Washington's voice is one of the most distinctive sounds in classic pop. While some casual listeners might have trouble distinguishing between, say, Margaret Whiting and Frances Langford, no one who has ever heard her would mistake the sound of Dinah Washington. Her tone was clear and bright, like a flute's, but with a nasty bite—a flute with an attitude problem. She had a strong alto voice with a range of two octaves, and she generally held it in check until she'd feel like barking a phrase or booming out a climactic chorus for dramatic impact. Her intonation was excellent, but she also knew how to bend and slide notes for interpretive emphasis. She swung, and liked to linger behind the beat like Billie Holiday. Of course, her most distinctive trait—the heart of the Dinah Washington sound—was her manner of clipping off the note at the end of a phrase and sliding into a *parlando* (talk-singing) voice. The technique gives her singing a sassy authority, a streetwise snap, as if every line ended with an unspoken "and I mean it, buster."

There is a lot of gospel fire in Washington's singing. Born Ruth Lee Jones to Alice Williams Jones and Ollie Jones on August 8, 1924, in Tuscaloosa, Alabama, she learned how to sing and play piano from her mother, a church pianist and choirmaster. After moving to Chicago, Ruth was already singing in the St. Luke's Baptist Church choir and playing duets with her mother by age eleven. At fifteen, Ruth won an amateur contest at Chicago's Regal Theater, singing "I Can't Face the Music" (which she would record in later years). At sixteen, Ruth Jones began her professional career, touring with gospel legend Sallie Martin as her pianist and singing in Martin's first-ever female gospel group, the Sallie Martin Colored Ladies Quartet.

A more skillful sinner than saint, the teenage Jones developed a reputation for liking nightlife, drink, and men, and in 1941 switched to singing in nightclubs, where vice was nearly as good for business as it was on the gospel circuit. Still performing as Ruth Jones, she started her secular singing career in Chicago clubs such as Dave's Rhumboogie Club and the Downbeat Room, appearing at the latter with Fats Waller in '42. At age eighteen, she was performing at Chicago's Garrick Bar when she caught the eye of booking agent Joe Glaser, who hooked her up with the Lionel Hampton band. It's Glaser who is usually credited with changing Ruth Jones's name to Dinah Washington, although Hampton and Chicago nightclub owner Joe Sherman have also made that claim.

Washington earned her third name, The Queen of the Blues, during the first decade of her secular career, when she emerged as a major rhythm-and-blues singer. Bucking some foot-dragging by Hampton, who seems to have feared that Washington would steal his spotlight, Leonard Feather arranged a recording session for Washington to sing some of his original blues numbers with a sextet culled from Hampton's band. Some recordings with the full Lionel Hampton orchestra followed before Washington went solo again, recording a series of R&B and novelty tunes, including "Chewin' Woman Blues" and "Me Voot Is Really Voot" and "Me Voot Is Boot."

Influenced by Bessie Smith and Ethel Waters, these early records show touches of the well-parceled emotion that would distinguish Washington's mature pop work, as well as the refined diction that would always complement her essential earthiness. Throughout the late 1940s and very early 1950s, recording for Mercury Records, Washington made the Top Ten in the R&B charts regularly with blues hits, including "Baby Get Lost," "Trouble in Mind," and "Long John Blues." She reveled in her success, particularly the parts that involved drinking, nightclubbing, and gambling.

Washington treasured her title, Queen of the Blues, according to her biographer James Haskins. After mistakenly boarding a chartered bus full of retarded adults, she was asked by the bus driver to identify herself. "I'm The Queen of the Blues," Washington told the driver, who said matter-of-factly, "You belong here."

A few producers at Mercury Records, including Bob Shad, were convinced that Dinah Washington belonged in both R&B *and* pop, and they began expanding her repertoire, arrangements, and accompaniment in the early 1950s. "I wanted to take her out of the R&B field," Shad explained to music historian Arnold Shaw. "But at that time, if you brought a record by a black artist to pop disk jockeys, they would refuse to play it. I would refuse to tell them who it was. I'd say, 'Just listen to the record.' "

Despite the efforts of Washington's record producers, most white radio stations refused to accept Dinah Washington as a mainstream pop artist, and they denied the general public exposure to dozens of records that would prove to be her greatest work. Interpreting more than a hundred pop standards with both orchestral and jazz-combo accompaniment, Washington brought a willful and womanly street wisdom to such songs as "Stormy Weather," "I'm a Fool to Want You," and "I Won't Cry Anymore." She seemed especially adept at Cole Porter (unlike Ella Fitzgerald), and had the perfect voice for his wryly bitter side in songs such as "Love for Sale." Washington brought out the "urban" in Porter's urbanity.

Following half a dozen now-classic pop albums, including *After Hours with Miss D, Dinah!,* and *In the Land of Hi-Fi*, Washington finally got her first—and last—Top Ten pop hit with "What a Diff'rence a Day Makes" in 1959. A sentimental ballad with a syrupy orchestral arrangement, the record sold a million copies, made number nine on the *Billboard* pop chart, won Washington a Grammy, and, as such hits tend to do, rocketed her straight into a rut of recording overblown ballads for the rest of her career. There were important exceptions, however, most notably a couple of sensuous duets with Brook Benton, her return to gospel with Mahalia Jackson, and Washington's R&B comeback, *Back to the Blues.*

Despite her commercial success, Dinah Washington appeared very rarely on television, in part because she refused to lip-sync and in part because she had become notorious for both her drinking and her refusal to rehearse. She did appear in a few R&B music-revue films: *Harlem Jazz Festival* (1955); *Harlem Rock 'n' Roll* (1955), and *Basin Street Revue* (1956), all virtually lost today, as well as in the classic documentary *Jazz on a Summer's Day* (1958), singing a snappy, self-assured rendition of "All of Me."

Using her royalties, Washington fulfilled a lifelong ambition and bought a restaurant in Detroit in 1962. She spent most of her time running it, tending the cash register, scheduling the help, and locking up at night, every night for most of 1962.

Returning to recording in '63, Washington made *eight* albums in one year, which is not quite as hard as it may seem when one never rehearses and sings only one take of each song. She was in the midst of trying to save money to step up from the restaurant business and buy a hotel when she had too many drinks in combination with the wrong pills and died in her sleep on December 14, 1963, at age thirty-nine.

No one close to her has ever publicly speculated that her death was a suicide, and there appear to be no sound reasons for such speculations. On the contrary, Dinah Washington seems to have died the same way that she lived and sang—defiantly, fast, and having a good time.

TONY BENNETT

The epitome of what entertainers
were put on earth for.
—JUDY GARLAND

Steadily revving for that big finale, Tony Bennett has worked his life
like he works a song. It has taken forty years from his start as a bobby-
soxer idol, but Bennett has come thundering into the 1990s at the
peak of his popularity and critical acclaim. At sixty-something, his
voice is sensually seasoned with age, and his stylized technique appeals
to both his longtime fans and the growing audience of over-thirty rock-
generation converts to classic pop. Moreover, Tony Bennett has become a self-styled symbol of much of what classic pop has come to
represent to both inveterate and crossover audiences—artistry, maturity, and sophistication.

"I was a poor kid, like everybody in New York in the Depression,
but there was great hope, skyscrapers were going up, and everybody
felt we were going toward something great. It was a unique era, and
it all still lives in the music that came out of that time," Bennett told
us enthusiastically. "The songs of the '20s, '30s, and '40s—especially
the songs by Gershwin, Kern, Arlen—are truly America's classical
music. At the time, it was considered nothing more than popular
music. But today we think of it as art music. It *is* art."

As a sketch artist and painter since childhood, Tony Bennett has
always been comfortable discussing music as art and art as an influence
on his music. In fact, after showing promise at New York's School of
Industrial Art, the future singer started planning a career as an artist—
a *commercial* artist, naturally, like a good Depression-bred boy gifted
with both an artist's flair and a laborer's work ethic. Bennett shelved
his smock when he was drafted into the Army infantry during World

War II, and he didn't slip it back on until many years later, when he earned the indulgence as a profitable *performing* artist.

"Singing and singing success came fairly easy to me," Bennett says coolly. The market for young Italian male pop singers was certainly ripe enough in the last days of the war, when the teenaged Anthony Benedetto started working the New York club circuit under the almost-Anglicized name Joe Bari. The big bands were starting to wane, the music we now know as classic pop still owned the national airwaves, home-front girls were in the mood to swoon, and Sinatra was the most recent Big Thing.

Nonetheless, the critics' early response to Bennett was not especially warm. Many of his earliest press notices described the artist as a young ham. In one scathing syndicated column, Harriet Van Horne wrote: "Bennett's singing was almost a parody of a cabaret act. The style was so overwrought as to make an audience look away in polite embarrassment . . . stiff-legged, wildly off-key, eye in a fine frenzy rolling. And those top notes! Pure screaming agony." In time, even Van Horne became one of Bennett's strongest advocates, although the shift didn't come until the mid-1960s, but she said it was Bennett's style, not her opinion, that had changed.

According to backstage myth, it was Bob Hope who gave Joe Bari his big break—and the name he's used ever since. Over the years, several versions of the Hope discovery story have circulated, all of which have been corroborated *and* contradicted by the singer himself at one time or another. One fact remains: Tony Bennett was the first major singer to break in on national television, rather than through radio or the nightclub circuit. It was 1950, on the cusp of radio days and the video age, when Bennett appeared on Arthur Godfrey's *Talent Scouts* show (finishing second to Rosemary Clooney), leading to a spot on Jan Murray's TV show *Songs for Sale*. The appearances launched Bennett's first national tour, with Bob Hope, as well as Bennett's first recording contract, with Columbia.

Despite his initial breakthrough on television, Bennett was never able to take full command of the medium, as did Perry Como, Andy Williams, Dinah Shore, Sinatra, and others. Evidently, if there were a picture next to Marshall McLuhan's definition of the "hot" TV type, it would be Tony Bennett—bellowing, body bobbing, grinning with the sheer joy of performing. The "cool" medium of TV just doesn't care for this sort of behavior, no matter how well it may work in the concert hall. Many rock singers, such as Mick Jagger, proved to have the same problem adapting their big, broad style to the small screen.

Nonetheless, Tony Bennett has done nearly a thousand national TV appearances over four decades, by his estimate. He also served as the host of Perry Como's summer replacement show, telling reporters in the 1950s, "Television is what I've been shooting for all along." His only series pilot—an unusual musical show called *The Wandering Minstrel*, in which Bennett was to sing on the streets of a different city each week—was never bought.

Recordings and performances have been Tony Bennett's best showcase since his first record, "The Boulevard of Broken Dreams," became a hit in 1950. Working under the rigid stewardship of Mitch Miller, Bennett displayed exceptional raw power amid the melodramatic material and ultramushy arrangements that were standard at Columbia at the time. Miller made two follow-up hits with Bennett, doing more tear-jerkers, "Because of You" and "Cold, Cold Heart." The latter, Bennett's first million-seller, was a groundbreaking mainstream pop treatment of a "hillbilly" song (by Hank Williams), and it cleared a path toward the huge country-pop craze to come.

Thanks to the unprecedented trilateral impact of TV, radio, and records in the early 1950s, Tony Bennett was able to become an almost instant singing star. But he was certainly an unorthodox one by pop standards of any period. At twenty-five in 1951, Bennett was older than Sinatra, Crosby, Vallee, and most others had been when they had hit the pop scene. Moreover, with his stocky build and craggy Mediterranean looks, the fellow just didn't look the part of an adolescent sex idol. After all, the largest record-buying market was (and still is) teenage girls. "Everybody told me to get a nose job, so I'd look like Tony Martin," grumbled Bennett, who declined the advice and sold about half a million more records than Martin in his first year on the charts. In doing so, Tony Bennett became one of the very rare "normal-looking" pop singing stars until rock arrived.

Like most crooners, Bennett was stunned and outraged at the sudden commercial success of rock 'n' roll in the mid-1950s—despite the fact that the Mitch Miller school of sappy pop had helped create a demand by young people for more lively, danceable music. "[Rock] is just noise. It has three chords, and two of them are wrong," cracked Bennett in 1957. Yet this noise turned out to trigger an important transition for Bennett as a singer. Suddenly Miller's style was out, and Bennett found himself free to develop a style of his own for the first time.

Unlike some lesser artists, Bennett avoided the temptation of lucrative but listless "middle of the road" music, as rock pulled pop away from young listeners. "I never went for that. Middle-of-the-road means it's neither this nor that—it's nothing," he told us. "That's the opposite of what music is supposed to be." Instead, Bennett chose "the music high road," as he calls it. He started refining the style that would distinguish Tony Bennett for the rest of his career.

By the turn of the decade, Bennett was employing a range of vocal textures and techniques rarely used in his big, full-bodied performances under Mitch Miller. He began letting more throat and head tones through, coloring his voice with natural character; there was some of the rasp that would practically consume his tone twenty-five years later. He manipulated his range, adding tension by stretching far above his natural baritone. His phrasing became more conversational, betraying his admitted debt to Mabel Mercer.

Bennett's repertoire at this stage was a typical mix of pop standards and then-recent tunes written in the style of standards, such as a number Bennett released as the "B" side of a single, "I Left My Heart . . ." everybody knows where. A simple showcase for the singer's liberated style, the ballad became Tony's Bennett's all-time biggest hit, his signature song, and proof of the ongoing appeal of standard pop in the "rock era." "I Left My Heart in San Francisco" peaked at number nineteen on the pop charts in '62; "Monster Mash" was number one.

For the next several years, Tony Bennett's career was charmed. "I Left My Heart in San Francisco" primed record-buyers for three more Top-40 hits: "I Wanna Be Around," "The Good Life," and "This Is All I Ask." All were custom Bennett vehicles—musically sophisticated, lyrically bittersweet. Moreover, Bennett's popularity lifted the singer beyond the nightclub circuit into the concert arena, beginning with a critically acclaimed '62 appearance at New York's Carnegie Hall, recorded for a now-classic Columbia album.

Bennett plowed through the 1960s with his popularity soaring, recording regularly and touring some forty weeks of the year, including about eighteen weeks in Las Vegas. The singer was a superstar. In fact, Bennett was famous enough to be offered a costarring role in a movie, *The Oscar*, without much prior (or subsequent) indication of acting ability. To Bennett's credit, he was natural on-camera, although in his case this means naturally awkward-looking. He never made another film and says simply, "I'm not an actor, really."

As a singer, really, Tony Bennett matured to become one of the most highly regarded artists in classic pop. By the end of the 1960s he had won two Grammies and the Variety Performer of the Year Award as well as the highest honor in his field—lionization by Sinatra. "[Tony Bennett is] the singer who gets across what the composer had in mind and possibly a little more," Sinatra wrote in a *Life* magazine article. "He's the best singer in the business."

Ray Charles echoed Sinatra's praise and commended Bennett's technical command. "Tony has such an even flow of all his notes, and they're so effortlessly produced," said Charles. "He has all the tools."

Thanks to meticulous maintenance, Bennett carefully controlled the rust on those vocal tools through the 1970s. He always followed a rigid schedule of practicing scales for twenty minutes, three times per day, every day. Also, after earning millions in his first thirty-five years as a singer, Bennett could afford to husband his performing resources. By the early 1980s Bennett had cut his concert schedule down to twenty or thirty weeks per year, spending most of the rest of his time painting. Many of the performances he chose to do were essentially labor-of-love shows at small clubs such as New York's Village Vanguard, or benefits for favorite causes such as civil rights and the Police Athletic League.

With the exception of a dry spell in the mid-1970s, Bennett recorded regularly through the late 1980s, though he chose his projects judiciously. Most of his late-period albums are finely wrought treatments of his favorite themes, such as *Bennett/Berlin*, his tribute to the composer Bennett considers "the heart and soul of American song." Among all his recordings, in fact, Bennett produced his most personal piece of work in the early 1990s. It's a memoir in song called *Astoria*, named for the Queens, New York, district of Bennett's childhood.

"At this stage in life, I think it's important to look back at where you came from," Bennett explains. "Tony Bennett can still learn something from Anthony Benedetto."

SYLVIA SYMS

*If every modern female vocalist would take a
one- or two-year hiatus from her work, sit down, and
study the vocalizing of Sylvia Syms, the world
would be better for it.*
—FRANK SINATRA

It's easy to act like a singer, mimicking the moves, the attitude, and,
thanks to modern electronics, even the sound of a pro. As a matter
of fact, there are pros who've been getting away with acting like singers
for years. But it's not so easy to sing like an actor, losing yourself in
the story of a song, tapping into the emotion at its heart, and making
that emotion meaningful to strangers. Sylvia Syms can do this, and
do it as well as or a little better than almost any other singer. She's
the Helen Hayes of classic pop.

Her singing doesn't have character; it has characters, and she seems
to adopt a different one to fit the story of each song. Her tone itself
may not vary much—it's consistently natural-sounding and sort of
plain, with a hint of a New York accent and a controlled vibrato.
Other singers have voices more powerful and fuller-bodied than
Syms's unadorned contralto. It's her versatility as an interpreter and
the emotional depth of her interpretations that distinguish Sylvia Syms
as a singer.

"To be honest, I don't have one of those classically trained voices.
I'm really a song interpreter," she admits. "It's like acting, but instead
of creating a character in two acts and two hours, I have to do it every
three or four minutes, with each new song."

Of course, Sylvia Syms has long done both kinds of acting, onstage
and in song. In fact, she's achieved nearly as much attention as an
actress in musical, comedy, and dramatic roles as she has as a vocalist.
She's appeared in musicals, including *South Pacific* and *Funny Girl*,
over the years, as well as in such dramas as *Camino Real*, in which
she costarred with Al Pacino and Jessica Tandy at New York's Lincoln

Center. Syms started out as a singer, however, and eventually gravitated back to her first love.

In her case, "first love" is no overstatement, either. Syms says her mother told her that she was singing while still in diapers, literally before she could talk. "Today they'd call that being a gifted child. In those days they thought I was bananas," jokes Syms. Born Sylvia Blagman in the Jewish ghetto of New York's Lower East Side, where her father worked in the garment trade, Syms was never encouraged to go into "the show business," as her parents called it. She agreed to study journalism at New York University, but went after summer jobs doing songs instead of interviews. Twenty-two years old in the summer of 1940, she was hired to sing with bandleader Benny Carter at a jazz club called Kelly's Stable for $25 per week, and never went back to college until middle age, when she was asked to *teach* singing at Norwood College in Dallas.

Syms became a regular on the Manhattan nightclub circuit at a time when that circuit was charged and peaking. She made close friends with Carter, Lester Young, and Art Tatum, who nicknamed her "Moonbeam Moscowitz" because of the two long braids she wore at the time. She club-hopped with Billie Holiday and says (as do a few others) that she slipped the first gardenia into Holiday's hair. And Syms drank with another young singer who would become one of her lifelong friends and biggest fans, Frank Sinatra.

By the early 1950s, as the veterans' generation settled down with their young families and the nightclub business slowed down around the country, Syms took on more and more work on the stage. She had been doing some theater since the early 1940s, when Mae West saw her act at the Cinderella Club in Greenwich Village and signed her to West's revival of *Diamond Lil*. Later Syms joined *Dream Girl* with Judy Holliday, followed by *Flower Drum Song* and *Rain* with June Havoc.

Many of Syms's roles were comic and/or ethnic in one way or another. "I've played Indians, Hawaiians, everything," she says, " 'cause I look funny, I guess."

Chubby, shortish, and plain-featured (Sinatra calls her "Buddha"), Sylvia Syms has the everyday looks that you don't see on a successful singer every day. Indeed, with her exquisite style of singing, it's possible that Syms might have become even more successful than she has if she neatly matched the music industry's conception of how a female singing star should look. Some other vocalists have certainly gone twice as far as Syms with half her talent.

She has a certain sex appeal, although it's an unconventional kind. "Third-person sex" is what she calls it. "If I can make a man find the woman he's with more desirable, that is what I want to do."

Her closest brush with international stardom came in 1956 when, after several years of recording, her release of "I Could Have Danced All Night" became a hit, selling a million records worldwide. None of Syms's follow-ups did quite as well with the public, although the quality of her work improved steadily through the years. At first her debt to Billie Holiday was perhaps a bit too evident. By the late 1950s and early 1960s, however, Syms was Syms completely, at the peak of her physical powers and emerging as a top interpreter of the classic-pop repertoire.

In 1969 Syms faced the first of several serious health problems that set her back for some time. She lost one complete lung, her spleen, and part of her intestines in cancer surgery, and could not breathe without a respirator. Sinatra paid the bills. Syms was not destitute, although she couldn't sing very well on a respirator, and she was self-supporting. Both of her marriages—the first to Bret Morrison, who played The Shadow on the radio, the second to Ed Begley, the dancer, *not* the actor whose son is now a TV star—had ended in divorce.

Within a year, after recovering smoothly, Syms was planning a comeback with a costarring role in the sitcom *Bridget Loves Bernie*, until both of her legs were broken in a car accident. Soon after, she came down with emphysema and asthma—and then found herself blind in one eye, with surgery required to save the other.

Syms decided to take it easy at this point, and spent her time in New York practicing her Chinese cooking and serving as a volunteer at the Children's Recreational Service at Bellevue Hospital. The therapy was effective, and Syms was working again by the early 1980s, capping her comeback with an album produced and conducted by Sinatra, *Syms by Sinatra*. She hasn't slowed down since, still recording and performing—still singing like an actor, and acting like she'll never stop.

BARBARA LEA

*One of the great pleasures of writing songs
is that someone with the talent, good taste,
and sincerity of Barbara Lea may sing them.*
—*JOHNNY MERCER*

The scene: The small, chic supper club called Jan Wallman's in New York. The room is filled mostly with other singers and musical "insiders." They listen attentively, completely mesmerized by the striking, copper-haired, porcelain-skinned singer on the club's tiny "stage-ette." She is Barbara Lea—and she is giving one of her weekly classic-pop "recitals," treating the well-known and not so well-known songs of Gershwin, Porter, Kern, Rodgers and Hart, Arlen, Berlin, Mercer, and many, many others with insights akin to what a classical *lieder* singer reveals with Schubert, Mozart, or Mahler. When she finishes to enthusiastic applause and shouts of "*Brava!*" the conversation in the room inevitably turns to why Barbara Lea isn't better known among the general public. After all, she continually wins rave reviews from all the top critics—such as Whitney Balliett of the *New Yorker*, bluntly declaring, "Barbara Lea has no superior among popular singers."

She's been winning such plaudits since the mid-1950s, when she finished college and was ready to begin her bid for a singing career. But rock was then taking over the pop-music industry, and hardly anyone in a position of power seemed interested in new singers of the "old" kind of stuff, even if they were as good as Barbara Lea. The result has been a career that has never made Lea a household name but has won her an admiring following of other singers and just plain lovers of first-class singing.

Barbara Lea has sometimes been called a jazz singer, an inaccurate label she has long tried to discourage but doesn't entirely object to, partly because it enables her (like her early idol Lee Wiley) to work and record with some of the country's best jazz musicians. She can swing with the best of them. But at heart Lea is a ballad singer—with a warm, smooth, sultry alto that she usually projects in a soft-toned, understated, yet never banal or boring way.

She has few equals today singing the songs of the great classic-pop composers—not just the standards that everyone knows, but also hundreds of their lesser-known and long-neglected gems. She has a way of quietly getting to the heart of such songs and making you believe you are *really* hearing them for the first time, on occasion even turning them into miniature psychodramas. When she sings such songs as "Smoke Gets in Your Eyes," "Time on My Hands," "But Not for Me," "I'll Follow My Secret Heart," and, most particularly, her languid, unexpectedly introspective version of "Begin the Beguine," they are transformed into fresh examples of insightful art.

What especially distinguishes Barbara Lea is her knack for capturing the exact meaning and feeling of a song's lyrics without altering the melodic line. "I really love songs the way they're written," she told us with typical Lea directness. "Alec Wilder once said that a certain song had 'an air of permissiveness about it.' Well, some songs do and some songs don't. And when they don't, I don't feel I have to impose myself and 'correct' what the songwriters have written." That doesn't mean Lea won't stretch a phrase when she feels it's appropriate or stress an unexpected word along the way. But unless it's a song with that air of permissiveness, she'll never do it at the expense of the melody as written.

Lea says she got serious about singing when she was six or seven, while going to school in the Detroit area in the late 1930s. Her name then was Barbara Leacock, which her family had Anglicized from its original LeCocq and traces back to French composer Alexandre Charles LeCocq. Both of her parents were musical—her mother a pianist and her lawyer-father a clarinetist who had played in the Broadway pit orchestra of Al Jolson's *Sinbad*. Her own musical interests developed mainly through radio and through her older brother, who played several instruments. "He had a friend who reviewed records for one of the Detroit papers," she recalls, "and she would pass some of the records on to us. I remember falling in love with Fats Waller's wartime V-discs that way, and Louis Armstrong and Jack Teagarden, and Tommy Dorsey and Glenn Miller, and a particularly wonderful album of *The Chamber Music Society of Lower Basin Street* with Dinah Shore and Lena Horne. And later, Billie Holiday and Lee Wiley."

"I knew I wanted to be a singer, but I was always very shy about it," Lea says. "I was terrified at first to even think about performing." But she started singing on weekends with small, local dance bands around Detroit. Then came college, via a scholarship to Wellesley. While earning her degree in music theory, she sang in the Wellesley choir and also "across the river with a Harvard Dixieland band called the Crimson Stompers."

After college, Lea eventually moved to New York. She cut a single record for a small company, and the head of Riverside Records liked it enough to invite Lea to make an LP with Billy Taylor and his trio. *The New York Times* critic John S. Wilson picked it as one of the best vocal albums of 1955. "I was the only unknown on the list," she notes. There were raves from others too, including *Down Beat*'s international critics' poll, naming her the Best New Singer of 1956.

"But the golden era of American popular song had passed," she says. "Music got out of the hands of the bandleaders and into the hands of the record companies' A&R men. They didn't seem to care about quality—only about making hits by appealing to the lowest common denominator." It was an unfortunate time for Lea, with her strong feelings about quality, to begin a career. In addition, her painful shyness made live performing difficult; her nightclub engagements were only moderately successful. And a husband-manager proved to be almost as much a hindrance as a help in getting her jobs.

After their divorce, she studied acting, determined to overcome her stage fright. "I did some Shakespeare, some Chekhov, a little this, a little that, with repertory theaters and summer-stock companies in the Midwest," she says. "I'd play different characters in six or seven shows a season and, of course, I thought it qualified me for Broadway. But the Broadway producers didn't have quite the same idea." Besides, the Broadway composers were not writing roles in her vocal range.

Lea moved to Los Angeles and over the course of six years did more regional theater, made a couple of minor movies that she calls "definitely forgettable," and went back to college to get her M.A., in theater. There were two more marriages, which also ended in divorce. It wasn't until the mid-1970s that, single again, she started singing regularly again. "I was in New York for a theater audition when I ran into a piano player I knew," she recalls. "He was working Thursdays in a small club on Fifteenth Street and suggested I come down and sit in. I did, and ended up singing two hours without stopping. And I kept going down on Thursdays and sitting in. Marian McPartland and Alec Wilder came in one night—and that's how I got invited to do one of the broadcasts in Wilder's National Public Radio series." That, in turn, led to several recording dates with longtime Wilder associate Loonis McGlohon and such top instrumentalists as Billy Butterfield, Vic Dickenson, Bob Dorough, and Richard Sudhalter. She also played Michael's Pub and other major New York clubs for the first time, as well as in a regional theater production of Stephen Sondheim's *Company* and in his *Follies* at the Equity Library Theater in New York. And she became the featured vocalist with Loren Schoenberg's big band.

"Although I had a lot of critical success, I still didn't really believe in myself for quite a while," she admits frankly. "I still felt like a kid who *wanted* to sing." To help develop her confidence, she began studying Actualism lightwork meditation (which she now teaches). And to indulge her passion for classic-pop songs, she began regular appearances one night a week at Jan Wallman's tiny New York club, first in Greenwich Village and then in the Broadway theater district. At first she developed duo acts with singer-pianists Brooks Morton and Larry Carr. Then, working primarily with the subtly imaginative Wes McAfee as her pianist, she quietly built up her reputation in the 1980s as one of the finest singers on the New York club scene.

At Jan Wallman's she delighted in changing her repertoire for each performance, with some wags describing the enormous scope of her programs as "Classic Pop 101." She also sought out the songs of worthy new or lesser-known songwriters she felt were building on the classic-pop tradition, such as Addy Fieger, Arthur Siegel, June Siegel, Ronny Whyte, Marshall Barer, Franklin Roosevelt Underwood, and Richard Rodney Bennett. But most impressive was the *way* Barbara Lea sang everything and communicated so completely with her listeners—with her smooth-as-satin tones, her ungimmicky, no-nonsense style, impeccable phrasing, clear but understated dramatic insights, and, where appropriate, her warm sense of humor.

After Jan Wallman gave up her club in 1990 (partly for health reasons), Lea branched out to perform in other New York rooms and at several major jazz concerts. She has also recently recorded a series of critically acclaimed albums with the legendary Yank Lawson–Bob Haggart jazz band (with an emphasis on long-neglected classic-pop ballads), winning a special *Stereo Review* citation for one of them among 1990's Best Vocal Albums. She insists she is no longer "bugged" by the fact that "big star" success has not yet come her way. "Being part of the music," she says, "is its own reward."

BARBRA STREISAND

*Barbra Streisand has one of the two or three best
voices in the world of singing songs. It's not just
her voice but her intensity, her passion and control.*
—STEPHEN SONDHEIM

Close enough in age to have gone to high school with Paul Simon,
Smokey Robinson, and Mick Jagger, Barbra Streisand is the only
performer of her generation to rank among the great singers of the
classic-pop repertoire. In fact, she was the first major singer of her
generation to buck convention and pass by the rock sounds of her
time in favor of music she saw as timeless. Before her, classic-pop
singers weren't such classicists; they were singing the contemporary
music of their generations. Streisand was the first singer of a new
generation to treat classic pop as repertory music, and she has helped
establish it as just that by keeping it on the top of the record charts.
She outrebelled the rock revolutionaries by rebelling against rock, at
least at first.

Although she is one of today's best singers in the classic-pop vein,
Streisand has actually recorded far more light-rock songs by contemporary songwriters than standards by the masters of Tin Pan Alley.
As a matter of fact, as she's grown older she's tried to adopt a progressively contemporary—that is, younger—sound, with occasional
exceptions, such as the serious-minded *Classical Barbra* album in 1976
and the *Broadway Album*, which, after more than twenty years,
brought her back to classic pop in 1985.

Streisand's singing has never fit neatly within the parameters of the
classic-pop style. It's a quirky hybrid of theatrical and rock singing—
she has a Broadway pro's power, intonation, and song-story sense
combined with the irreverence and imagination of a rock singer. She
refuses to come down hard on the beat as a true rock singer must,

but she does wilder things with a melody than a traditional theatrical singer would dare.

In short, she sings much as she does everything else in life—however she damn well pleases. This is Barbra Streisand's quest, to follow that whim. And who could blame her? She's trusted her instincts and used her own individuality as the driving force of her whole career, and it's gotten her farther than any singer of her time. She's tackled more aspects of entertainment than any woman before her, including singing, acting, songwriting, directing, and producing. Successful at them all, she's won more major awards than any pop singer ever—two Oscars, a Tony, an Emmy, seven Grammies, and eleven Golden Globe Awards, as well as a French Legion of Honor medal and more than a dozen other honors.

Ironically, Streisand attributes the individuality that has fueled her extraordinary success to feelings of deficiency as a girl. "I believe my individuality—because, let's face it, I am a personality and not just a singer or actress—comes from the feeling of social inadequacy that plagued me as a kid," she recalls. "I was unsure of myself, so I wore white makeup and made myself look like a nut, so people would notice me."

Blessed with the natural survivor's instinct for turning seeming liabilities into strengths, Streisand played up her New York Jewish accent and strong features, and crafted a "kooky" persona to set her apart from the WASPy cookie-cutter dolls competing with her when she first tried breaking into show business in 1960. Born Barbara Joan Streisand in 1942, she cooked up the "Barbra" spelling as a young adult, to give her individuality a name. The accent was as natural as her features. Streisand grew up in the working-class Williamsburg section of Brooklyn and was raised by her mother and two other siblings after her father, a teacher, died at age thirty-four, when she was fifteen months old. "We weren't *poor* poor," Streisand explains, "but we didn't have anything."

One of the intangibles she didn't have was formal music training when she entered a Greenwich Village talent contest as a singer in 1961—and won. From her start, evidently, she had that ability to plow into something entirely new with no experience or expertise and to prevail by the power of her will and personality. Encouraged by the talent contest (assuming she ever needed encouragement), Streisand auditioned to sing at a *très chic* joint in Greenwich Village called the Bon Soir, got the job, and played eleven straight weeks to a fast-growing following of influential New York show people.

By late '61, she had landed her first part in a play, an Off-Broadway musical called *Another Evening with Harry Stoones*. Well-named if not well-written, the show lasted one evening, but it got Streisand enough attention for her to be booked at New York's hottest nightclub, the Blue Angel, where producer David Merrick caught her act and signed her for her first Broadway role, as the lonely secretary Miss Marmelstein in Jerome Weidman's *I Can Get It for You Wholesale*. The leading man of the show was Elliot Gould, to whom Streisand was briefly married. (The couple had a son, Jason Emmanuel, Streisand's only child.)

Her koo-koo Greenwich Village spirit and shameless mock-theatricality were at the heart of Barbra Streisand's appeal initially. Yet neither nightclubs nor Broadway really launched her career. Although many latter-day accounts of her life fail to note this, she was already a star by the time she debuted in her first major Broadway role, as Fanny Brice in *Funny Girl* in March 1964. In the days when most TV variety and talk shows were still based in New York and drew from local nightclub acts for new talent, Streisand gained national exposure on the *Garry Moore*, *Jack Paar*, and *Tonight* shows. But it was her LP records that made her a famous name—her first solo release, *The Barbra Streisand Album*, was a number-one hit and multimillion-dollar-seller a full year before *Funny Girl* opened. As a matter of fact, two follow-ups, *The Second Barbra Streisand Album* and *The Third Barbra Streisand Album*, were also smash hits before the curtain rose on *Funny Girl*.

With these three early albums, Streisand not only rose to stardom as a singer but also established her lasting reputation as a highly individualistic interpreter of classic pop. She was drawn to very dramatic material and novelty numbers—"Cry Me a River," "Happy Days Are Here Again" flipped around as an ironic dirge, and Harold Arlen and Truman Capote's "Sleeping Bee" on her first album; "Lover Come Back to Me," "Any Place I Hang My Hat Is Home," and "Down with Love" on her second album; and "Melancholy Baby," "As Time Goes By," and "Never Will I Marry" on her third. Like some others of her generation, she revealed a preference for the work of Harold Arlen, whose blues-based work has a certain affinity with rock 'n' roll. Performed with still-startling boldness and youthful exuberance (Streisand recorded them between ages nineteen and twenty-one), these albums are the cornerstone of Barbra Streisand's reputation as a classic-pop stylist.

With *Funny Girl* on Broadway, however, Streisand's transition from singing star to all-around superperson began. From this show onward, she would spend her career marching from entertainment medium to medium, the great show-business conqueror. Her first number in the Jule Styne–Bob Merrill show, "I'm the Greatest Star," sung when her character was anything but, seemed to set the tone for everything to follow. Never having heard a record or seen a film of Fanny Brice, she used her role in *Funny Girl* as a Barbra Streisand showpiece. She collected a Tony for this first starring stage performance and moved on to concerts, television, and films, never returning to a Broadway show. Even so, Streisand won a special Tony in 1970 as "Actress of the Decade."

Conquering the concert hall next, Streisand barnstormed the country in a twenty-city national tour in 1966, setting a new record for concert earnings by a solo performer—she earned $50,000 per show, nearly twice as much as Frank Sinatra at the time. As a topper, she set another record for highest attendance at a concert by a single performer, attracting an estimated 135,000 listeners for a free concert in New York's Central Park in 1967. Afterward she virtually disappeared from the concert stage and concentrated on television and films.

As something of a dry run for her movie career, the twenty-three year-old Streisand had demanded and was given virtually complete creative control over a series of ten TV specials that were originally contracted to air over the course of ten years. Beginning with the Emmy-winning *My Name Is Barbra* (1965), Streisand went on to produce, write, star in (with no guests stars allowed), and oversee the set design, lighting, and sound for a series of consistently high-rated and generally critically acclaimed specials—*Color Me Barbra* (1966), *The Belle of 14th Street* (1967), *A Happening in Central Park* (1968), and *Barbra Streisand . . . and Other Musical Instruments* (1973). Of course, once she felt she had outgrown network TV, she moved on again and never made half of the specials she had originally planned.

By the time she made her screen debut in 1968, reprising her portrayal of Fanny Brice in the movie version of *Funny Girl*, Streisand was clearly accustomed to instant success and power. She got her usual instant success, earning a Best Actress Oscar (in a tie with Katharine Hepburn for *The Lion in Winter*), and she steadily built up her power in Hollywood. After a string of roles demonstrating her versatility, including solid comedic and dramatic performances in *The Owl and the Pussycat* (1970), *What's Up, Doc?* (1972), and *The Way We Were* (1973), Streisand started flexing her well-exercised creative muscles in her film productions. She took to writing her own movie theme songs, winning her second Oscar for her theme to the 1977 *A Star Is Born*, "Evergreen" (co-composed with Paul Williams).

Streisand began developing a reputation as one of the more arrogant and egomaniacal figures in a town and a business fueled by arrogance and egomania. She is certainly, at the very least, an obsessive taskmaster determined to meddle in every possible aspect of a production, no matter how minute. By 1982, when she decided to be her own director for *Yentl* (based on an Isaac Bashevis Singer story about an Orthodox Jewish girl who disguises herself as a boy to pursue an education), Streisand had become the first woman ever to produce, direct, write, and star in a major Hollywood film.

In a typical story about Streisand's obsessive approach to filmmaking, she is said to have insisted on personally overseeing the transfer of *Yentl* from film to videotape for release on home cassette. As the technician working with her tells the anecdote, Streisand was displeased with the sound of the tape but uncertain of the precise problem. After a few hours of work, she finally announced the solution: She wanted the volume of the entire movie raised a few decibels. The technician did as told, without asking if Streisand had considered that when cassettes are watched at home, viewers turn their TVs to whatever volume they want.

Recording regularly through the years, Streisand built up a catalog of some forty LPs, from her 1963 debut to the early 1990s. While more than half of her output lies outside classic pop, her first half-dozen records, of mostly Broadway and Tin Pan Alley material, remain models of individualistic interpretation—personality pop. There are plenty of clunkers in her light-rock output, including a sweet-and-sour duet with Neil Diamond and a sweet-and-sourer one with her onetime lover Don Johnson. But there are also interesting moments in all these contemporary albums, including her lounge-act-at-the-space-station rendition of David Bowie's "Is There Life on Mars?" and her points-for-effort attempt at reggae, doing Bob Marley's "Guava Jelly" on her much-maligned *Butterfly* album, produced and art-directed by her lover at the time, Jon Peters. (Looking back on Streisand's overpublicized elevation of Peters from hairdresser to record and film producer, it's clear that she wasn't as love-blind as some of her critics claimed at the time. Long after he slipped out from under Streisand's wing, he continued rising until he became one of the most successful film producers in Hollywood.)

After more than fifteen years, Streisand finally returned to classic pop in 1985 with *The Broadway Album*, a collection of songs from such shows as *Carousel*, *Show Boat*, *West Side Story*, and *Sunday in the Park with George*. Even arranger Peter Matz was back from Streisand's early days, contributing pretty arrangements for "Can't Help Lovin' That Man" and a medley of Sondheim's "Pretty Woman" and "Ladies Who Lunch." Replacing Harold Arlen, Streisand's new composer of choice was Sondheim, who wrote or cowrote (and in some cases *re*wrote at Streisand's request) eight of the album's fifteen songs. Far more restrained and subtle than Streisand's youthful classic-pop records, with her voice less reedy-pure but more maturely disciplined, *The Broadway Album* was a definite comeback for Barbra Streisand as a singer. "It was time for me to do something I truly believe in," she explains. "This is the music I love. It is where I came from. It is my roots."

LIZA MINNELLI

*I was with Vincente Minnelli at the
hospital when Liza was born. I can tell
you that she had a beautiful voice then—
and it gets better all the time.*
—*FRANK SINATRA*

It's not often that the son or daughter of a superstar becomes a superstar in his or her own right. But Liza Minnelli has become one—and definitely in her own right. As the daughter of singer-actress Judy Garland and film director–designer Vincente Minnelli, it could be said that she was born with "show biz" in her veins. But the same could be said about the offspring of many other talented performers who have never attained the heights Liza has—including an Academy Award for her movie work, three Tonys for Broadway productions, and several Emmys and a Golden Globe Award for television. In 1986 she became the first popular singer in the then ninety-six-year history of New York's Carnegie Hall to play a sold-out engagement for three consecutive weeks at that prestigious house.

At Carnegie Hall and in most of her other concert engagements, Minnelli is one of the few nonrock performers who gets an ovation from the audience as soon as she steps on the stage. "It scares me when I haven't done anything yet," she says, "because then I feel I have to live up to this adulation. Mind you," she quickly adds, "I'm always thrilled." And so, usually, is the audience with the performance that follows.

With fewer natural vocal gifts than a dozen other contemporary singers, and certainly fewer than her legendary mother, the gaminelike Minnelli has learned how to go beyond most of them in really *delivering* a song. She does it with a combination of rhythmic incisiveness, an exceptionally expressive style of delivery (some would say overexpressive), and sheer showstopping energy. Whether the song is serious or lighthearted, torchy or comic, she conveys the impression that you are hearing it fully exposed. At the same time, she can sometimes give the impression that there is more bravado and more calculated mannerisms than sincere involvement in her performances.

For a while, she seemed locked into a formula of beginning a song fairly quietly and building and building to a *pow* finale of riveting intensity, as her mother frequently did. And, indeed, the songs with which Minnelli has become most identified follow that formula: "Cabaret," "Ring Them Bells," "Maybe This Time," "New York, New York," and "City Lights." But she has also proved herself an expert at projecting many songs with soft understatement and delicacy, such as "More Than You Know," "Try to Remember," "It Amazes Me," and "I Never Have Seen Snow."

The classic pop songs of her mother's and father's musicals were, of course, part of Liza Minnelli from her birth in 1946. She was named after the Gershwin song "Liza," which both her parents loved. Its lyricist Ira Gershwin, in fact, was her godfather. "I knew every Gershwin song by the time I was thirteen," Liza once told an interviewer. "I decided to learn them all." Virtually every Minnelli program still includes a Gershwin song or two. Her godmother was also famous: Kay Thompson, then a top MGM arranger and vocal coach as well as a radio and nightclub star and author. Thompson's famous fictional character Eloise (the little girl who lived at the Plaza Hotel in New York) was based in part on Liza. "Kay would tease me about how, at six, I knew how to dial room service and quote Oscar Wilde," she has reported.

Growing up in such a sophisticated show-business environment, in between attending schools in Switzerland and France as well as the United States, Liza Minnelli matured early. "I was born old," she once told an interviewer. After Garland's film career collapsed and her concert career was plagued with illnesses resulting from her pill dependencies, Liza found herself virtually propelled into the role of mothering her mother and Judy's two younger children by Sid Luft. Somehow, unlike the children of Bette Davis and Joan Crawford, Liza "didn't turn her childhood traumas into gothic revenge," as Bob Colacello so aptly expressed it in a 1987 *Vanity Fair* profile. Instead, "she chose the initially easy but almost impossible route of going into the family business."

Liza has always been the first to admit that a good part of her approach to singing comes from her mother. After her parents' divorce in 1950, Liza traveled extensively with her mother during that part of Garland's post-MGM career devoted almost exclusively to singing.

Inevitably, Liza picked up some of her mother's vocal mannerisms as well as some of her insights into performance practices. "She taught me that a lyric needs to be approached just like a script," Minnelli once told Friars Club interviewer Greg Morris for the newsletter of that well-known entertainers' organization. " 'Just because you're holding a note,' Mom said, 'don't think the emotion of the word is over. Never lose the thought behind the word.' "

Yet Liza Minnelli has never been just warmed-over Judy Garland. Except for her big, brown, expressive eyes, Minnelli shares few physical similarities to her mother. Some critics have not been particularly kind in pointing out that her face is not conventionally pretty or cute in the way Garland was in her movie days (although, as we mentioned in our Garland chapter, Judy's appearance certainly had its ups and downs in her later years). But like Streisand, Merman, Sinatra, Astaire, and a number of other major musical stars, Minnelli developed a unique personality and "show-biz magnetism" that have more than compensated for whatever limitations she may have had in meeting the Hollywood "looks" standard. Moreover, the electricity of her performances must surely be the envy of thousands of beautiful dolls who will never be much more than background decorations.

Early on, Liza determined to be her own person, taking the best she could from her roots and her parents' experience but then going her own way. At the beginning, it wasn't easy. Many people assumed either Vincente Minnelli or Judy Garland was pressuring colleagues into opening doors for her, and resented Liza for it. Others, of course, were intrigued to see what the only offspring of such a supertalented couple could do. Somewhat awkward appearances on Garland's New York Palace Theater programs in the mid-1950s and on her CBS television series in the early 1960s brought mixed critical notices. Liza's response was to work harder than anyone around her to *prove* her talent.

That she did decisively at age seventeen, when, after a series of regional theater productions, she took on Broadway, where her parents then had the fewest connections. First, in a secondary role in the 1963 Off-Broadway revival of the early-1940s musical *Best Foot Forward* and then in the lead of the 1965 Broadway musical *Flora the Red Menace*, Minnelli began winning audiences over. She won her first Tony for *Flora*—the youngest actress ever to win in the Best Actress in a Musical category. *Flora* also marked her first professional association with the songwriting team of John Kander and Fred Ebb, who soon thereafter began working regularly with her, writing songs

and special material for most of her television and concert appearances
as well as several later Broadway shows (including *The Act* and *The
Rink*). Ebb, in fact, became perhaps her most influential mentor.

In 1967 Minnelli made her movie debut (not counting a "walk-on"
bit at age three in the final scene of her mother's *In the Good Old
Summertime*)—not, however, as a singer and not at MGM, but as a
somewhat kooky young secretary in the British-made drama *Charlie
Bubbles*. She followed that with two other nonmusical parts at Paramount, *The Sterile Cuckoo* (about a lonely girl who forces her at-
tentions on a reluctant college student) and *Tell Me That You Love
Me, Junie Moon* (about a facially scarred young woman living with
two disabled young men). Each of these parts helped establish an
identity much different from her mother's, and for each of them Liza
won generally glowing critical notices. For *The Sterile Cuckoo* she got
her first Oscar nomination (Maggie Smith won that year for *The Prime
of Miss Jean Brodie*).

It was not until after her mother's death that Liza Minnelli made
her first movie musical, Bob Fosse's *Cabaret*. As Christopher Isherwood's stagestruck Sally Bowles (trying desperately to be "divinely
decadent" in early-1930s Berlin), she finally established a screen identity completely distinct from her mother's. Liza also turned Kander
and Ebb's title song into a bigger hit than it had ever been in *Cabaret*'s
Broadway version, and permanently made it "hers" as far as audience
identification goes. Her performance was warm, funny, kookily serious, touching, and, above all, lovably vulnerable, while her singing
combined sweetness, intensity, and vocal power in a way that moviegoers had not seen in anyone else of her generation. To crown all
her work to that time, Minnelli won the 1972 Academy Award as Best
Actress for *Cabaret*.

Despite *Cabaret*'s success, movie musicals were pretty much out of
fashion with audiences in the 1970s, so Minnelli's singing was limited
mostly to recordings and to television specials, including Bob Fosse's
Emmy-winning *Liza with a Z*. Then, after a couple of nonmusical
movie flops (including her father's Rome-made *A Matter of Time* with
Ingrid Bergman), Minnelli took on Martin Scorsese's *New York, New
York*, essentially a drama with interspersed songs (since the two leading characters, Robert DeNiro and Minnelli, are both musicians).
Daringly, and with a confidence born of her own independent stardom,
Minnelli didn't hesitate in the musical numbers to emulate elements
of her mother's style. It was as if Liza were saying, "Yes, folks, I *can*
sing like my mother, so let's do it once and for all, and get it out of

the way." Out of *New York, New York* came another permanent cornerstone of Minnelli-the-singer's repertoire, the title song.

Whatever Minnelli's considerable success as an actress in movies and on Broadway, there is still nothing to compare with a Minnelli concert performance, as several of them now preserved on video will attest for years to come. As Fred Ebb has commented, "She doesn't simply sing a song, she inhabits it." Her programs are usually a mixture of songs she has made famous, songs from the classic-pop repertory, and songs newly written for her that are clearly modeled on the classic-pop style. Perhaps in reaction to her mother's often erratic record in terms of late appearances and cancellations, she has sometimes carried "the show must go on" tradition to extremes, working with a sore throat and a high temperature, throwing her head back and raising an arm high above her head in typically full-speed-ahead Minnelli gestures.

Meanwhile, Minnelli's personal life for many years could best be described as a roller coaster. Three marriages (to singer Peter Allen in 1967; producer Jack Haley, Jr., in 1974; and sculptor Mark Gero in 1979) ended in divorce, and she has suffered at least one miscarriage. There were also widely publicized romances with Desi Arnaz, Jr., Peter Sellers, and Martin Scorsese. She also inherited her mother's scoliosis, a painful curvature of the spine whose severity is often intensified by dancing. That was primarily why she started taking Valium a number of years ago rather than abandon the dancing she loves and that was such a key part of her act. But her addiction to that drug, as well as abuse of alcohol and what she has called "party drugs," escalated to such an extent in the 1980s that she resorted to prerecording some of her numbers for the Broadway show *The Rink* (just miming to the tape during some performances) and eventually dropped out of the show to enter the Betty Ford Center for treatment.

"I think I'm calmer and more secure than I was," she told an interviewer in 1989 after returning to concert appearances. "I don't depend on things that aren't real anymore." Friends say that doesn't mean she's become stodgy or a recluse in her private life—far from it. And onstage, her energy and intensity now seem much less on automatic pilot and more sharply in focus. She has insisted, moreover, on changing one line of her signature song, "Cabaret"—the line that refers to a pal who succumbed to pills and liquor. Liza now sings, "I made my mind up back in Chelsea, when I go I'm *not* going like Elsie."

NOT TO BE FORGOTTEN

Many other fine singers of classic pop also rose to major levels of fame and success in the years during and following World War II. Here are miniprofiles of just a few more who were, and in most cases still are, particularly distinctive and memorable.

Helen Forrest

Perhaps more than any one else, Helen Forrest epitomized the big-band singer of the swing era. She sang with three of the best bands during their heyday: Artie Shaw's, Benny Goodman's, and Harry James's. Her warm, sweet, flexible voice could handle just about any expressive mood or rhythmic style. She sang ballads with a kind of understated sincerity that gave them a real one-to-one feeling without ever losing the basic dance beat of a number, in contrast to so many other, matter-of-fact band singers, whose concentration on the beat gave them a more detached feeling. In up-tempo tunes she had a natural lilt that seemed to have a built-in smile. Although not "Hollywood pretty" in the conventional sense of the day (which kept her from a major movie career despite occasional guest appearances), Forrest always came across as a classy lady who could draw whistles from the males in the audience, especially when wearing one of her form-fitting gowns.

She started singing as a teenager with her brother's small band in her hometown of Atlantic City, New Jersey—then principally a town of fashionable summer-resort hotels rather than the gambling-casino town it's become in recent years. She also sang on local radio stations, at one point singing on six different programs under as many different names—Helen Trees, Helen Farraday, Fran Helene, Hilda Farrar, and Bonnie Blue among them.

A two-week singing engagement at the Mardillon Room in Washington, D.C., in 1937 got extended to two years. While there, Forrest auditioned for Benny Goodman, but he turned her down. She got a different reaction from Artie Shaw and in 1939 became Shaw's lead vocalist for what she still calls fifteen of the most memorable months of her life. But then, suddenly, Shaw decided to disband and quit the business—leaving Forrest, the orchestra and Shaw's millions of fans in shock.

Goodman, obviously having changed his mind about her in the interim, was the first to contact her with a job offer. Ten days after Shaw's orchestra disbanded, Forrest joined the Goodman orchestra. She stayed twenty months, but, as she says in her 1982 autobiography *I Had the Craziest Dream*, "they felt like twenty years." Although she admired "The King of Swing" as a great musician (and still does), she found him a cold, difficult man to work for. Finally she could take no more and quit, telling a reporter, "I wasn't angry with him, I just couldn't take his needling anymore. He's a perfectionist and he drives people crazy."

She wasn't out of work for long. Trumpeter Harry James, who had previously left Goodman to form his own band, promptly hired Forrest. She and James's male vocalist Dick Haymes divided the ballads and occasionally teamed up for romantic duets. But it wasn't for Haymes that Forrest pined romantically; it was for James himself. They became lovers for most of the two years she sang with his band, and he gave her an engagement ring at one point. But then, as she later told columnist Earl Wilson, "He met Betty Grable—and how could I compete with the pinup girl of the world? The next thing I knew I was standing outside the window of my apartment on a ledge about three stories high and people were yelling at me not to do anything foolish." As she says in her autobiography, "I'm glad I didn't. I've had a pretty good life and a lot of laughs since then."

It was during her years with the James band that Forrest recorded her biggest hits—"I Had the Craziest Dream," "Skylark," "I Cried for You," "I've Heard That Song Before," "Mister Five by Five," and "I Don't Want to Walk Without You" among them. In 1942 and 1943 she won both the *Down Beat* and *Metronome* polls as the number-one female singer in the country—ahead of Helen O'Connell, Peggy Lee, Jo Stafford, Dinah Shore, Billie Holiday, Mildred Bailey, Lena Horne, and Ella Fitzgerald.

After James and Grable eloped in 1943, Forrest quit the band to go out on her own the way Jo Stafford, Peggy Lee, and others were doing. At first, instead of the $250 to $450 a week she'd earned with James (depending on recording sessions and radio shows), she was now making $2,000 a week playing theaters and nightclubs. She changed her hair color from brunette to blond and had cosmetic surgery on her nose and chin. But aside from a successful fifteen-minute radio show she did with Dick Haymes from 1944 to 1947, Forrest never hit it as big on her own as some of the other former band singers. She has sometimes blamed it on not being beautiful enough, and sometimes on the way the music business changed with the coming of rock 'n' roll.

Forrest settled in Hollywood for a time and married actor Paul Hogan. Like her first youthful marriage, to drummer Al Spieldock, it ended in divorce, as did a third marriage, in 1959, to businessman Charlie Feinman. Forrest gave up show business altogether in the mid-1960s, when she moved to Phoenix, Arizona, because her son (by Feinman) required a dry climate for a serious sinus condition. In Phoenix she ran an Indian jewelry shop for a time. But in 1979 she realized that she was happiest only when she could perform as a singer. She returned to Hollywood and began taking part in big-band fund-raisers for public-television stations, and rejoined Dick Haymes for a tour of *The Fabulous '40s*. A year later she suffered a mild stroke. Fully recovered, she was back singing two months later, though on a more limited schedule.

"Let's face it, the old girl is no kid now," she says. "I think every time I step on a stage I am young again. I think my performances prove I can still sing with anyone, even those many years younger. What scares me is being alone."

Helen O'Connell

Of all the big-band canaries who rose to popularity in the 1940s, Helen O'Connell was clearly the sunniest. The infectious smile that always seemed to be on her face beautifully matched her clear, bright, lilting singing style. The New York *Sunday News'* Homer Peters summed it up unforgettably when he wrote, "The dimples around her mouth are as two quote marks around a happy phrase."

Pert, blond O'Connell was not the only singer in the Irish-American family into which she was born in Lima, Ohio, on May 23, 1920. Helen's older sister, Alice, got a head start on her, singing with small dance bands in the Ohio area to help support the family after the death of their father. Then, one night, Alice decided to elope. "I won custody of her two evening gowns," Helen recalls, "and I showed up that night on the bandstand in one." Helen got to keep the job.

Several years and several bands later, she was heard one night in a Greenwich Village club in New York by bandleader Jimmy Dorsey. He signed her the following day. O'Connell became a mainstay of the Dorsey orchestra from 1939 to 1943, the band's "golden years" as an almost endless hitmaker. Most critics of the day weren't wild about her ballad-singing, but they liked her good looks, her bouncy personality, and the infectious way she handled novelty tunes. Together with Dorsey's handsome male vocalist Bob Eberly (brother of Glenn Miller vocalist Ray Eberle), O'Connell began an early-1940s' vogue for boy-girl duets—in which Eberly would first croon the song in a straight-forward, romantic way, and then O'Connell would belt out the second chorus in a more rhythmic, up-tempo style. When their first such duet, "Green Eyes," quickly became a multimillion-seller, it was followed by "Tangerine" and others. Soon O'Connell and Eberly, rather than the instrumental soloists who shared the spotlight with the singers of most other big bands, were the biggest audience draws for the Dorsey orchestra. Their fans were forever trying to link them romantically, but Eberly was already happily married, so their relationship was limited strictly to the bandstand and the recording studio.

"An overwhelming number of high-school and college kids flocked to see the bands in those days," Helen later noted, "and a couple of hundred young men proposed to me by mail." She politely turned down all proposals until she met a young Navy aviator from Boston, whom she married in 1941. Two years later, at the peak of her popularity, she quit the Dorsey orchestra to concentrate on raising her children while her husband was away in service. "I got tired of all the traveling around by bus and train, and all the one-nighters," she told John S. Wilson of *The New York Times*. "I love music and show business, and it's done a lot for me. But when you have children to raise, it's not a healthy life." She also felt she was being underpaid by Dorsey—$200 a week, with no royalties on her recordings, just $25 extra per recording.

O'Connell settled in Los Angeles and, determined to get the high-school diploma she had lost by dropping out in her sophomore year in Ohio, enrolled at Hollywood High under her married name. She also stopped singing altogether, until after her divorce in 1950. She then cut several records for Capitol in the early 1950s that showed her voice to be as bright and chipper as ever.

In 1957 O'Connell moved to New York to become Dave Garroway's on-the-air "girl Friday" on TV's *Today Show* for two years. Garroway told reporters he hired her because she "is the sunniest girl imaginable" for an early-morning show. She did the weather and special features but sang only occasionally, contending that it was hard to warm up her voice so early in the day. On one of the shows she met author Thomas T. Chamales, who was promoting his new book, *Never So Few*. Two weeks later they were married. Their life together turned into a soap opera, however. Several times she had him arrested for beating up both her and her daughter—with the headlines, of course, playing up the singer of "Green Eyes" now having black eyes. She and Chamales were living apart when he died in 1960.

After a subsequent marriage to a musician ended in divorce, O'Connell resumed her career once again in the late '70s and early '80s, when nostalgia for the '30s and '40s was "in" in various parts of the country. As she told UPI reporter Vernon Scott at the time, "When I go on the road, I pass out my arrangements to the orchestra, which varies from three pieces to fifteen. We have a two-hour rehearsal, and then I cross my fingers and say a lot of prayers. My repertoire isn't nostalgic. I sing a medley of the old tunes to keep the audience happy, but most of my songs are contemporary or standards." She also joined Rosemary Clooney, Margaret Whiting, and Rose Marie in a tour of the show *4 Girls 4* for several years.

But it's the four years she sang so breezily with Jimmy Dorsey's orchestra, from 1939 to 1943, that still give Helen O'Connell's name its greatest resonance in the history of classic pop.

Bobby Short

Virtually synonymous with the sassy elegance of Manhattan nightlife, or, more accurately, its myth, Bobby Short has been performing at the same tony Upper East Side night spot, the Café Carlyle, since 1968. Stepping into his domain—a gilded boudoir with wall-to-wall murals by French designer Marcel Vertès—is like zapping right into a scene from an old Cary Grant movie. You don't feel comfortable without a martini and formal wear, and the only music that could possibly fit the scene would have to be by Cole Porter or Noel Coward.

As a matter of fact, Bobby Short is very much the Cary Grant of classic pop. Like Grant, who was born a poor kid named Archibald Leach and concocted his aristocratic persona from whole cloth, Short was the ninth of ten children born to Myrtle and Rodman Short, in Kentucky, in 1924. After his father died in a coal-mining accident, Bobby Short used his natural musical ability to help support his family, hitting the vaudeville circuit in 1936 as a piano player. At age twelve, he dolled himself up in evening garb and billed himself as "The Midget King of Swing."

By the late 1940s, Short had graduated from honky-tonks such as the Lookout House in Covington, Kentucky, to the chicest nightclubs of Manhattan—the Blue Angel, the Living Room, Le Cupidon, and others. He started recording for Atlantic Records in the 1950s, cutting more than a dozen albums of elegant readings of Broadway show music, including rarely heard tunes from the '20s and '30s. (Highlights of this rich period of recording have been compiled in a set of LPs, *Fifty by Bobby Short*.)

Something of a specialty performer, Short has never become a major recording star, despite the warmth and polish of his singing on records. He is at his best and has enjoyed extraordinary longevity as a nightclub singer and pianist. In the intimacy of a club, his effervescence and infectious love for his material help counterweight his somewhat over-refined diction and sometimes off-putting vocal mannerisms, particularly his voluptuous vibrato.

Another deterrent to becoming a Top Ten recording artist has certainly been his rarefied choice of material. Short is a singing archivist. He loves to unearth obscure or forgotten works by great songwriters, such as Cole Porter's "I Worship You" from *Fifty Million Frenchmen* or the Gershwins' "Nashville Nightingale" from *Nifties of 1923*.

As the nightclub scene diminished in the 1960s, Short found himself practically broke and hungry for work, playing at exclusive cocktail parties for a modest fee. Yet during the same period, he appeared annually on lists of The Ten Best-Dressed Men in America.

Weathering the slump of the '60s, Short was able to start a new career as a concert-hall performer as classic pop began to be accepted in a new light, as repertory music. He played a critically acclaimed concert with his longtime friend Mabel Mercer at New York's Town Hall, followed by increasingly prestigious concerts over the ensuing decade at New York's Carnegie Hall and Avery Fisher Hall.

Short reached something of a career peak in the early '70s, with his Café Carlyle shows a sold-out attraction, his album *Bobby Short Loves Cole Porter* well accepted, and the publication of his autobiography, *Black and White Baby*. Through his book, in particular, Short attracted new fans by clearing the air about a controversial element of his work. He had been criticized, especially by some African-American separatists, for seemingly abandoning his African roots by performing "white" music in a "white" style. Short explained that his approach is "color-blind." After all, as he often notes, classic pop has been influenced by a variety of cultures, including African-American, Italian, Jewish, and many others, and he certainly plays it all.

Steve Lawrence and Eydie Gormé

There have been other married-couple singers in pop music, going back to nineteenth-century vaudeville, but none in recent times have quite matched the popularity of Steve and Eydie as separate singing talents or Steve&Eydie as a team. Although they came onto the pop-music scene at about the same time as Elvis Presley, they have stuck steadfastly—and successfully—to the classic-pop style of music for more than four decades.

Both have strong, attractive voices—he a warm, mellow, two-octave baritone with overtones of Crosby's easygoing style, she a bright, buoyant alto capable of shaking the rafters in the Garland manner. What they lack in musical originality is usually offset by their polished, straightforward, satisfying performances of good songs in the classic-pop manner. There may be a sameness to their musical approaches to most songs—he crooning in a soothing, romantic way, she building to a more emotional, all-stops-out wrap-up—but it almost always works in an audience-pleasing way, even when her sound tends to overwhelm his in the climaxes of their duets.

Each hails from New York City—he was born in Brooklyn (July 8, 1935), she in the Bronx (August 16, 1932). The son of a cantor, Lawrence began singing at an early age in the choir of his father's synagogue, and then at local clubs and private parties for $5 to $100 a night. It became a routine family gag for him to come home late from such gigs and hide the money in the refrigerator so he could say, "I'm giving Mom cold cash."

Gormé, meanwhile, started singing at school assemblies and then for brief periods with such name bands as Tommy Tucker's and Tex Beneke's. The daughter of Sephardic Jews who spoke Spanish at home, Gormé was also able to put her bilingualism to work broadcasting for the Voice of America, ending up with her own program, *Cita con Eydie* (A Date with Eydie), beamed to Spanish-speaking countries throughout the world.

They met when Steve Allen hired them, independently, to sing on NBC's *Tonight Show* in 1953. Gormé says it was love at first sight. But at twenty, Lawrence was in no rush to get married. So they kept most of their colleagues guessing until December 1957, when they finally tied the knot. Allen, meanwhile, teamed them frequently in duets as well as in solo numbers.

They began their nightclub singing careers separately—Gormé in 1954, as a last-minute substitute at New York's Copacabana for an indisposed Billy Daniels, Lawrence in 1956, also at the Copa. Lawrence, however, still had his eye on an eventual acting career, hoping to become a singing movie star like Gordon MacRae. Steve Allen gave Lawrence plenty of opportunities to polish his acting skills in *The Tonight Show*'s sketches, where he proved himself an adept, witty ad-libber (just as he was later to do as a frequent guest on *The Carol Burnett Show*). But no movie offers came, partly because most producers thought him too short (he's five-nine) and slightly on the chunky side.

Soon after their marriage, Lawrence was drafted into the Army for eighteen months. It was not until after his discharge that the couple decided to do a club act together, and from then on they have alternated joint appearances with solo ones throughout the country. The same has been true about their recording dates and their frequent TV guest appearances—some together, some separately. Jointly they have won two Emmys for their TV work: one for *Steve and Eydie Celebrate Irving Berlin* and another for their Gershwin tribute *Our Love Is Here to Stay*. They won a Grammy for their joint album *We've Got Us*, and Gormé won a Grammy on her own for her heartrending recording of "If He Walked into My Life" from Jerry Herman's score for the Broadway musical *Mame*. Each has had more than a dozen recordings reach hit status on the Top Hundred charts (mostly in the late '50s and early '60s), including her "Blame It on the Bossa Nova" and "Too Close for Comfort" and his "Pretty Blue Eyes" and "Go Away, Little Girl."

Over the years, Steve and Eydie have been called the Lucy and Desi of popular music. Once, when an interviewer asked Lawrence if they ever fight, he replied, "Of course we fight. What kind of married couple doesn't fight? In fact, we have a 7:00 P.M. bout scheduled for tonight."

In 1964 Lawrence finally won a major acting role, starring in the Broadway musical *What Makes Sammy Run?* He won the New York Drama Circle Award for his performance and also a Tony nomination, but the show enjoyed only a limited run. Four years later Gormé joined him as the costar of another short-lived Broadway show, *Golden Rainbow*. Thereafter they decided to stick to clubs, concerts, and television—averaging six months a year on the road performing and six months at home in California. A highlight was their eight-day engagement at New York's Carnegie Hall in 1981.

In 1986 they almost quit for good when their twenty-three-year-old son died of a heart attack without any previous history of heart trouble. They could not bring themselves to perform for months but finally were coaxed back to concert appearances by friends and colleagues who insisted they still had something to say through their music—not only to their own generation but to younger ones as well. Lawrence himself had previously summed up somewhat philosophically their commitment to classic pop when he told a *New York Post* interviewer, "Kids today hang on to catchphrases. How can they know where it's at when they don't know where it's been?"

Andy Williams

Next to Perry Como, Andy Williams is the singer who most owes his celebrity as a crooner of popular songs to television stardom. Although his TV success came after rock began to dominate the music scene but before the ascendancy of MTV and music videos, Williams has generally specialized in intimate romantic ballads in the classic-pop tradition. "I've ignored rock 'n' roll," he said a number of years ago, "because I think ballads are more welcome on TV, but now and then I get on the fringe of rock 'n' roll for my recordings."

The five-foot-nine, sandy-haired Williams has a smoky-toned high baritone, which he usually uses in an easygoing, unforced way but which he can also let loose in the climax of a song for a much stronger effect than, say, Perry Como or Steve Lawrence. "Smooth" and "tasteful' are the adjectives most often used to describe Williams's singing of such songs as "Moon River," "Canadian Sunset," "In the Village of Saint Bernadette," "Love Story (Where Do I Begin?)," and the many others he introduced or helped along the road to Top Ten status.

Williams was born on December 3, 1930, in the small Iowa town of Wall Lake (population under one thousand at the time). His father was a railroad mail clerk and amateur musician who trained Andy and his three older brothers to sing in the choir of the local Presbyterian church. Andy was eight when the Williams Brothers began singing on radio in Des Moines and then Chicago—which, in turn, led to a movie contract with MGM. But before any film work actually materialized, the two oldest brothers were drafted into military service. Andy settled down to finish high school in Los Angeles, occasionally free-lancing in choruses or as a back-up singer for movies and recordings. He is, for example, in the background on Bing Crosby's best-selling 1943 recording of "Swinging on a Star" from *Going My Way*, and the following year (at age thirteen) he dubbed the singing voice of Lauren Bacall in her debut movie, *To Have and Have Not*.

After the war, the Williams Brothers became a part of Kay Thompson's popular nightclub act and then, with Thompson, a regular on such radio and TV shows as Bing Crosby's. In 1953, when two of the brothers decided to try other lines of work, Andy moved out on his own. Within a year he had a recording contract with Cadence Records and was signed for a two-week stint on Steve Allen's *Tonight Show*. "After the two weeks, no one said anything, and I just reported each week and kept singing—and they kept paying me," Williams has said. He remained on the show for two and a half years, meanwhile guesting occasionally on other shows, including Dinah Shore's.

In 1958 ABC offered Williams a prime-time summer show of his own. "It is a lazy, good-natured show with an extremely pleasant host in Williams," reported the *New York Herald-Tribune*'s TV critic, adding, "He sings in a casual style and doesn't attempt to overpower you with personality." It wasn't long before NBC decided that was just what it needed for its regular-season line-up, and the hour-long *Andy Williams Show* became a popular fixture on its schedule throughout the rest of the 1960s. Williams became known on the show for his dependably pleasing versions of popular standards from Broadway and Hollywood, plus new songs modeled mostly on nonrock styles. However, with those styles in decline among younger listeners by the late '60s, the show's producers made occasional attempts to attract a less graying audience with psychedelic lighting and guest rock acts, but they didn't help the show's eventual slide in the ratings, and it went off the air in 1971.

Throughout his career, Williams has kept his "nice guy" image— or, as a *New York World-Telegram* reporter once commented, "He looks and acts like just what he is: a country boy from the Midwest who has made good in the big city." His private life has occasionally been in the news due to his close friendship with Ethel Kennedy and his standing by his ex-wife, actress Claudine Longet, during her involvement in a murder investigation. Except for sporadic TV guest appearances and recording dates, Williams has quietly cut back on singing engagements in recent years, preferring to pursue his longtime interests, modern painting (especially collecting French Impressionists) and sponsoring golf events.

Julius LaRosa

That ephemeral something called star quality—if there ever was living proof that it's real, that proof is Julius LaRosa. Watch LaRosa in a nightclub, singing masterfully, magnificently, and you'll appreciate star quality. It's the thing that's missing.

We can't explain this phenomenon any further, other than to add that it is entirely irrelevant in the case of LaRosa. Pop music has plenty of stars; one fewer probably doesn't matter much. But there's always room for more artists—performers who work from a love of the work itself, risk failure and frequently achieve it, and sometimes manage to change the way we look at things (including the way we look at the artists themselves). Julius LaRosa is this kind of a classic-pop artist.

Of course, he did have his fifteen minutes of fame, which is different from stardom. As everybody over forty knows, LaRosa is the fellow who earned a place as a footnote in television history for being the first performer to be fired on the air. Arthur Godfrey decided to drop the singer from his popular TV show in 1953, and his special way of breaking the news to LaRosa was by announcing it to America on live TV.

The event, which took all of seventeen seconds more than thirty-five years ago, is so integrally associated with LaRosa that he has rarely been seen in purely musical terms. In a clear-eyed assessment of the singer, however, his uncommon ability is striking. His voice is one of the most direct, unpretentious, and understated baritones in pop, with a hint of vibrato and a full, masculine tone. The sheer simplicity of LaRosa's singing is a marvel of control and a wonderful vehicle for the plaintive lyrics and naturally flowing melodies of classic pop. Like Sinatra, LaRosa's phrasing is acutely attentive to the lyrical meaning of a song, albeit sometimes at the expense of the melody. As a matter of fact, there is a great deal of Sinatra in LaRosa—more than there is in Vic Damone, and that's a lot indeed.

Watching Sinatra at New York's Paramount Theater in the '40s (as Damone also did), LaRosa was heavily influenced by his admitted idol while still a school kid in Brooklyn. But he didn't think of singing professionally himself, he says. He was planning to join his father's radio-repair business, and only joined the Grover Cleveland High glee club "to get out of classes."

It was in the Navy, singing in a company show, that LaRosa was heard—and snatched up—by Arthur Godfrey, who dropkicked him into his show while LaRosa was still in navy uniform. "I guess I was the first nonentity ever to appear on TV," recalls LaRosa, who had never sung in a nightclub, in a theater, or with a band. LaRosa was one of the first test cases of the theory that TV doesn't need celebrities, it makes them. And unmakes them. When Godfrey discovered that LaRosa had hired a personal manager and had been skipping the ballet lessons Godfrey required for all members of his cast, he decided LaRosa had lost his "humility" and kicked him off his show.

In turn, LaRosa was immediately signed for a $185,000 concert tour and told *Life* magazine that being fired was the best thing that had ever happened to him. LaRosa was no media martyr. "I got jobs because of the publicity," he glowed at the time. "A *dog* could get jobs with headlines like that." LaRosa landed all sorts of jobs in the decades after the Godfrey incident—as the lead in the play *A Broadway Musical*, as the star of the "B" musical movie *Let's Rock*, as a disc jockey for New York's WNEW-AM Radio. His problem was that those jobs didn't work out, either, or they didn't lead to anything bigger in the future.

All along, though, LaRosa has steadily improved as an artist. "I kept channeling any frustrations I had into my craft," he explains, and it has showed. The singer surprised both audiences and critics with a powerful "comeback" performance at New York's Carnegie Hall in November 1974, followed over the ensuing years by several acclaimed cabaret performances in New York, including an incisively delivered show of songs with lyrics by Oscar Hammerstein II at Michael's Pub.

By the close of the '80s, LaRosa had developed a loyal if relatively modest following among pop connoisseurs, and they were buying enough tickets to keep him busy in nightclubs around the country.

Moreover, as he approached his sixties, he was performing at the mature top of his form, clearly comfortable with himself and his role as an important classic-pop artist, if not necessarily a star.

Teddi King

Few singers who first came to the fore in the 1950s won such unanimous critical kudos as Teddi King. Jazz critic Nat Hentoff went so far as to declare that she had "the most impressive vocal equipment in pop music." Yet Teddi King was never able to win the kind of major public recognition she deserved. Part of the problem was the time of her arrival on the scene, just as rock 'n' roll took over the popular music industry. Another obstacle proved even more formidable, when she contracted a degenerative disease of the connective tissue that curtailed her performances for many years and was a factor in her sudden death in November 1977 at age forty-seven.

Teddi (originally Theodora) King was a tiny lady, just under five feet tall. She had tiny hands and tiny feet; short, dark hair; a pretty face highlighted by deep brown, magically alive eyes; and an openly warm personality. Petite as she may have been, when she opened her mouth to sing, out came a big voice—a strong, rich, bright soprano that seemed to flow effortlessly, especially in long-lined ballads. Her phrasing, too, seemed effortless and natural, and she had an instinctive regard for the value of understatement, as is evident in her recordings of such Gershwin songs as "Isn't It a Pity" and "Bidin' My Time," and Alec Wilder's "Blackberry Winter."

Because she could swing so easily and frequently worked with jazz instrumentalists, some identified Teddi King as a jazz singer. She rejected that designation. "Most jazz singers change many of the notes," she said. "I don't. And I really care about the words of a song."

Her flowingly clear diction was also distinctive, a carryover from her original plans to be an actress. While in high school in her native Boston, she was active in its dramatic club. After graduation, she tried out for a regional theater company that specialized in Shakespeare, O'Casey, and classic American plays. When they discovered that she could also sing, they gave her the role of a singing mermaid in a musical *Peter Pan*. Although she wasn't listed in the program, she was singled out by Elliot Norton, one of Boston's top critics, who wrote, "An unidentified young lady in a mermaid costume sang 'Song of the Lorelei.' It was hauntingly beautiful." That convinced King that perhaps she should concentrate on a singing career.

Growing up in Boston, King had rarely missed any of the stage shows that appeared then at the city's leading first-run movie houses and that were frequently headlined by touring big bands or singers. As she later recounted to Whitney Balliett for a *New Yorker* profile: "I'd sit in the front row with my lunch to see Frank Sinatra, Jo Stafford, Helen Forrest, and Helen O'Connell. When the RKO had a Dinah Shore sing-alike contest, I entered it and beat out five hundred girls." King's singing career was under way.

For three years, King sang mainly in clubs in the Boston area, including the fabled Storyville. She worked regularly with Nat Pierce's orchestra, made recordings with him, and also appeared on local radio and television shows. An engagement at the Copley Square Hotel with George Shearing led to an invitation to tour with him for two years beginning in 1952 (the only singer he's ever employed) and to make recordings with Shearing's quintet. Then King and her husband, Boston society-band drummer Josh Gerber, decided it was time to strike out on her own. To her regret, she hired a manager who put her in sequined gowns and packed her off to Las Vegas. As she told Whitney Balliett, "It wasn't me. I was doing pop pap, and I was in musical despair. Rock arrived, Elvis Presley got bigger and bigger, and I got very depressed and thought of quitting." Still, she hung on, making recordings for RCA Victor that sold decently if never rising to top spots on the charts, and singing to consistently glowing reviews in most of the major clubs throughout the country that still featured classic pop throughout the late '50s and early '60s. After she and her husband decided to settle in New York, she began a long association with the New York Playboy Club.

Then, in 1970, King began having problems with simple maneuvering. She spent most of that summer in and out of hospitals undergoing tests before doctors at Boston's Pratt Clinic finally diagnosed her affliction as systemic lupus erythematosus, or, as it is commonly called, lupus. She was told that it could be controlled with drugs for certain periods of time but that its long-term prognosis was uncertain. As physically and emotionally drained as the disease made her, she worked hard to keep her spirits up. "I was bedridden quite a while," she later said, "and my main concern was whether I'd be able to sing again." But as she began to mend, she found her voice was still in fine shape, even if the cortisone and other drugs she'd been taking had given her a swollen-looking face and body. Gradually she took on singing engagements again, participating in Alec Wilder's public radio series on American popular song, then a number of music festivals, and finally six weeks at New York's fashionable Café Carlyle to some of the best reviews of her career. She also began recording again for small, independent labels with pianists Marian McPartland and Dave McKenna.

She was halfway through recording an album with McKenna in the fall of 1977 and planning a new club engagement when a sudden illness sent her to the emergency room of a nearby hospital, where she died the next day. As Sam Parkins, producer of that uncompleted last album, wrote for the album's liner notes when it was released, her needless death "put a sudden end to a comeback which had lifted her from artistic near-oblivion into the select front-rank of American singers."

Nancy Wilson

The only African-American woman in classic pop to earn her own network TV music series, Nancy Wilson was a popular sensation in the 1960s.

She came up through jazz, touring the country with saxophonist Rusty Bryant as a teenager in 1956–57. Returning to her hometown of Columbus, Ohio, in 1958, she was working as a single in local clubs when she caught Cannonball Adderly's eye. An important jazz talent scout as well as a leading alto saxophonist, Adderly encouraged Wilson to try the big time and come to New York. Through his intercession and contracts, she landed a recording contract with Capitol Records, the label for which she was to record for the bulk of her career. But Wilson was practical as well as beautiful and talented, and she kept a comfortable secretarial job as a hedge against failure, holding on to it until her first Capitol release was in the stores and selling well.

Wilson's singing is distinguished by a straightforward but soulful, gentle but emphatic, pitch-perfect delivery and impeccable diction. Her first albums—a collaboration with Cannonball Adderly's quintet, a pair of upbeat Billy May–arranged LPs, and a team-up with George Shearing (a big early booster)—were critically acclaimed and respectable sellers. Wilson's good looks and accessible singing style encouraged Capitol to steer her toward pop and away from jazz, and her album of Broadway show tunes (directed by the overlooked Ellington associate Jimmy Jones) turned out to be a hit. It was followed closely by a similar collection of movie songs and an album of contemporary pop tunes, both also arranged and conducted with tasteful economy and flair by Jimmy Jones. With these recordings, Wilson emerged from jazz to establish herself as one of the most popular club and concert attractions of the '60s. As a result, she was tapped to host her own network TV variety series, the mid-1960s *Nancy Wilson Show*.

Her strongest influence is clearly Dinah Washington. But Wilson is able to convey the biting, sweet-and-sour edge that was Washington's trademark without the trebly nasal stridency that is sometimes associated with Washington. Of the singers who descend stylistically from Washington, Esther Phillips built her style around that reedy, feline Washington nasality, whereas Wilson is able to suggest it without coming off as brassy or overbearing.

Her versatility is such that she can move between pop and straight-ahead jazz, between small combo backings and lush orchestration, between Latin rhythms and contemporary beats with an assurance and grace that keep the focus on the essence of the song. In Wilson's hands, a song of betrayed love, such as her big hit "Guess Who I Saw Today," is treated with knowing, womanly depth, but the buoyant quality and resilient positivity that makes her "I Believe in You" so credible is never far from the surface. Her readings are always soulful, but even at her most drenchingly blue, the desolation of Billie Holiday and the haughty, brazen quality of Dinah Washington are never to be found in her voice.

Wilson is also among the most deft of popular singers at delivering a story line. From Berlin's "You Can Have Him" to Arlen's "Happiness Is a Thing Called Joe," she often uses an intimate, half-spoken style to reveal the verse. The body of the song is delivered with the dramatic intensity of a first-rank musical-theater star, although Wilson's training ground was the nightclub.

One of Wilson's vocal trademarks is her frequent but tasteful use of a falsetto descending "catch" or grace note at the beginning of a phrase, a vocal mannerism often used by the R&B harmony groups of the '50s. High-tenor leads such as Clyde McPhatter, Tony Williams, and Jackie Wilson, among others, have used a similar "catch" in the voice to telegraph seething passion or sadness. But Wilson's use of the same vocal device seems meant less to convey melodrama than to vary the texture of her voice, as a saxophonist or trumpeter might choose to apply a bit of growl.

Since ending her long association with Capitol in the late '60s, Wilson has recorded for several labels and renewed her association with jazz, recording and appearing with an all-star quintet sometimes known as the Griffith Park Collection, featuring saxophone great Joe Henderson and keyboardist Chick Corea. Her substantial interpretive powers have only deepened, and she seems to have become a looser, more open-to-impulse performer than she was at the peak of her popular success. Perhaps she feels most at home with the jazz sounds with which she started out as a singer.

JACK JONES

Of all the singers in the rock 'n' roll era who have strived to carry on the classic-pop tradition, Jack Jones has been one of the most successful, both artistically and commercially.

He started out as something of a musical clone of his father, Allan Jones, who starred in movies and had a few hit records in the '30s and '40s singing in the broad, theatrical style. At age nineteen in 1957, Jack Jones made his show-business debut singing with the elder Jones on the Nevada nightclub circuit. But he seemed to strike both critics and audiences—the way Frank Sinatra, Jr., and Tina Martin would in the '60s—as a pleasant but essentially redundant curiosity. Jack Jones retreated to the Air Force and, while still in the service in 1959, cut a demo singing in his own more casual style, and submitted it blind to a record company. The song, "Lollipops and Roses," became a Top Ten hit.

The tone of Jones's warm baritone voice is clear and natural—in fact it's perilously close to being as bland as both Jack Jones's name and his '50s prom-king looks. But Jones's singing is saved, to some degree, by a good sense of swing time, rare among singers of his age. More distinctively, Jones has a confident, almost cocky way of phrasing. He sings with an unseen smirk that makes much of his work seem subtly self-mocking.

Jones's flawed taste in material has always hurt his reputation as a singer. He first hit the charts in the early 1960s, the age of social rebellion and enlightenment, singing some of the most demeaningly sexist songs in the pop repertoire. His first hit, "Lollipops and Roses," treats adult women as infants who can be thrown token gifts to keep them complacent. As a follow-up, Jones released "Wives and Lovers," which makes "Lollipops and Roses" sound like *The Hite Report* by ordering a woman (called "little girl") to treat her makeup and hairdo as her top priorities.

For a while in the early 1960s, Jones seemed braced to become an important singer. In 1962 he was voted Most Promising Male Vocalist by a *Cashbox* magazine deejay poll, and Sinatra called him "the next major singing star of show business." But polarized from his own generation by the sheer regression of his material, Jones ended up appealing mainly to the audience of his father's generation, after all.

Over the years since his early commercial success, Jones has matured, achieving more and more success as a performing artist. In his club dates and concerts in the '80s and '90s he often omitted 'Lollipops" and "Wives and Lovers"—or sang them with self-deprecating introductions acknowledging the songs' sexism. He's turned increasingly to up-tempo standards that suit his casually cocksure style, including concert highlights such as "All Right, Okay, You Win," and "Just One of Those Things." As *New York Times* jazz critic John S. Wilson remarked in a review of Jones in the '80s, "He has a deeper feeling for jazz and a more wry sense of humor than [his hits] 'The Impossible Dream' and 'The Love Boat' suggest."

PART THREE

Selected Discographies and Videographies

S INGERS are, first and foremost, meant to be heard. The following pages offer a selective listing of each singer's best or most
representative audio recordings, plus a selective listing of concert videos, movies, documentaries, or other types of programs on which they
can be seen as well as heard on home-video tapes or laserdiscs.

The emphasis in these listings is on discs and tapes now available
in record or video stores. In the case of audio recordings, this means
primarily *compact discs*, since CDs have become the leading audio
format for home listening since the late 1980s. There has been a steady
(some would say explosive) procession of digitally remastered transfers
to CDs, involving hundreds of original recordings of the past seventy
years, many of them superbly engineered in the transfer to surpass
their original 78-rpm or LP editions. But we also list important pre-
1990 *long-playing discs* (LPs) that may still be available in the specialty
shops that continue to stock LPs—or, perhaps more likely, that may
still be found in public or college libraries. In some cases, audiocassette
editions of these releases may also be available, and can be checked
in the latest edition of the Schwann Catalogs' *Spectrum*, available in
most record stores.

Our video listings are of VHS cassettes and/or video laserdiscs.
Although most video shops limit their stock to the latest best-selling
movies, music, and special-interest releases from the major distributors,
they will order tapes or discs that are not in stock if you ask them.
And, once again, many may be available from public or college libraries.

For easy reference, these listings are arranged alphabetically by
singer rather than in the order of the preceding chapters.

LOUIS ARMSTRONG

SELECTED DISCOGRAPHY

The Hot Fives and Hot Sevens, Vols. I–III Three-volume CD compilation of seminal Armstrong sides: *Vol. I* includes "Potato Head Blues" and "You Made Me Love You"; *Vol. II* includes "Muskrat Ramble" and "My Heart"; *Vol. III* includes "The Last Time" and "Skip the Gutter." (Columbia, mono)

The Silver Collection CD compilation of pop standards with jazz-pop arrangements by Russ Garcia; includes "Top Hat, White Tie and Tails," "Have You Met Miss Jones," "You're Blasé," "You're the Top," and "Don't Do Nothin' Till You Hear From Me." (Verve/Polygram, stereo)

Ella and Louis First of three albums by Armstrong and Ella Fitzgerald (including *Ella and Louis Again* and *Porgy and Bess*, all available on CD). Songs include "They Can't Take That Away from Me," "A Fine Romance," "A Foggy Day," and "Cheek to Cheek"; featuring Oscar Peterson, Ray Brown, Herb Ellis, Buddy Rich, and Louis Bellson. (Verve, stereo)

Louis Armstrong July 4, 1900–July 7, 1971 LP compilation of selections from 1932 to 1956, including "You'll Wish You'd Never Been Born," "Some Sweet Day," "Lovely Weather We're Having," and "I Never Saw a Better Day." (RCA, mono and stereo)

Louis Armstrong and His Orchestra LP compilation of mid-'40's recordings, including "Blues in the Night," "A Pretty Girl Is Like a Melody," "Ac-cent-tchu-ate the Positive," and "Always." (Joker, mono)

The Essential Louis Armstrong 1965 Paris concert performance on LP; includes "Lover," "When It's Sleepy Time Down South," "When I Grow Too Old to Dream," "Perdido," and "Cabaret"; with pianist Billy Kyle and others. (Vanguard, stereo)

Hello, Dolly! All-Armstrong LP from the mid-'60s (not the movie sound track); includes "A Lot of Livin' to Do," "A Kiss to Build a Dream On," "Moon River," "You Are Woman, I Am Man," and title song. (Kapp, mono)

SELECTED VIDEOGRAPHY

Satchmo Comprehensive documentary written and codirected (with Kendrick Simmons) by Armstrong scholar Gary Giddins (based on his biography); with performances from 1932 to the 1960s, including rare footage of Chicago nightclub appearance in 1935; narrated by Hattie Winston. (Sony Music Video tape)

High Society 1956 Cole Porter musical version of *The Philadelphia Story* with Bing Crosby, Frank Sinatra, and Grace Kelly, and with Armstrong in a small but memorable role, singing "Samantha" and "Now You Has Jazz" in a duet with Crosby. (Paramount tape and laserdisc)

Jazz on a Summer Day Bert Stern's classic documentary about the 1958 Newport Jazz Festival, featuring Armstrong, Dinah Washington, Gerry Mulligan, and Thelonious Monk, among others. (New Yorker tape)

Hello, Dolly! 1969 musical adaptation of Thornton Wilder's *The Matchmaker* with Jerry Herman score; starring Barbra Streisand, Walter Matthau, Michael Crawford, and Armstrong, and directed by Gene Kelly. (CBS/Fox tape and laserdisc)

FRED ASTAIRE

SELECTED DISCOGRAPHY

The Astaire Story Two-CD edition of a 1952 LP set, with six members of Norman Granz's Jazz at the Philharmonic concert troupe headed by pianist Oscar Peterson; includes thirty-four of Astaire's Broadway and Hollywood songs plus several originals. (Verve/PolyGram, mono)

Starring Fred Astaire Two-CD or two-LP compilation of studio (not soundtrack) recordings of thirty-six songs from 1935 to 1940 with the orchestras of Johnny Green, Leo Reisman, Ray Noble, and Benny Goodman—mostly the best-known movie songs of the Astaire-Rogers period, plus two Astaire originals: "I'm Building Up to an Awful Letdown" and "Just Like Taking Candy from a Baby." (Columbia/Sony, mono)

A Fine Romance—Fred Astaire CD compilation of twenty Astaire studio recordings from 1931 to 1937, with the orchestras of Leo Reisman and Johnny Green; duplicates many of the post-1935 Astaire-Rogers songs from the Columbia collection above, but also includes several earlier Astaire recordings from Broadway's *The Band Wagon*. (ProArte, mono)

Best of Fred Astaire from MGM Classic Films CD compilation of sound-track selections from Astaire's MGM musicals of 1946 to 1957, including *Easter Parade*, *The Band Wagon*, *The Barkleys of Broadway*, and *Silk Stockings*. (MCA, mono)

Fred Astaire Rarities CD compilation of songs dating from 1931 (a medley from Broadway's *The Band Wagon* with Fred and Adele) to 1955 (*Daddy Long Legs'* "Slue Foot" and "Something's Gotta Give"); also includes two Ginger Rogers solo recordings from 1938 (both from *Carefree*). (RCA/BMG, mono)

Astaireable Fred 1987 LP compilation of six Astaire originals (including "Sweet Sorrow," "There's No Time Like the Present," and "Just Like Taking Candy from a Baby"); four Gershwin songs from the movie version of *Funny Face*; and five lesser-known movie and TV songs recorded in the late 1950s and early 1960s with the orchestras of Buddy Bregman, Dick Hazard, and Russ Garcia. (DRG, mono)

SELECTED VIDEOGRAPHY

The Fred Astaire Songbook David Heeley and Joan Kramer's 1991 PBS-TV *Great Performances* tribute to Astaire-the-singer, with complete-song movie and TV film clips and on-camera comments by Audrey Hepburn, Melissa Manchester, Liza Minnelli, Hermes Pan, Richard Schickel, and others. (Turner tape)

That's Entertainment MGM's 1972 compilation classic, with Astaire as one of eleven host-narrators; includes Astaire songs (and dances) from *Dancing Lady*, *Broadway Melody of 1940*, *Ziegfeld Follies*, *The Barkleys of Broadway*, *Royal Wedding*, and *The Band Wagon*. (MGM/UA tape; MGM/UA laserdisc)

That's Entertainment, Part 2 MGM's 1974 follow-up compilation feature, with Astaire and Gene Kelly as narrators (including newly filmed musical "framing sequences"); includes songs (and dances) from *Easter Parade*, *Belle of New York*, *Silk Stockings*, and *The Band Wagon*. (MGM/UA tape)

The Gay Divorcee 1934 movie adaptation of Broadway's *Gay Divorce*; with Astaire and Ginger Rogers, Cole Porter's "Night and Day," and Conrad and Magidson's Oscar-winning "The Continental." (RKO/Turner tape)

Top Hat 1935 movie musical with Ginger Rogers and an Irving Berlin score; Astaire sings "No Strings," "Cheek to Cheek," "Isn't This a Lovely Day to Be Caught in the Rain," and "Top Hat, White Tie and Tails." (RKO/Turner tape)

Swing Time 1936 Astaire-Rogers musical with a Jerome Kern–Dorothy Fields score; Astaire sings "The Way You Look Tonight," "A Fine Romance," and "Never Gonna Dance." (RKO/Turner tape; Criterion Collection laserdisc)

You Were Never Lovelier 1942 Jerome Kern–Johnny Mercer musical with Astaire and Rita Hayworth; Astaire sings "Dearly Beloved" and the title song. (RCA/Columbia tape)

Easter Parade 1948 musical with Judy Garland, Astaire, Ann Miller, and Peter Lawford, and songs by Irving Berlin; Astaire sings "Steppin' Out with My Baby," "It Only Happens When I Dance with You," "Drum Crazy," "Snooky Ookums," and the title song. (MGM/UA tape and laserdisc)

The Band Wagon 1953 movie adaptation (with a new plot) of the 1931 Arthur Schwartz–Howard Dietz Broadway revue, with Astaire, Cyd Charisse, Nanette Fabray, Jack Buchanan, and Oscar Levant; Astaire sings "A Shine on Your Shoes," "By Myself," "Triplets," and "That's Entertainment." (MGM/UA tape and laserdisc)

Funny Face 1957 movie adaptation of a George and Ira Gershwin Broadway musical (with a new plot), with Astaire, Audrey Hepburn, and Kay Thompson; Astaire sings " 'S Wonderful," "He Loves and She Loves," "Clap Yo' Hands," and the title song. (Paramount tape)

MILDRED BAILEY

SELECTED DISCOGRAPHY

Mildred Bailey: That Ol' Rockin' Chair Lady CD compilation of twenty-eight selections taken from 1943 to 1951 broadcasts and from 1943 to 1944 V-disc recording sessions (for the wartime armed forces); accompaniments include the Red Norvo Quintet, Benny Goodman, and the All-Star Band, and the Delta Rhythm Boys; includes "Ol' Rockin' Chair," "More Than You Know," "Sunday, Monday and Always," "Right As the Rain," "It's So Peaceful in the Country," and "Georgia on My Mind." (Vintage Jazz Classics, mono)

Mildred Bailey: Harlem Lullaby CD compilation of twenty songs recorded by Bailey between 1931 and 1938; includes the title song, "Rockin' Chair," "Georgia on My Mind," "Please Be Kind," "I Let a Song Go Out of My Heart," and "Thanks for the Memory."

Mildred Bailey, Her Greatest Performances, 1929–1946 1981 two-LP compilation of forty-eight commercially recorded selections, with accompaniments led by the Dorsey Brothers, Benny Goodman, Red Norvo, Alec Wilder, and others; includes "Ol' Rockin' Chair," "I'm Nobody's Baby," "Old Folks," "Darn That Dream," "A Ghost of a Chance," "Prisoner of Love," "I've Got My Love to Keep Me Warm," "Thanks for the Memory," "Harlem Lullaby," "Downhearted Blues," "Lover Come Back to Me," and "Hold On." (Columbia, mono)

SELECTIVE VIDEOGRAPHY

At publication time there were no known videocasettes or videodiscs with Mildred Bailey.

TONY BENNETT

SELECTED DISCOGRAPHY

Tony Bennett Sings His All-Time Hall of Fame Hits 1970 greatest-hits compilation, on CD and LP; includes "Because of You," "Cold, Cold Heart," "I Left My Heart in San Francisco," and "I Wanna Be Around." (Columbia, stereo)

Art of Excellence The 1986 album that brought Bennett back to the public eye, on CD and LP; includes "Why Do People Fall in Love," "Moments Like This," "What Are You Afraid of?" and "When Love Was All We Had." (Columbia, stereo)

Bennett/Berlin 1988 tribute to Irving Berlin on CD and LP; includes "They Say It's Wonderful," "Cheek to Cheek," "Let's Face the Music and Dance," and "White Christmas." (Columbia, stereo)

Astoria: Portrait of the Artist 1990 album of songs inspired by Bennett's boyhood in 1930s New York, on CD and LP; includes "Just a Little Street Where Old Friends Meet," "Antonia," "Where Do You Go from Love," and "I've Come Home Again." (Columbia, stereo)

The Beat of My Heart 1958 LP with Ralph Sharon and orchestra, featuring Art Blakey, Jo Jones, Chico Hamilton, and others; includes "Let's Begin," "Love for Sale," "Crazy Rhythm," and "Let's Face the Music and Dance." (Columbia, stereo)

Tony Bennett Sings the Rodgers and Hart Songbook 1973 LP with the Ruby Braff–George Barnes Quartet; includes "Lover," "Isn't It Romantic," "I Could Write a Book," and "There's a Small Hotel." (DRG, stereo)

Tony Bennett, the McPartlands and Friends Make Magnificent Music 1977 LP with Marian McPartland and Jimmy McPartland; includes "Watch What Happens," "Let's Do It," and "Softly as in a Morning Sunrise." (DRG, stereo)

SELECTED VIDEOGRAPHY

Tony Bennett Sings 1981 concert performance with Ralph Sharon conducting the ITV Concert Orchestra; includes "My Funny Valentine," "Just in Time," and "Lullaby of Broadway." (Sony tape)

The Oscar Bennett's only dramatic movie performance, with Stephen Boyd and Elke Sommer; directed by Russell Rouse in 1966. Bennett sings "Maybe September." (Nelson tape)

CONNEE BOSWELL

SELECTED DISCOGRAPHY

Connie Boswell—Sand in My Shoes 1976 LP compilation of six Boswell Sisters tracks from the early 1930s, twelve of Connee's best solo recordings from the late 1930s and early 1940s, and two duets with Bing Crosby from 1939 and 1940; includes the title song, "Blueberry Hill," "Sunrise Serenade," "That Old Feeling," "I Hear a Rhapsody," "Yes Indeed," and "I'm Putting All My Eggs in One Basket." (MCA, mono)

Connee Boswell and the Boswell Sisters on the Air 1977 LP compilation of previously unreleased air checks from Rudy Vallee's "Fleischmann Hour" (1935) and the "Kraft Music Hall" (1941), plus four broadcast transcriptions with Freddy Rich's orchestra (1936). Connee's solos include "I Can't Give You Anything But Love, Baby," "I Hear a Rhapsody," "Amapola," and "Manhattan." (Totem, mono)

The Boswell Sisters, 1932–34 1972 LP compilation, including two previously unissued takes ("Mood Indigo" and "Crazy People"). Also includes "Was That the Human Thing to Do?" "Hand Me Down My Walkin' Cane," "Minnie the Moocher's Wedding Day," "The Object of My Affection," "We Just Couldn't Say Goodbye." (Biograph, mono)

The Boswell Sisters, 1932–34, Vol. 2 1982 LP compilation of twelve recordings, including previously unissued takes of "Rock and Roll" and "If I Had a Million Dollars"; also includes "42nd Street," "Shuffle Off to Buffalo," "It Don't Mean a Thing," "Alexander's Ragtime Band," "Heebie Jeebies," and "Way Back Home." (Biograph, mono)

SELECTED VIDEOGRAPHY

Transatlantic Merry-Go-Round The Boswell Sisters have only one complete number in this 1934 mixture of detective story and musical romance on an ocean liner, and that number (by today's standards) is sheer camp, as they sing Richard Whiting's "Rock and Roll" in a kitschy setting. (Video Late Show tape)

BUDDY CLARK

SELECTED DISCOGRAPHY

The Buddy Clark Collection, 1942–1949 1987 LP compilation of twenty representative selections from the more than 150 songs Clark recorded in the 1940s for Columbia, with accompaniments by the orchestras of Mitchell Ayres, Ted

Dale, and Sonny Burke; includes "Linda," "You're Too Dangerous, Cherie," "I'll See You in My Dreams," "Peg o' My Heart," "Ballerina," "If This Isn't Love," "Just One More Chance," and "You'd Be So Nice to Come Home To." (Murray Hill, mono)

Buddy Clark—The Early Years, 1935–1937 1980 LP compilation of fourteen selections taken from broadcast air checks and transcription discs, with accompaniments led by Eddy Duchin, Lud Gluskin, Mark Warnow, and others; includes "I'm Shooting High," "Midnight in Paris," "The Magic of You," "I've Got My Fingers Crossed," and "But Definitely." (Take Two, mono)

Favorites By Buddy Clark, Vols. 1 & 2 Two separate mid-1980s LP compilations of mostly 1948 broadcast air checks; includes "Come Rain or Come Shine," "These Foolish Things," "Blues in the Night," "If There Is Someone Lovelier Than You," "Lullaby of Broadway," "But Not for Me," "All the Things You Are," "It's a Big, Wide, Wonderful World," "On a Slow Boat to China," and fifteen others. (Take Two, mono)

SELECTED VIDEOGRAPHY

Seven Day's Leave A 1942 wartime comedy with Lucille Ball, Victor Mature, Ginny Simms, Mel Tormé, and the orchestras of Freddy Martin and Les Brown. Clark has a small role as a sailor buddy of Mature's and has no solo songs. Score by Jimmy McHugh and Frank Loesser. (RKO/Turner tape)

ROSEMARY CLOONEY

SELECTED DISCOGRAPHY

Rosemary Clooney Sings the Music of . . . A series of albums (on CD and LP) dedicated to the music of the great classic-pop composers, recorded in the 1980s with small jazz bands. Highlights:

Cole Porter Includes "In the Still of the Night," "It's De-Lovely," and "My Heart Belongs to Daddy." (Concord, stereo)

Rodgers, Hart & Hammerstein Includes "Oh, What a Beautiful Morning," "People Will Say We're in Love," and "The Gentleman Is a Dope." With the Los Angeles Jazz Choir. (Concord, stereo)

Johnny Mercer Includes "Laura," "Skylark," and "Something's Got to Give." (Concord, stereo)

Irving Berlin Includes "Cheek to Cheek," "What'll I Do," and "Let's Face the Music and Dance." (Concord, stereo)

Blue Rose 1956 collaboration with Duke Ellington and Billy Strayhorn (available on CD and LP); includes "Passion Flower," "It Don't Mean a Thing (If It Ain't Got That Swing)," "I Got It Bad (And That Ain't Good)," and "Mood Indigo." (Columbia/Mobile Fidelity Sound Labs, stereo)

Rosemary Clooney Sings Ballads 1985 album with jazz sextette featuring Scott Hamilton (available on CD and LP); includes "Thanks for the Memory," "Here's That Rainy Day," "It Never Entered My Mind," and "A Nightingale Sang in Berkeley Square." (Concord, stereo)

SELECTED VIDEOGRAPHY

White Christmas 1954 Irving Berlin film musical about a pair of former GIs (Bing Crosby and Danny Kaye) trying to help their old general (Dean Jagger), who runs a winter resort. As Kaye's love interest, Clooney sings "Sisters," "Snow," and "Love, You Didn't Do Right By Me." Directed by Michael Curtiz. (Paramount tape and laserdisc)

NAT "KING" COLE

SELECTED DISCOGRAPHY

Nat "King" Cole: Collectors Series CD compilation of Cole hits from the course of his career. Includes "Straighten Up and Fly Right," "Route 66," "The Christmas Song," "Nature Boy," "Mona Lisa," and "Too Young." (Capitol, stereo)

Nat "King" Cole and the King Cole Trio CD compilation of vintage Cole and rarities, with vocal numbers from 1938 to 1939, including "Jumping Jitters" and "Let's Do Things." (Savoy Jazz, mono)

Nat "King" Cole Trio: The Vocal Sides CD compilation of recordings from 1943 to 1949; includes "Too Marvelous for Words," "You're the Cream in My Coffee," and "Embraceable You." (Laserlight, mono)

Crazy Rhythm CD compilation of Cole trio radio broadcasts from 1947 to 1948; includes "For Sentimental Reasons" and "What'll I Do," plus oddities such as a Wild Root Cream Oil commercial. With guest appearances by Pearl Bailey, Duke Ellington, and Woody Herman. (Vintage Jazz Classics, mono)

SELECTED VIDEOGRAPHY

Nat "King" Cole: Unforgettable 1989 documentary about Cole's life and career, with recollections by Frank Sinatra, Mel Tormé, Ella Fitzgerald, and Oscar Peterson. Songs include "These Foolish Things," "It's Only a Paper Moon," "The Christmas Song," and "The Very Thought of You." (MPI tape)

RUSS COLUMBO

SELECTED DISCOGRAPHY

Russ Columbo—A Legendary Performer 1976 LP compilation of recordings made between September 1931 and August 1932; includes "You Call It Madness (But I Call It Love)," "Time on My Hands," "Just Another Dream of You," "Where the Blue of the Night Meets the Gold of the Day," "Prisoner of Love," and "Just Friends." (RCA, mono)

Russ Columbo—Prisoner of Love 1975 LP compilation of recordings made between 1930 and his last recording session in June 1934; includes "Street of Dreams," "Guilty," "A Peach of a Pair," "I See Two Lovers," "Prisoner of Love," "My Love," and "Goodnight Sweetheart." (Pelican, mono)

The Films of Russ Columbo 1970s sound-track compilation with variable-quality sound, with excerpts from the short subject *That Goes Double* and the feature films *Broadway Thru a Keyhole, Moulin Rouge,* and *Wake Up and Dream.* (Golden Legends, mono)

Gone But Not Forgotten—Russ Columbo Poorly documented 1982 four-LP compilation of fifty-one reputed air checks and recordings by Columbo and/or his orchestra; the authenticity of a dozen or so of the tracks has been challenged as possibly involving Harlan Thompson, Billy Ekstine, or others, not Columbo. But the album does include much genuine Columbo material not otherwise available. (Russ Columbo Archives, Inc., mono)

SELECTED VIDEOGRAPHY

No Russ Columbo movies or documentary footage are known to be available on either videotape or videodisc.

PERRY COMO

SELECTED DISCOGRAPHY

Perry Como—Pure Gold CD edition of a 1975 LP compilation from the 1940s and 1950s, including "Till the End of Time," "It's Impossible," "Prisoner of Love," "Papa Loves Mambo," "Because," and five others. (RCA/BMG, stereo)

Perry Como All-Time Greatest Hits CD edition of a 1976 LP compilation of fifteen recordings from the 1940s to the 1970s; includes "No Other Love," "Papa Loves Mambo," "Till the End of Time," "It's Impossible," "Temptation," and "Dream a Little Dream of Me." (RCA/BMG, stereo)

Perry Como Today 1987 compilation for CD of ten recordings from the 1980s, including "Sing Along with Me," "Making Love to You," "You're Nearer," "My Heart Stood Still," "Bless the Beasts and Children," and "Dreaming of Hawaii." (RCA/BMG, stereo)

Young Perry Como 1984 LP compilation of sixteen recordings Como made between 1936 and 1941 as a singer with Ted Weems' dance band, including his first recording, "Lazy Weather." (MCA, British import, mono)

SELECTED VIDEOGRAPHY

Words and Music Como plays a small role in this highly fictionalized 1948 movie biography of Rodgers and Hart. Como sings "With a Song in My Heart," "Blue Room," and "Mountain Greenery." (MGM/UA tape and laserdisc)

The Perry Como Show Taken from kinescopes of an October 1951 telecast, with Peggy Lee as Como's guest. The tape also includes other '50s programs with Tony Martin, Eddie Fisher, and Freddy Martin. (Shokus tape)

BING CROSBY

SELECTED DISCOGRAPHY

Bing Crosby the Crooner—The Columbia Years 1928–1934 Three-CD or three-LP 1988 compilation of sixty-five songs recorded with the orchestras of Paul Whiteman, the Dorsey Brothers, Gus Arnheim, Jimmy Grier, Lennie Hayton, and others; includes "Oh, Miss Hannah," "I've Got the World on a String," "Brother, Can You Spare a Dime?" "Try a Little Tenderness," "Learn to Croon," "Paradise," "Love, You Funny Thing," "Let's Put Out the Lights and Go to Sleep," "Lazy Day," and "May I?" (CBS/Sony, mono)

Bix 'n' Bing CD compilation of twenty songs recorded between 1927 and 1930 with Paul Whiteman's orchestra, with the legendary Bix Beiderbecke on cornet; includes "Changes," "Mississippi Mud," "From Monday On," "Sunshine," " 'Tain't So, Honey, 'Tain't So," and "Waiting at the End of the Road." (Academy, English import, mono)

The Best of Bing Two-CD edition of a 1965 two-LP compilation of twenty-four recordings from the 1930s and 1940s, with the orchestras of Victor Young, Georgie Stoll, John Scott Trotter, and others; includes "June in January," "Where the Blue of the Night (Meets the Gold of the Day)," "I'm an Old Cowhand," "Pennies from Heaven," "Swingin' on a Star," "White Christmas," and "Now Is the Hour." (MCA, mono)

The All-Time Best of Bing Crosby CD compilation of ten recordings from the 1930s and 1940s, including "Where the Blue of the Night (Meets the Gold of the Day)," "Easter Parade," "Swingin' on a Star," "Don't Fence Me In" and "Accent-tchu-ate the Positive" (with the Andrews Sisters), and "Lazy River," and "Bye Bye Blues" (with Louis Armstrong). (MCA/Curb, mono)

Bing Crosby—On the Sentimental Side CD compilation of twenty recordings from 1931 to 1938, including "Stardust," "Black Moonlight," "How Deep Is the Ocean?" "Sweet Is the Word for You," and "I Have Eyes." (Living Era/Academy, mono)

Bing Crosby in Hollywood 1967 LP compilation of studio recordings of thirty-one songs from Crosby movies of 1930 to 1934; includes "Happy Feet," "Please," "Temptation," "Moonstruck," "Love Thy Neighbor," and "Love in Bloom." (Columbia/CBS Hall of Fame Series, mono)

SELECTED VIDEOGRAPHY

King of Jazz An all-star, 1930 Technicolor revue starring Paul Whiteman's orchestra; Crosby's first movie, as part of Whiteman's Rhythm Boys; his songs include "Happy Feet," "Mississippi Mud," and "The Bluebirds and the Blackbirds." (MCA/Universal tape and laserdisc)

Blue of the Night and *I Surrender, Dear* Two of the Mack Sennett musical shorts Crosby filmed in 1931 as his radio popularity began to soar; his songs include "My Silent Love," "Where the Blue of the Night (Meets the Gold of the Day)," "I Surrender, Dear," "Wrap Your Troubles in Dreams," and "One More Chance." (Video Ten tape)

Holiday Inn 1942 Paramount musical classic costarring Crosby and Fred Astaire, with songs by Irving Berlin; Crosby's songs include "White Christmas," "Be Careful, It's My Heart," "Abraham," "Let's Start the New Year Right," and "Happy Holiday." (MCA/Universal tape and laserdisc)

Road to Morocco Third (1942) and one of the best musically of Crosby's popular *Road* pictures with Bob Hope and Dorothy Lamour; Crosby's songs include "Moonlight Becomes You," "Constantly," and "(We're Off on) The Road to Morocco." (MCA/Universal tape)

White Christmas Another all-Irving Berlin musical (1954), costarring Crosby this time with Danny Kaye and Rosemary Clooney; Crosby's songs include "Count Your Blessings," "Snow," "Heat Wave," "Blue Skies," and the title song. (Paramount tape and laserdisc)

High Society MGM's 1956 musical remake of *The Philadelphia Story*, with Crosby, Frank Sinatra, Grace Kelly, and Louis Armstrong; Crosby's songs include "True Love," "Well, Did You Evah!" "Now You Has Jazz," and "Samantha." (MGM/UA tape and laserdisc)

VIC DAMONE

SELECTED DISCOGRAPHY

Vic Damone Sings the Great Songs CD compilation includes "Softly as I Leave You," "Come Back to Me," and "Over the Rainbow." (Pickwick International, stereo)

A Dreamer's Holiday CD compilation of romantic ballads; includes "The Look of Love," "A Day in the Life of a Fool," and "Mean to Me," with arrangements by Nelson Riddle. (MCS Ltd., Swiss import, stereo)

The Best of Vic Damone Live 1970 concert performance with orchestra conducted and with arrangements by Norm Geller; includes "In the Still of the Night," "On the Street Where You Live," and "Here's That Rainy Day." (Rainwood, stereo)

SELECTED VIDEOGRAPHY

Kismet Lavish MGM musical version of the Broadway musical by Robert Wright and George Forrest. Damone sings "And This Is My Beloved." Howard Keel, Delores Gray, and Ann Blyth star; Vincente Minnelli directed. (MGM/UA tape and laserdisc)

DORIS DAY

SELECTED DISCOGRAPHY

Best of the Big Bands: Doris Day with Les Brown CD compilation of singles from the early 1940s; includes "While the Music Plays On," "It Could Happen to You," "We'll Be Together Again," and "Let's Be Buddies." (Columbia, mono)

One Night Stand with Doris Day CD compilation of 1940s radio broadcasts with Les Brown; includes "Sentimental Journey" and "Saturday Night (Is the Loneliest Night of the Week)." (Sandy Hook Records, mono)

Doris Day Sings 22 Original Recordings CD compilation of radio broadcasts from the early 1950s, with the Van Alexander Orchestra and the Page Cavanaugh Trio; includes "My Blue Heaven," "I Could Write a Book," and "I Can't Give You Anything but Love." (Hindsight, mono)

SELECTED VIDEOGRAPHY

Young at Heart Day 1954 melodramatic musical based on Fannie Hurst's *Four Daughters*, directed by Gordon Douglas. Sinatra plays Day's love interest, and Gig Young and Ethel Barrymore costar. (Republic Pictures tape)

Love Me or Leave Me Portraying singer Ruth Etting (with whom she has little in common), Day sings "I'll Never Stop Loving You," "Ten Cents a Dance," "Mean to Me," "Shaking the Blues Away," and the title song. James Cagney costars in this 1955 bio-pic, directed by Charles Vidor. (MGM/UA tape and laserdisc)

The Man Who Knew Too Much Day delivers one of her best-regarded non-musical performances (although she does sing one song, her hit "Que Sera, Sera") in this 1956 Alfred Hitchcock remake of his own 1934 suspense film. James Stewart costars. (MCA/Universal tape and laserdisc)

Pajama Game Playing a prefeminism feminist caught between her principles and her passions, Day stars in this George Abbott musical from 1957, with songs by Richard Adler and Jerry Ross. Day sings "I'm Not at All in Love," "Once-a-Year Day!" "Small Talk," and "There Once Was a Man." Bob Fosse choreographed, and Abbott codirected with Stanley Donen. (Warner tape and laserdisc)

RUTH ETTING

SELECTED DISCOGRAPHY

The Original Recordings of Ruth Etting LP compilation of early '30s recordings, released to tie in with the 1955 movie *Love Me or Leave Me*; includes the title song, "Ten Cents a Dance," "Shaking the Blues Away," "Mean to Me," "Take Me in Your Arms," and "I'll Never Be the Same." (Columbia, mono)

Hello, Baby A collection of 1926–1931 recordings, transferred to LP with Etting's blessing in 1973; includes "I'll Be Blue Thinking of You," "Just One More Chance," "Ain't Misbehavin'," "Body and Soul," "If I Could Be With You One Hour Tonight," and "Now That You're Gone." (Biograph, mono)

Ruth Etting—Queen of the Torch Singers 1987 LP compilation of recordings, radio transcriptions, and movie sound tracks, mostly from 1927 to 1936; includes "My Man," "Happy Days and Lonely Nights," "It's a Sin to Tell a Lie," "Dancing With Tears in My Eyes," "Trying to Live My Life Without You," and "There Ought to Be a Moonlight Saving Time." (Broadway Intermission, mono)

Ruth Etting—Reflections 1927–1935 1979 LP compilation; includes "All of Me," "A Faded Summer Love," "With My Eyes Wide Open I'm Dreaming," "What About Me?" and "Why Dream?" (Take Two, mono)

Ruth Etting Encores 1981 LP compilation, including "Happy Days and Lonely Nights," "I'm Nobody's Baby," "More Than You Know," "Out of Nowhere," and "Dancing in the Moonlight." (Take Two, mono)

Ruth Etting—America's Radio Sweetheart 1978 compilation of radio transcriptions—side one from the '30s, side two from Etting's brief comeback year of 1947; includes "Somebody Loves Me," "All of Me," "You Took Me Out of This World," "Shine On Harvest Moon," "Whose Honey Are You?" and "Zing Went the Strings of My Heart." (Totem, mono)

SELECTED VIDEOGRAPHY

Roman Scandals 1933 musical comedy starring Eddie Cantor, with production numbers staged by Busby Berkeley; Etting plays a deposed Roman courtesan who ends up in the slave market singing "No More Love." (Nelson tape)

Hips, Hips, Hooray 1934 musical comedy featuring the vaudeville-based comedy of Bert Wheeler and Robert Woolsey; Etting appears only in the opening number, singing "Keep Romance Alive." (RKO/Turner tape)

ALICE FAYE

SELECTED DISCOGRAPHY

Alice Faye in Hollywood 1969 LP compilation of sixteen songs Faye recorded commercially in the mid-1930s from such films as *George White's Scandals of 1935, 365 Nights in Hollywood, Every Night at Eight, King of Burlesque*, and *On the Avenue*; includes "Wake Up and Live," "Never in a Million Years," "I've Got My Love to Keep Me Warm," "Slumming on Park Avenue," "I'm Shooting High," "Goodnight, My Love" and "According to the Moonlight." (Columbia, mono)

Alice Faye—Outtakes and Alternates 1985 LP compilation mostly taken from discarded recordings made for film sound tracks between 1938 and 1941, such as *Rose of Washington Square, Tin Pan Alley, Barricade, The Great American Broadcast, Sally, Irene, and Mary*, and *Weekend in Havana*; includes "I Never Knew

Heaven Could Speak," "Half Moon on the Hudson," "I Could Use a Dream," and "Are You in the Mood for Mischief?"—some in different versions from those used in the final films, some not used at all. (George Ulrich Productions, mono)

SELECTED VIDEOGRAPHY

The only three Alice Faye movies now available in video formats are two in which she plays supporting roles to child star Shirley Temple—*Stowaway* and *Poor Little Rich Girl* (both 1936)—and one in which she returned to the screen briefly in 1962 to play a supporting role as Pat Boone and Ann-Margret's mother in the remake of Rodgers and Hammerstein's *State Fair*. (All three, CBS/Fox tape)

ELLA FITZGERALD

SELECTED DISCOGRAPHY

The "Songbook" Series (available in multidisc and multirecord sets on CD and LP):

Harold Arlen Includes "Come Rain or Come Shine," "Blues in the Night," "It's Only a Paper Moon," "Get Happy," and "Stormy Weather." Arranged and conducted by Billy May. (Verve, stereo)

Irving Berlin Includes "Puttin' on the Ritz," "Always," "Alexander's Ragtime Band," "All By Myself," and "Cheek to Cheek." Arranged and conducted by Paul Weston. (Verve, stereo)

Duke Ellington Includes "Take the 'A' Train," "Cottontail," "Perdido," "Satin Doll," "In a Sophisticated Mood," and "Lush Life." Arranged by Billy Strayhorn and Duke Ellington, conducted by Duke Ellington. (Verve, stereo)

George and Ira Gershwin Includes "They All Laughed," "But Not for Me," "Oh, Lady Be Good," and "How Long Has This Been Going On?" Arranged and conducted by Nelson Riddle. (Verve, stereo)

Jerome Kern Includes "The Way You Look Tonight," "A Fine Romance," "I'm Old-Fashioned," "Yesterdays," and "Remind Me." Arranged and conducted by Nelson Riddle. (Verve, stereo)

Johnny Mercer Includes "Too Marvelous for Words," "Day In, Day Out," "Laura," "Skylark," and "Travelin' Light." Arranged and conducted by Nelson Riddle. (Verve, stereo)

Cole Porter Includes "Anything Goes," "I Get a Kick Out of You," "Just One of Those Things," "Begin the Beguine," and "From This Moment On." Arranged and conducted by Buddy Bregman. (Verve, stereo)

Rodgers and Hart Includes "A Ship Without a Sail," "Bewitched, Bothered, and Bewildered," "Have You Met Miss Jones?" and "I Didn't Know What Time It Was." Arranged and conducted by Buddy Bregman. (Verve, stereo)

The Chronological Ella Fitzgerald Three-CD series of early recordings with Chick Webb, Teddy Wilson, Taft Jordan, Sandy Williams, and others. *1935–1937* includes "Love and Kisses," "Crying My Heart Out for You," "Vote for Mr. Rhythm," and "Goodnight, My Love"; *1937–1938* includes "Dedicated to You,"

"All or Nothing at All," "Just a Simple Melody," and "If Dreams Come True"; *1938–1939* includes "This Heart of Mine," "Saving Myself for You," "Wacky Dust," and "Woe Is Me." (Classics, mono)

On the Sunny Side of the Street Collaboration with Count Basie (arrangements by Quincy Jones), on CD and LP; includes "Honeysuckle Rose," "Them There Eyes," "I'm Beginning to See the Light." (PolyGram, stereo)

The Intimate Ella Ballad album with solo piano accompaniment by Paul Smith, on CD and LP; includes "Misty," "I'm Getting Sentimental Over You," "September Song," and "Angel Eyes." (PolyGram, stereo)

Ella Swings Gently with Nelson 1962 LP arranged and conducted by Nelson Riddle; includes "Sweet and Low," "I Can't Get Started," "Street of Dreams," and "Imagination." (Verve, stereo)

Ella and Duke at the Cote d'Azur 1967 concert performance with the Duke Ellington orchestra and the Jimmy Jones Trio, on LP; includes "Mack the Knife," "Lullaby of Birdland," "Going Out of My Head," and "Misty." (Verve, stereo)

Thirty by Ella 1968 LP with Benny Carter's Magnificent Seven; includes "My Mother's Eyes," "Try a Little Tenderness," "It's a Wonderful World," and "No Regrets." (Capitol, stereo)

SELECTED VIDEOGRAPHY

Ride 'Em Cowboy 1942 Abbott and Costello Western comedy includes Fitzgerald singing "A-Tisket A-Tasket" with the Merry Macs. (MCA/Universal tape)

Pete Kelly's Blues 1955 Jack Webb drama about early jazz, with Fitzgerald and Peggy Lee in the cast, along with Janet Leigh, Edmond O'Brien, and Jayne Mansfield. (Warner tape)

Frank Sinatra: The Reprise Collection Three tape (or two-disc) set of three Sinatra TV specials from the 1960s and 1970s. Fitzgerald costars on one special, *A Man and His Music + Ella + Jobim*. She solos on "Body and Soul," "It's All Right with Me," and "Don't Be That Way," and sings medleys and duets with Sinatra, including "How High the Moon," "Ode to Billy Joe," and "The Lady Is a Tramp." Arrangements by Nelson Riddle. (Warner/Reprise tape and laserdisc)

HELEN FORREST

SELECTED DISCOGRAPHY

Helen Forrest—On the Sunny Side of the Street 1985 LP compilation of fourteen songs recorded in 1949 and 1950 for World Transcriptions (a broadcast transcription service) and released commercially for the first time by Audiophile in 1985; includes the title song, "I Hadn't Anyone Till You," "I Can't Get Started," "Paradise," "My Man," "How High the Moon," and "Too Marvelous for Words." (Audiophile, mono)

Helen Forrest and Dick Haymes—Long Ago and Far Away 1983 LP compilation of ten songs recorded with the orchestras of Victor Young, Earl Hagen, and Toots Camarata between 1944 and 1946, eight of them duets with Haymes; includes the title song, "It Had to Be You," "I'll Buy That Dream," "Time Waits for No One," "Together," and "Come Rain or Come Shine." (MCA, mono)

SELECTED VIDEOGRAPHY

Springtime in the Rockies 1942 Betty Grable musical, also featuring Carmen Miranda, John Payne, Charlotte Greenwood, and Harry James's orchestra; Forrest sings "I Had the Craziest Dream" with James's orchestra. (CBS/Fox tape and CBS/Fox/Image laserdisc)

Bathing Beauty 1944 MGM movie musical with Esther Williams, Red Skelton, and Harry James's orchestra; Forrest sings "I Cried for You" with James's orchestra. (MGM/UA tape)

JUDY GARLAND

SELECTED DISCOGRAPHY

Judy at Carnegie Hall The legendary New York concert of April 23, 1961, with Mort Lindsey's orchestra, remastered in 1989 for a two-CD set; includes "Come Rain or Come Shine," "I Can't Give You Anything But Love," "The Man That Got Away," "You're Nearer," "Swanee," "San Francisco," "Chicago," and "Over the Rainbow." (Capitol, stereo)

Judy Originally recorded in 1956 with Nelson Riddle's orchestra and remastered for CD in 1989 with an additional track ("I'm Old-Fashioned"); includes "I Feel a Song Coming On," "Last Night When We Were Young," "Lucky Day," "Dirty Hands, Dirty Face," and "Come Rain or Come Shine." (Capitol, mono)

Judy in Love Late-1950s LP with Nelson Riddle's orchestra, reissued in 1988; includes "This Is It," "Do I Love You?" "I Can't Give You Anything But Love," "I Concentrate on You," and "Day In, Day Out." (Capitol, mono)

The Best of Judy Garland from MGM Classic Films (1938–1950) CD compilation and exactly what the title says; includes "Over the Rainbow," "Singin' in the Rain," "I'm Nobody's Baby," "Johnny One Note," "Love of My Life," and "Get Happy." (MCA, mono)

Judy Garland—The Best of the Decca Years CD compilation of recordings from the 1930s and 1940s, including "Dear Mr. Gable/You Made Me Love You," "Zing! Went the Strings of My Heart," "Over the Rainbow," "Embraceable You," "The Boy Next Door," "The Trolley Song," "On the Atchison, Topeka and Santa Fe," and "Yah-Ta-Ta, Yah-Ta-Ta" (duet with Bing Crosby). (MCA, mono)

Judy Garland Collector's Items (1936–1945) 1970 two-LP compilation of 78-rpm records not previously issued on LP, with the orchestras of David Rose, Bob Crosby, Victor Young, Georgie Stoll, and others; includes "Stompin' at the Savoy," "Swing, Mr. Charlie," "Everybody Sing," "No Love, No Nothin'," "Blues in the Night," "Buds Won't Bud," "I Got Rhythm," and "A Journey to a Star." (Decca/MCA, simulated stereo)

The Great Garland Duets An LP of uneven technical quality, primarily sound track excerpts from Garland's 1963–64 TV series, offering her in unique duets with Barbra Streisand, Ethel Merman, Frank Sinatra, Jack Jones, Liza Minnelli, and others. (Paragon, mono)

SELECTED VIDEOGRAPHY

Judy Garland in Concert, Vols. 1 & 2 Each volume includes a complete TV program from Garland's 1963-64 CBS series; includes "Once in a Lifetime," "I Feel a Song Coming On," "The Boy Next Door," "Alexander's Ragtime Band," "Be a Clown," "The Man That Got Away," "Liza," "He's Got the Whole World in His Hands," "Rockabye Your Baby With a Dixie Melody," and "America the Beautiful." (RKO tapes)

A Star Is Born Nearly complete 1983 "restored" version of the 1954 movie musical. Garland's songs include "The Man That Got Away," "Lose That Long Face," "It's a New World," "Gotta Have You Go with Me," "Here's What I'm Here For," "My Melancholy Baby," and "Swanee." (Warner tape and laserdisc)

The Wizard of Oz The classic 1939 MGM fantasy that introduced "Over the Rainbow" and won Garland a special Oscar(cttc). (MGM/UA tape and laserdisc)

Meet Me in St. Louis The classic 1944 MGM family musical, directed by Vincente Minnelli. Garland's songs include "The Boy Next Door," "The Trolley Song," and "Have Yourself a Merry Little Christmas." The 1990 video editions include an audio supplement of Garland singing Rodgers and Hammerstein's "Boys and Girls Like You and Me," cut from the original release print. (MGM/UA tape and laserdisc)

Easter Parade 1948 MGM musical with Garland and Fred Astaire, songs by Irving Berlin; Garland's songs include "A Fella with An Umbrella," "Better Luck Next Time," "Snooky Ookums," "I Love a Piano," and "We're a Couple of Swells." (MGM/UA tape and laserdisc)

The Pirate (1948) Directed by husband Minnelli, with a Cole Porter score and costarring Gene Kelly; Garland sings "Love of My Life," "Mack the Black," "You Can Do No Wrong," and "Be a Clown." (MGM/UA tape and laserdisc)

DICK HAYMES

SELECTED DISCOGRAPHY

James and Haymes CD compilation of sixteen songs recorded in 1941 by Harry James's orchestra for World Transcriptions (a radio transcription service) and never before released commercially; the seven Haymes vocals include "All or Nothing at All," "The Things I Love," "Here Comes the Night," "Maria Elena," and "Spring Will Be So Sad."

Dick Haymes Sings Irving Berlin 1983 LP compilation of songs recorded between the late 1940s and early 1960s, including "How Deep Is the Ocean," "Let's Take an Old-Fashioned Walk," "Say It Isn't So," "Say It with Music," "Soft Lights and Sweet Music," and "The Song Is Ended (but the Melody Lingers On)." (MCA, mono)

Dick Haymes—For You, For Me, For Evermore 1976 LP recording with small combo accompaniment; includes the title song, "They Can't Take That Away from Me," "Someone to Watch Over Me," "How Long Has This Been Going On?" "Bidin' My Time," "Where's the Child I Used to Hold?" "Jeepers Creepers," and "It Had to Be You." (Audiophile, stereo)

SELECTED VIDEOGRAPHY

State Fair The 1945 Rodgers and Hammerstein movie version, also with Jeanne Crain, Vivian Blaine, Dana Andrews, and Charles Winninger; Haymes's songs include "That's for Me," "Isn't It Kinda Fun?" and "It's a Grand Night for Singing." (CBS/Fox tape)

DuBarry Was a Lady 1943 MGM movie version of Cole Porter's Broadway musical, with Lucille Ball, Gene Kelly, Red Skelton, and Tommy Dorsey's orchestra. Haymes is seen and heard briefly with Dorsey's orchestra. (MGM/UA tape)

BILLIE HOLIDAY

SELECTED DISCOGRAPHY

The Quintessential Billie Holiday Seven-volume CD compilation of Holiday recordings from 1933 to 1939: *Vol. 1* (1933–35) includes "What a Little Moonlight Can Do" and "Miss Brown to You"; *Vol. 2* (1935) includes "These Foolish Things" and "The Way You Look Tonight"; *Vol. 3* (1936–37) includes "I Must Have That Man" and "I've Got My Love to Keep Me Warm"; *Vol. 4* (1937) includes "Let's Call the Whole Thing Off" and "Carelessly"; *Vol. 5* (1937–38) includes "He's Funny That Way" and "Nice Work If You Can Get It"; *Vol. 6* (1938) includes "You Go to My Head" and "The Very Thought of You"; *Vol. 7* (1938–39) includes "Long Gone Blues" and "More Than You Know." (Columbia, mono)

The Complete 1951 Storyville Club Sessions Live recording at Boston's Storyville nightclub on CD, featuring Stan Getz; includes "Lover, Come Back to Me," "Crazy He Calls Me," and "Them There Eyes." (Freshsound, mono)

The Last Recording From 1959, with Ray Ellis and his orchestra, on LP and CD; includes "All of You," "You Took Advantage of Me," "Don't Worry 'Bout Me," and "All the Way." (Verve, stereo)

Lady Day LP compilation of 1935–37 recordings; includes "Miss Brown to You," "I Wished On the Moon," "What a Little Moonlight Can Do," "Summertime," and "Easy Living." (Matrix, mono)

Teddy Wilson–Billie Holiday LP compilation of mid-'30s sessions with Teddy Wilson and his orchestra, covering Holiday's entire career; includes "Miss Brown to You," "I Wished On the Moon," "If You Were Mine," and "I Must Have That Man." (Columbia, mono)

Fraternity Rush 1957 LP includes "Solitude," "Get Out of Town," "Willow Weep for Me," and "I'll See You in My Dreams." With Boyd Raeburn and his orchestra. (Matrix, stereo)

SELECTED VIDEOGRAPHY

The Sound of Jazz Rare Holiday TV appearance on Robert Herridge's jazz performance series, shot live in 1958. Holiday sings "Fine and Mellow" with weary elegance. (Laser Island laser disc, Japanese import only)

LENA HORNE

SELECTED DISCOGRAPHY

Stormy Weather—The Legendary Lena CD compilation of twenty-two songs recorded between 1941 and 1958, including two with Charlie Barnet's orchestra ("Good-for-Nothin' Joe" and "You're My Thrill") and two with Artie Shaw's orchestra ("Love Me a Little" and "Don't Take Your Love from Me"); also includes "What Is This Thing Called Love?" "The Man I Love," "I Gotta Right to Sing the Blues," "Moanin' Low," and "Where or When." (RCA/BMG, mono)

The One and Only Lena Horne 1982 LP reissue of previously released MGM Records material with uncredited orchestras and no dates (but presumably from the 1960s); includes "Take Love Easy," "I Got the World on a String," "Pass Me By," "Love of My Life," and " 'Deed I Do." (PolyGram, stereo)

Lena, Lovely & Alive 1960s LP devoted primarily to popular standards, with arrangements by Marty Paitch; includes "I Concentrate on You," "I Let a Song Go Out of My Heart," "I Get the Blues When it Rains," "I'm Confessin' (That I Love You)," "I Surrender, Dear," and "I've Grown Accustomed to His Face." (RCA/BMG, stereo)

Lena Horne—Give the Lady What She Wants A late-1950s LP, with Lennie Hayton's orchestra and arrangements by Hayton and Ralph Burns; includes "Honey in the Honeycomb," "Speak Low," "Love," "At Long Last Love," "Get Out of Town," and "Let's Put Out the Lights and Go to Sleep." (RCA International, stereo)

SELECTED VIDEOGRAPHY

The Lady and Her Music Taped-for-cable-TV version of Horne's 1981 one-woman Broadway show, essentially a concert of her best-known songs with autobiographical comment and reminiscences along the way. (HBO tape)

Cabin in the Sky 1943 all-black film version of the Vernon Duke–John Latouche Broadway show, with additional songs by Harold Arlen and E. H. (Yip) Harburg. Horne sings "Honey in the Honeycomb" and "Life's Full o' Consequence." (MGM/UA tape)

Girl Crazy Although Horne is not in the 1943 Judy Garland–Mickey Rooney movie version of this Gershwin musical, the 1990 laserdisc edition also contains a 1944 MGM "Pete Smith Specialty" short subject, *Studio Visit*, which includes footage cut from *Cabin in the Sky* with Horne singing "Ain't It de Truth" (written for the film version by Arlen and Harburg). (MGM/UA laserdisc)

Till the Clouds Roll By Highly fictionalized, all-star 1946 MGM musical biography of Jerome Kern; the opening sequence presents extended excerpts from *Show Boat* with Horne in the role of Julie, singing "Can't Help Lovin' Dat Man." (MGM/UA tape)

Stormy Weather Horne's most famous movie (1943), with an all-black cast that also includes Bill Robinson, Fats Waller, and Cab Calloway. (CBS/Fox Tape)

AL JOLSON

SELECTED DISCOGRAPHY

Al Jolson: Stage Highlights, 1911–1925 CD compilation of early Jolson recordings, some never on LP; includes "Sister Susie's Sewing Shirts for Soldiers," "Where Did Robinson Crusoe Go with Friday on Saturday Night?" "Keep Smiling at Trouble," "Yakka Hula Hickey Dula," "Give Me My Mammy." (Pearl, Mono)

Al Jolson (The World's Greatest Entertainer): The Jazz Singer CD compilation of Jolson songs from 1924 to 1932, mostly from movie sound tracks (*The Jazz Singer, The Singing Fool, Say It With Songs,* and others); includes "April Showers," "I'm Sitting on Top of the World," "My Mammy," "Sonny Boy," and "Rock-a-Bye Your Baby with a Dixie Melody." Orchestras include Guy Lombardo and His Royal Canadians, and Bill Wirges and His Orchestra. (Halcyon, mono)

Mammy CD compilation; includes "Sonny Boy," "Swanee," "California, Here I Come," and "There's a Rainbow 'Round My Shoulder." (Intersound International, mono)

World's Greatest Entertainer LP of selections from Kraft Music Hall radio broadcasts from the 1930s; includes "Baby Face," "I'll Be Seeing You," "Albany Bound," and "Bright Eyes," with orchestra and chorus directed by Lou Bring. (MCA, mono)

Best of Al Jolson LP compilation of 1940s recordings; includes "Toot, Toot Tootsie (Goo'bye)," "April Showers," "My Mammy," and "Swanee." (MCA, mono)

SELECTED VIDEOGRAPHY

The Jazz Singer Historic early talkie from 1927, mostly silent, with Jolson doing a few songs, including "My Mammy," "Toot, Toot Tootsie (Goo'bye)," and "Blue Skies." Costarring May McAvoy, Myrna Loy, Eugenie Besserer, and Warner Oland. Directed by Alan Crosland. (CBS/Fox tape and laserdisc, mono)

The Jolson Story Entertaining if mostly inaccurate screen bio from 1946, starring Larry Parks in acclaimed portrayal of Jolson. Oscar-nominated Parks lip-syncs to Jolson's voice in updated renditions of Jolson classics newly recorded for the movie. (RCA/Columbia Pictures tape and laserdisc, mono)

Jolson Sings Again Parks lip-syncs to Jolson's singing voice again in this 1949 sequel to *The Jolson Story* that is even more fanciful than the first entry. (RCA/Columbia Pictures tape and laserdisc, mono)

JACK JONES

SELECTED DISCOGRAPHY

Jack Jones in Person at the Sands Hotel 1970 LP recorded live in Las Vegas; includes "God Bless the Child," "The More I See You," and a medley of "Lollipops and Roses"/"Wives and Lovers." (RCA, stereo)
Jack Jones Sings Michel Legrand 1971 LP arranged and conducted by Legrand; includes "What Are You Doing the Rest of Your Life," "The Years of My Youth," and "Pieces of Dreams." (RCA, stereo)

SELECTED VIDEOGRAPHY

No movies or other programs in which Jack Jones has appeared as a singer are known to be available on video.

TEDDI KING

SELECTED DISCOGRAPHY

Teddi King Sings Ira Gershwin . . . This Is New The LP King was working on with pianist Dave McKenna when she died suddenly in 1977. She completed eight of the planned thirteen tracks, including the title song, "I Can't Be Bothered Now," "Fun to Be Fooled," "Here's What I'm Here For," and "Isn't It a Pity." McKenna plays solo piano versions of the remaining five songs. (Inner City, stereo)
Someone to Light Up My Life An LP recorded a year before King's death, with an instrumental trio led by pianist-arranger Loonis McGlohon; includes Jobim's title song, "I Let a Song Go Out of My Heart," "Two for the Road," "You Turned the Tables on Me," "There's a Lull in My Life," and "It Never Entered My Mind." (Audiophile, stereo)
Bidin' My Time A 1972 reissue of a 1950 LP with Al Cohn's orchestra, representing King at an early peak; includes the title song, "That Old Feeling," "For All We Know," "Love Walked In," "I Poured My Heart Into a Song," and "Taking a Chance on Love." (RCA Victor, mono)
Nat Pierce Orchestra, Featuring Teddi King, Charlie Mariano and Ralph Burns A 1977 LP reissue of recordings made by Boston-based Pierce's orchestra between 1948 and 1950; King sings "Oh, You Crazy Moon," "You Don't Know What Love Is," and "Goodbye, Mr. Chops." (Zim Records, mono)

SELECTED VIDEOGRAPHY

Teddi King made no movies, and no TV appearances are known to have been released on video.

FRANCES LANGFORD

SELECTED DISCOGRAPHY

Frances Langford—Getting Sentimental 1989 LP compilation of twenty songs originally recorded between 1935 and 1937; includes "I'm in the Mood for Love," "Once in a While," "Sweet Someone," "I've Got You Under My Skin," "You Are My Lucky Star," and "I'm Getting Sentimental Over You." (Conifer, mono)

Frances Langford—I Feel a Song Coming On 1982 LP compilation of fourteen songs from the same 1935–37 period as above; duplicates six songs but also includes the title song, "Then You've Never Been Blue," "You Hit the Spot," "Easy to Love," "Swinging the Jinx Away," and "It's Like Reaching for the Moon." (Take Two, mono)

The Return of the Bickersons Three-cassette set of six 1947–48 programs from the radio series starring Langford and Don Ameche. (Radiola, mono) Also: a 1960s LP titled *The Bickersons* was long ago withdrawn but may still be available in some stores or libraries. (Columbia/CBS, mono)

SELECTED VIDEOGRAPHY

Yankee Doodle Dandy The James Cagney Oscar-winning movie biography of George M. Cohan. Langford sings seven songs, including "The Love Nest," "Little Nelly Kelly," "In a Kingdom of Our Own," "The Man Who Owns Broadway," and "Over There." (MGM/UA tape and laserdisc)

Too Many Girls 1940 movie version of Rodgers and Hart's "collegiate" Broadway musical featuring Lucille Ball, Richard Carlson, Ann Miller, Eddie Bracken, Desi Arnaz, Van Johnson, and Langford. Her songs include "You're Nearer," "Love Never Went to College," and " 'Cause We Got Cake." (RKO/Turner tape)

The Glenn Miller Story 1954 movie biography of the popular bandleader (starring James Stewart), with a cameo by Langford as herself. (MCA/Universal tape)

JULIUS LAROSA

SELECTED DISCOGRAPHY

Julius LaRosa 1988 CD includes "Don't Go to Strangers," "Jeepers Creepers," "That Old Feeling," and "But Not for Me." (Project 3, stereo)

Julius LaRosa Early 1960s LP with Joe Reisman and his orchestra; includes "But Not for Me," "Don't You Know I Care," and "A Fellow Needs a Girl." (Mercury, stereo)

SELECTED VIDEOGRAPHY

No movies or other programs in which Julius LaRosa has appeared as a singer are known to be available on video.

STEVE LAWRENCE AND EYDIE GORMÉ

SELECTED DISCOGRAPHY

The Best of Steve & Eydie CD compilation of ten songs recorded in the 1960s, including "Bésame Mucho," "And the Angels Sing," "I've Got a Girl in Kalamazoo," and "Bei Mir Bist du Schoen." (Curb/MCA, stereo)

Steve Lawrence CD compilation of twelve songs of uncredited origin (presumably 1970s, possibly 1980s), including "Poinciana," "Say It Isn't True," "With Every Breath I Take," and "How Many Stars Have to Shine?" (King, stereo)

If He Walked into My Life LP compilation from the 1960s; includes the title song, "Ev'ry Time We Say Goodbye," "As Long as He Needs Me," "What Did I Have I Don't Have Now," and "No One to Cry To." (CBS/Sony Special Products, stereo)

The World of Steve & Eydie 1972 LP of songs from ten different countries, recorded with the Mike Curb Congregation and Don Costa's orchestra; includes "Tristeza," "Rose d'Irlande (It Was a Good Time)," "Bashana Haba-ah," "Du Sollst Nichen Weinen," and "E Fini." (MGM/MCA, stereo)

Golden Rainbow The original Broadway cast recording of the 1958 show in which Lawrence and Gormé starred; songs include "For Once in Your Life," "All in Fun," "Desert Moon," and "We Got Us." (Calendar/Kirschner Entertainment, stereo)

SELECTED VIDEOGRAPHY

The Lonely Guy 1984 comedy-drama with Steve Martin, Charles Grodin, Judith Ivey, Merv Griffin, and (in a non-singing role) Steve Lawrence. (MCA/Universal tape)

BARBARA LEA

SELECTED DISCOGRAPHY

You're the Cats—Barbara Lea & the Legendary Lawson-Haggart Jazz Band CD album of thirteen songs, including the title song, "I'm Building Up to an Awful Letdown," "Do What You Do," "True Blue Lou," "Waiting at the End of the Road," "Love's Got Me in a Lazy Mood," and "For You, For Me, For Evermore." (Audiophile, stereo)

Sweet and Slow—Barbara Lea & the Legendary Lawson-Haggart Jazz Band CD of thirteen songs; includes the title song, "Sleepy Head," "Baby's Blue," "Soon," "With Every Breath I Take," "Maybe My Baby Loves Me." "Lonesome Me," and "Everyone Loves You (When You Sleep)." (Audiophile, stereo)

Barbara Lea—Lea in Love Remastering for CD of a 1957 Prestige LP with the Jimmy Lyon Trio, Dick Cary, Johnny Windhurst, Ernie Caceres, and others; includes "More Than You Know," "I've Got My Eyes on You," "Ain't Misbehavin'," "We Could Make Such Beautiful Music Together," and "The Very Thought of You." (Prestige, stereo)

Barbara Lea—A Woman in Love A 1981 LP compilation of eight songs recorded in 1955 and four in 1978 with the same instrumental accompanists, featuring Billy Taylor and Johnny Windhurst; includes "Come Rain or Come Shine," "Love Is Here to Stay," "A Woman Alone with the Blues," "I'm Old-Fashioned," and "I See Your Face Before Me." (Audiophile, stereo)

Barbara Lea—Do It Again A 1983 LP, with an instrumental accompaniment featuring Larry Eanet, Billy Butterfield, Vic Dickenson, Johnny Mince, and Tommy Cecil; includes "Make Believe," "You're Nearer," "Like a Straw in the Wind," "That Certain Feeling," and "Where or When." (Audiophile, stereo)

SELECTED VIDEOGRAPHY

No movies or TV programs with Barbara Lea are known to have been transferred to video.

PEGGY LEE

SELECTED DISCOGRAPHY

Peggy Lee: Collectors Series CD compilation of recordings from Lee's prime in the 1950s; includes "I Don't Know Enough About You," "Golden Earrings," "Mañana," " 'Deed I Do," and "The Old Master Painter" (a duet with Mel Tormé). (Capitol, stereo)

All-Time Greatest Hits CD compilation of hits from Lee's career; includes "It's a Good Day," "Is That All There Is," "My Man," "Fever," and "I'm a Woman." (DCC Jazz, stereo)

There'll Be Another Spring: The Peggy Lee Songbook 1990 recording of Lee's original songs, old and new; includes "He's a Tramp," "Johnny Guitar," "Sans Souci," and "I Just Want to Dance All Night," with arrangements by John Chiondini, Mike Renzi, Victor Young, and Gordon Jenkins (available on CD and LP). (Music Masters, stereo)

SELECTED VIDEOGRAPHY

Pete Kelly's Blues Lee was nominated for an Oscar as Best Supporting Actress in this 1955 Jack Webb drama about early jazz, which also featured Ella Fitzgerald, Jayne Mansfield, Janet Leigh, and Edmond O'Brien. (Warner tape)

Lady and the Tramp The real star of this romantic 1955 Disney animated feature, Lee cowrote the song score with Sonny Burke—and supplied voices for four characters (Peg, Darling, Si, and Am). (Disney tape and laserdisc)

MABEL MERCER

SELECTED DISCOGRAPHY

Mabel Mercer Sings Cole Porter 1955 LP includes "Ev'rytime We Say Goodbye," "Experiment," "It's All Right with Me," and "I'm Ashamed That Women Are So Simple." (Atlantic, stereo)

Merely Marvelous 1960 LP includes "Merely Marvelous," "Let's Begin," "All in Fun," and "The Fifth of July"; with the Jimmy Lyon Trio. (Atlantic, stereo)

Midnight at Mabel Mercer's 1962 LP includes "Just Once Around the Clock," "Young und Foolish," "It's a Lie, It's a Fake," and "Blame It on My Youth." (Atlantic, stereo)

Mabel Mercer and Bobby Short at Town Hall Mercer sings "All of You," "You Should See Yourself," "Lazy Afternoon," "Confession," and others in this 1969 concert performance on LP. Includes two duets with Short, "Here's to Us" and "The 59th Street Bridge Song." (Atlantic, stereo)

SELECTED VIDEOGRAPHY

Mabel Mercer: Cabaret Artist The last filmed performance of Mercer, captured at Cleo's cabaret in New York shortly before the singer's death in 1984; includes "Where, Oh Where," "Chase Me, Charlie," "Confession," "Someone to Light Up My Life," and "Down in the Depths," with Jimmy Lyons on piano. (VIEW Video tape)

ETHEL MERMAN

SELECTED DISCOGRAPHY

You're the Top CD compilation of songs from Merman shows (*Anything Goes*, *Red, Hot and Blue*, *DuBarry Was a Lady*, *Panama Hattie*, and others), recorded from 1934 to 1940; songs include "You're the Top," "How Deep Is the Ocean," "I Gotta Right to Sing the Blues," "Heat Wave," and "Eadie Was a Lady." (Fanfare, mono)

The World Is Your Balloon LP compilation of songs recorded by Merman from 1950 to 1954, including duets with Ray Bolger; songs include "Diamonds Are a Girl's Best Friend," "Dearie," "It's So Nice to Have a Man Around the House," and "Calico Sal." (MCA, mono)

Gypsy: Original Cast Album 1959 recording on LP featuring Merman, Jack Klugman, and Sandra Church. Merman sings "Some People," "Mr. Goldstone, I Love You," "Everything's Coming Up Roses," "Rose's Turn," and, with Klugman, "Small World" and "You'll Never Get Away from Me." (Columbia, stereo)

SELECTED VIDEOGRAPHY

Call Me Madam 1953 movie version of the Irving Berlin musical play, with Merman singing "Hostess with the Mostes' on the Ball" and "The Best Thing for You Would Be Me." Directed by Walter Lang, the only director who let Merman really be Merman. (CBS/Fox tape and laserdisc)

There's No Business Like Show Business 1954 Walter Lang musical whose numbers include the definitively Mermanesque title tune. Merman stars with Dan Dailey, Johnnie Ray, Mitzi Gaynor, Donald O'Connor, and Marilyn Monroe. (CBS/Fox tape and laserdisc)

LIZA MINNELLI

SELECTED DISCOGRAPHY

Liza Minnelli at Carnegie Hall Two-CD compilation of thirty-five songs recorded live during Minnelli's May–June 1987 performances in New York; includes "Some People," "Lonely Feet," "The Sweetest Sounds," "Ring Them Bells," "But the World Goes Round," "New York, New York," and a medley from *Cabaret*. (Teldec, stereo)

The Liza Minnelli Four-Sider CD reissue of a 1970s double-LP set of nineteen songs, including "The Man I Love," "I Will Wait for You," "God Bless the Child," "Come Rain or Come Shine," and "Liza with a Z." (A&M, stereo)

Liza with a Z CD reissue of the 1972 sound track LP from a TV special staged by Bob Fosse; includes the title song, "It Was a Good Time," "Ring Them Bells," "Bye, Bye, Blackbird," and a *Cabaret* medley. (CBS/Sony)

Liza Minnelli—Maybe This Time CD compilation of songs recorded in the late 1960s and early 1970s, including the title song, "Try to Remember," "Meantime," "Don't Ever Leave Me," "Blue Moon," and "Maybe Soon." (Capitol, stereo)

The Judy Garland/Liza Minnelli Concert at the London Palladium Two-LP album of thirty-six songs (some in medleys), abridged from 1973 live performances; Minnelli's songs include "Gypsy in My Soul," "By Myself," "Pass That Peace Pipe," and "Who's Sorry Now?"; her duets with her mother include "Together Wherever We Go," "Hooray for Love," "How About You?" "San Francisco," "Swanee," and "When the Saints Go Marching In." (Capitol, stereo)

SELECTED VIDEOGRAPHY

Liza Minnelli in Concert Taped-for-cable-TV highlights of a show Minnelli presented during a 1979–80 concert tour with Roger Minami and Obba Babtunde; includes "Come Rain or Come Shine," "Some People," "City Lights," "New York, New York," "Cabaret," and "But the World Goes Round." (Pioneer Artists laserdisc)

Cabaret 1972 movie directed by Bob Fosse and for which Minnelli won a Best Actress Oscar; adapted from the Broadway musical and based on Christopher Isherwood's *Berlin Stories*; Minnelli's songs include the title song, "Maybe This Time," "Money, Money," and "Mein Herr." (CBS/Fox tape and CBS/Fox/Image laserdisc)

New York, New York 1977 movie directed by Martin Scorsese, costarring Minnelli and Robert DeNiro, Minnelli's songs include the title song, "But the World Goes Round," "You Brought a New Kind of Love to Me," "Once in a While," "The Man I Love," and "Just You, Just Me." The video version includes the complete "Happy Endings" production number cut from the theatrical release and most TV showings. (CBS/Fox tape and laserdisc)

HELEN MORGAN

SELECTED DISCOGRAPHY

Helen Morgan—The Legacy of a Torch Singer, 1927–35 1986 LP compilation of 14 lesser-known Morgan songs. Includes "The Little Things You Used to Do," "I See Two Lovers," "(I've Got) Sand in My Shoes," "Mean to Me," "Where's That Rainbow?" "Do-Do-Do," and "Just Like a Butterfly That's Caught in the Rain." (Take Two, mono)

Helen Morgan & Fanny Brice 1969 LP compilation divided equally between the two ladies; Morgan's eight-tracks include her best-known songs, such as "Bill," "Can't Help Lovin' Dat Man," "Frankie and Johnny," "Body and Soul," "What Wouldn't I Do for That Man," "Don't Ever Leave Me," "More Than You Know," and "Give Me a Heart to Sing To." (RCA Vintage series, mono)

Show Boat The classic 1936 film version of the Kern-Hammerstein musical play, with Irene Dunne, Allan Jones, Paul Robeson, Hattie McDaniel, Charles Winninger, and Morgan. Her songs: "Bill" and "Can't Help Lovin' Dat Man." (MGM/UA tape; Criterion Collection/Voyager laserdisc)

HELEN O'CONNELL

SELECTED DISCOGRAPHY

Jimmy Dorsey & His Orchestra—Greatest Hits CD compilation of mono recordings from the 1940s in electronically "enhanced stereo"; O'Connell's songs include "Green Eyes," "Tangerine," "Amapola," and "Star Eyes." (MCA/Curb, stereo)

Helen O'Connell with the Page Cavanaugh Trio 1986 LP collection of early 1950s recordings; includes "Too Marvelous for Words," "As Time Goes By," "Blue Moon," "Ain't Misbehavin'," "I've Got the World on a String," and "All the Things You Are." (Hindsight, mono)

This Is Helen O'Connell 1985 two-LP collection of songs recorded in the early 1950s; includes "All of Me," "Amapola," "Green Eyes," "Tangerine," "Saturday Night (Is the Loneliest Night in the Week)," and "Star Eyes." (RCA, mono)

Helen O'Connell Sings Great Songs in High Style LP compilation of songs recorded in the 1950s; includes "My Old Flame," "I Cried for You," "Green Eyes," "I'm Getting Sentimental Over You," and "Ten Cents a Dance." (Audiophile, mono)

SELECTED VIDEOGRAPHY

The Fabulous Dorseys Partly fictionalized 1947 movie biography of Jimmy and Tommy Dorsey, with the brothers playing themselves; O'Connell also appears as herself and sings "Green Eyes" with Bob Eberly. (Republic tape)

Leonard Maltin's Movie Memories—Soundies, Vol. 2 1990 compilation of Soundies (musical shorts made in the 1940s for early motion-picture jukeboxes known as Panorams); O'Connell sings "All Reet" with the Jimmy Dorsey orchestra, filmed in 1943. (BMG tape)

DICK POWELL

SELECTED DISCOGRAPHY

Dick Powell in Hollywood, 1933–1935 Two-LP compilation of twenty-nine original studio (not sound-track) recordings, including "Lullaby of Broadway,"

"I'll String Along with You," "Flirtation Walk," "By a Waterfall," "Shadow Waltz," "Honeymoon Hotel," and "Pettin' in the Park." (Columbia Hall of Fame series, mono)

Dick Powell—Lullaby of Broadway 1986 British LP compilation of sixteen original studio (not sound-track) recordings from 1932 to 1936, including some of the titles on the Columbia set above, but also "Thanks a Million," "I Only Have Eyes for You," "Mr. and Mrs. Is the Name," and others. (Living Era, English import, mono)

Dick Powell—Love Is on the Air Tonight 1982 LP compilation of eight studio (not sound-track) recordings from the late 1930s, including the title song, "Have You Got Any Castles, Baby?" " 'Cause My Baby Says It's So," "I Know Now," "You Can't Stop Me from Dreaming," and others. (MCA, mono)

SELECTED VIDEOGRAPHY

42nd Street The movie that made Powell a singing star, and the granddaddy of backstage musicals; also with Warner Baxter, Ruby Keeler, Ginger Rogers, and Bebe Daniels. Powell sings the title song and "Young and Healthy." (MGM/UA tape and laserdisc)

Gold Diggers of 1933 With Powell, Joan Blondell, Ruby Keeler, Ginger Rogers, and Warren William, and with Busby Berkeley production numbers. Powell sings "The Shadow Waltz," "I've Got to Sing a Torch Song," and "Pettin' in the Park." (MGM/UA tape and laserdisc)

Footlight Parade With James Cagney, Joan Blondell, Ruby Keeler, and Powell, who sings "Honeymoon Hotel," "Ah, The Moon Is Here," and "By a Waterfall." Production numbers by Busby Berkeley. (MGM/UA tape and laserdisc)

Gold Diggers of 1935 Includes Busby Berkeley's own favorite among his production numbers, "The Lullaby of Broadway"—actually a self-contained mini-musical with Powell and Wini Shaw. Powell also sings "The Words Are in My Heart" and "I'm Going Shopping with You." (MGM/UA tape and laserdisc)

SHIRLEY ROSS

SELECTED DISCOGRAPHY

Bob Hope in Hollywood with Shirley Ross, Bing Crosby & Peggy Lee 1984 LP compilation of Hope duets (actually one track is a trio with Crosby and Lee), including four he recorded in the late 1930s with Ross: "Thanks for the Memory," "Two Sleepy People," "The Lady's in Love with You," and "Penthouse Serenade." (MCA, mono)

Rodgers and Hart, 1927–1942 1970s LP compilation of original-cast versions of songs from Rodgers and Hart's Broadway and Hollywood musicals; includes Ross's 1940 commercial recordings of four songs from *Higher and Higher*: "It Never Entered My Mind," "Nothing but You," "Ev'ry Sunday Afternoon," and "From Another World"; also includes other material featuring Helen Morgan, Frances Langford, Mary Jane Walsh, Audrey Christie, and others. (Music Masters/Box Office series, mono)

SELECTED VIDEOGRAPHY

San Francisco The 1936 drama-with-music (with Clark Gable, Jeanette MacDonald, Spencer Tracy, and the proverbial cast of thousands in the climactic earthquake sequences); Ross appears briefly near the beginning as a music-hall singer. (MGM/UA tape and laserdisc)

At publication time, none of Ross's Paramount films—representing her best movie work—is yet available on videocassette or videodisc.

DINAH SHORE

SELECTED DISCOGRAPHY

Dinah Shore—Love Songs CD edition of late-1940s recordings, including "Dream a Little Dream of Me," "A Cottage for Sale," "Once in a While," "I'm Yours," "They Didn't Believe Me," and "Scarlet Ribbons." (Columbia/Sony, mono)

The Best of Dinah Shore 1977 LP compilation of recordings from the late 1940s and early 1950s, including "Buttons and Bows," "Dear Hearts and Gentle People," "Shoo-Fly Pie and Apple-Pan Dowdy," "Lavender Blue," "I Love You (for Sentimental Reasons)," "My Romance" (duet with Frank Sinatra), and "Baby, It's Cold Outside" (duet with Buddy Clark). (Columbia, mono)

The Best of Dinah Shore 1989 compilation of eighteen songs recorded between 1959 and 1962 with the orchestras of Nelson Riddle, Jack Marshall, André Previn, and others; includes "I'm Old-Fashioned," "Our Love Is Here to Stay," "I Only Have Eyes for You," "Easy to Remember," "Buttons and Bows," "Somebody Loves Me," and "Sentimental Journey." (Capitol, stereo)

SELECTED VIDEOGRAPHY

Up in Arms Shore costars with Danny Kaye in this 1944 wartime comedy; her songs include "Now I Know" and "Tess's Torch Song." (Nelson tape)

Till the Clouds Roll By MGM's highly fictionalized, 1946 all-star musical biography of Jerome Kern; Shore sings "They Didn't Believe Me" and "The Last Time I Saw Paris." (MGM/UA tape)

BOBBY SHORT

SELECTED DISCOGRAPHY

Bobby Short Is C-Ra-Zy for Gershwin CD compilation of Short interpretations of Gershwin, including little-known songs. Includes "Love Walked In," "Hi-Ho," "That Certain Feeling," and "Drifting with the Tide." (Atlantic, stereo)

50 by Bobby Short CD compilation of recordings from the course of Short's career; includes "I Like the Likes of You," "Manhattan," "Lydia the Tattooed Lady," "Losing My Mind," and "A Room with a View." (Atlantic, stereo)

Bobby, Noel & Cole Two LPs (*Bobby Short Loves Cole Porter* and *Bobby Short Is Mad About Noel Coward*) on one CD. Porter selections include "You Don't Know Parée," "At Long Last Love," "I Hate You, Darling," and "Why Don't We Try Staying Home." By Coward: "I Travel Alone," "Matelot," "My Little Fish," and "Let's Fly Away." (Atlantic, stereo)

SELECTED VIDEOGRAPHY

Hannah and Her Sisters 1989 Woody Allen film includes a scene with Bobby Short performing "I'm in Love Again" at the Café Carlyle. (Orion tape and laser disc)

FRANK SINATRA

SELECTED DISCOGRAPHY

The Frank Sinatra Story in Music Two-CD compilation of Columbia 78s from the 1940s and early 1950s; includes "All or Nothing at All," "Nancy," "You Go to My Head," "The House I Live In," "Ol' Man River," "I've Got a Crush on You," and "Begin the Beguine." (CBS Special Products, mono)

Frank Sinatra: The Capitol Years Three-CD boxed set of seventy-five recordings from Sinatra's prime in the 1950s and early 1960s; includes "I Get a Kick Out of You," "You Make Me Feel So Young," "The Lady Is a Tramp," "Night and Day," "Chicago," and "High Hopes." Arrangers include Nelson Riddle, Billy May, and Gordon Jenkins. (Capitol, stereo)

Frank Sinatra: The Reprise Collection Four-CD boxed set of eighty-one recordings from Sinatra's later years on his own record label, with Basie, Ellington, Jobim, Riddle, and other musicians and arrangers; includes unreleased tracks, singles, and live recordings such as a duet with Sammy Davis, Jr., of "Me and My Shadow" and a spare studio version of "Send in the Clowns" with solo piano. (Reprise, stereo)

Songs for Swingin' Lovers 1956 album (available on CD and LP) with Sinatra at the prime of his vocal powers; includes "You Make Me Feel So Young," "I've Got You Under My Skin," and "Anything Goes," with arrangements by Nelson Riddle. (Capitol, stereo)

(Frank Sinatra Sings for) Only the Lonely A somber companion piece to *Swingin' Lovers*, recorded in 1958 with Nelson Riddle in an uncommonly reflective spirit (available on CD and LP); includes "One for My Baby," "Blues in the Night," and "Angel Eyes." (Sinatra won a Grammy as art director of the cover painting, which portrays the singer as a mournful clown.) (Capitol, stereo)

Sinatra and Basie One of the most successful collaborations of many Sinatra initiated on his own record label. This 1963 album (available on CD and LP) includes "Pennies from Heaven," "I Won't Dance," and "Please Be Kind," with arrangements by Neal Hefti (uncredited). (Reprise, stereo)

The Concert Sinatra Not a live album, but a 1963 collection of ballads, mostly by Richard Rodgers, sung with consistent intensity (available on CD and LP); includes "I Have Dreamed," "Bewitched, Bothered and Bewildered," and "My Heart Stood Still," with arrangements by Nelson Riddle. (Reprise, stereo)

September of My Years Facing middle age (on his fiftieth birthday) in 1965, Sinatra looks back in song (available on CD and LP); includes "September Song," "This Is All I Ask," "How Old Am I," and "Don't Wait Too Long," with arrangements by Gordon Jenkins. (Reprise, stereo)

Francis Albert Sinatra & Antonio Carlos Jobim Sweet-and-sour pairing of Sinatra and bossa-nova innovator Jobim from 1967 (available on CD and LP); includes "Quiet Nights of Quiet Stars," "How Insensitive," and "Dindi," with arrangements by Claus Ogerman and with Jobim sharing vocals on four songs. (Reprise, stereo)

She Shot Me Down Recorded in 1981, Sinatra's last top-shelf album (available on CD and LP)—a meditation on loss, with the loss of Sinatra's physical abilities its unspoken theme; includes "A Long Night," "Thanks for the Memory," and "The Gal That Got Away"/"It Never Entered My Mind" (medley), with arrangements by Don Costa, Gordon Jenkins, and Nelson Riddle. (Reprise, stereo)

SELECTED VIDEOGRAPHY

Frank Sinatra: The Reprise Collection Three of Sinatra's best TV specials from the 1960s and 1970s on three cassettes (or two laserdiscs): *A Man and His Music*, *A Man and His Music + Ella + Jobim* (with Ella Fitzgerald and Antonio Carlos Jobim), and *Ol' Blue Eyes Is Back* (with Gene Kelly). Among the many high points: "Don't Worry 'Bout Me" and "Nancy," with arrangements by Nelson Riddle; medleys with Jobim ("I Concentrate on You" and "The Girl from Ipanema"), Fitzgerald ("How High the Moon" and "The Lady Is a Tramp"), and Kelly ("Take Me Out to the Ball Game" and "Nice and Easy"). (Warner/Reprise tape and laserdisc)

On the Town Shot on location in New York in 1949, this is the third—and best—of three MGM musicals in which Sinatra costarred with Gene Kelly (who also codirected with Stanley Donen). Sinatra's performance as a girl-shy sailor in the big city is tongue-in-cheek, his dancing is energetic (if sometimes clunky), and his singing of the Leonard Bernstein–Betty Comden–Adolph Green tunes is sprightly. (MGM/UA tape and laserdisc)

From Here to Eternity The film to watch to see that Sinatra really could act (1954's *Suddenly* and 1955's *Man with the Golden Arm* are next on the list). Of course, his performance as Maggio in this Pearl Harbor drama won him the Best Supporting Actor Oscar—and helped him win back his career. Starring Burt Lancaster and Montgomery Clift (who helped Sinatra with his lines) and directed by Fred Zinnemann. (RCA/Columbia Pictures tape and laserdisc)

Guys and Dolls Star Marlon Brando got all the best songs, but Sinatra sings the dickens out of the few tunes he has as Nathan Detroit ("Sue Me," "Adelaide," and "Good Ol' Reliable Nathan"). Jean Simmons and Vivian Blaine costar in this 1955 version of the Frank Loesser musical (based on Damon Runyon stories), directed by Joseph L. Mankiewicz. (CBS/Fox tape and laserdisc)

Pal Joey In the film role that's closest to his own public persona, Sinatra stars as a talented rat with a soft spot. The Rodgers and Hart songs ("I Could Write a Book," "The Lady Is a Tramp," and "What Do I Care for a Dame") are among the team's best, and Sinatra sings them in the prime of his powers, in 1957.

Costarring Rita Hayworth and Kim Novak and directed by George Sidney. (RCA/Columbia Pictures tape and laserdisc)

KATE SMITH

SELECTED DISCOGRAPHY

Kate Smith—God Bless America CD compilation of twenty-one songs recorded between 1931 and 1939, accompanying orchestras uncredited, including "When the Moon Comes Over the Mountain," "Moanin' Low," "I Got Rhythm," "All of Me," "When My Ship Comes In," "Twenty Million People," and "God Bless America." (Pro Arte, mono)

Kate Smith, Legendary Performer 1978 LP compilation of sixteen songs recorded between 1963 and 1966, with orchestras led by Skitch Henderson, Peter Matz, and Claus Ogerman; includes "When the Moon Comes Over the Mountain," "The White Cliffs of Dover," "Fine and Dandy," "The Impossible Dream," "This Is All I Ask," and "God Bless America." (RCA Victor, mono)

Sincerely, Miss Kate Smith 1984 LP compilation of early 1930s recordings, with orchestras led by Ben Selvin and Guy Lombardo; includes "River, Stay 'Way from My Door," "There's Nothing Like an Old-Fashioned Waltz," "College Rhythm," "Dancing with Tears in My Eyes," and "When My Ship Comes In." (Sunbeam, mono)

Kate Smith On the Air 1983 LP compilation of air checks of variable quality from the late 1930s and the 1940s of seventeen songs, including "It Was So Beautiful," "Blues in the Night," "September Song," "Coming In on a Wing and a Prayer," "I'll Be Seeing You," "Why Don't You Do Right?" and Smith's first broadcast performance of "God Bless America." (Sandy Hook, mono)

SELECTED VIDEOGRAPHY

The Kate Smith Program Four half-hour television shows from 1951 and 1952, taken from black-and-white kinescopes; guests include Xavier Cugat, Ann Sheridan, Eddie Condon, and Myron Cohen. (Shokus tape)

This Is the Army The 1943 movie version of Irving Berlin's wartime servicemen's revue, in which Smith and a chorus sing "God Bless America." Also stars Ronald Reagan, Joan Leslie, George Murphy, and Alan Hale. Since rights to the movie have fallen into the public domain, prints in circulation are of variable quality—and some from small companies cut "God Bless America" to avoid paying royalties on the song, under Berlin's terms, to the Boy Scouts and Girls Scouts of America. (Video Yesteryear tape)

JO STAFFORD

SELECTED DISCOGRAPHY

Jo Stafford's Greatest Hits CD compilation of fourteen recordings from the 1950s with Paul Weston's orchestra, including "I'll Be Seeing You," "Come Rain or Come Shine," "You Belong to Me," "Embraceable You," "The Gentleman Is a Dope," "Stardust," and "Blues in the Night." (Corinthian, mono)

Jo Stafford, Collectors Series CD compilation of twenty-six recordings from 1943 to 1950, arranged chronologically; includes "Long Ago (and Far Away)," "The Trolley Song" (with the Pied Pipers), "Tim-Tayshun," "Symphony," and "Ridin' on the Gravy Train" (with Nat "King" Cole). (Capitol, mono)

Jo + Jazz CD reissue of an LP recorded in the 1960s in pop-jazz arrangements by Johnny Mandel, with Johnny Hodges, Ben Webster, Ray Nance, and other top jazzmen; includes "I've Got the World on a String," "S'posin'," "Just Squeeze Me," "I Didn't Know About You," and "Midnight Sun." (Corinthian, stereo)

GI Jo CD reissue of an LP of popular World War II–era favorites recorded in the 1960s with Paul Weston's orchestra; includes "I Don't Want to Walk Without You," "I Left My Heart at the Stage Door Canteen," "No Love, No Nothin'," "I'll Walk Alone," "I'll Be Seeing You," and "You'll Never Know." (Corinthian, stereo)

Jonathan and Darlene's Greatest Hits CD compilation of fourteen tracks from 1950s and 1960s recorded by Jonathan and Darlene Edwards (alias Weston and Stafford); includes "The Last Time I Saw Paris," "I Love Paris," "You're Blasé," "Take the 'A' Train," "Autumn in New York," and "Don't Get Around Much Anymore," plus one newly recorded track of "Staying Alive." (Corinthian, stereo)

SELECTED VIDEOGRAPHY

DuBarry Was a Lady The 1943 MGM adaptation of a Cole Porter Broadway musical comedy, with Lucille Ball, Gene Kelly, Red Skelton, and Tommy Dorsey's orchestra; Stafford sings "Katie Went to Haiti" with Dorsey's band and the Pied Pipers. (MGM/UA tape)

BARBRA STREISAND

SELECTED DISCOGRAPHY

My Name Is Barbra First of three studio albums that introduced Streisand as a singer of both contemporary and classic-pop songs (available on CD and LP), with arrangements by Peter Matz; includes "My Man," "I've Got No Strings," and "Someone to Watch Over Me." (Columbia, stereo)

My Name Is Barbra, Two Follow-up collaboration with Peter Matz (available on CD and LP); includes "Second-Hand Rose," "Give Me the Simple Life," "I Got Plenty of Nothing," and "Nobody Loves You When You're Down and Out." (Columbia, stereo)

Color Me Barbra More contemporary-oriented album, with some classic-pop tunes, including "Yesterdays" and "Where or When" (available on CD and LP). (Columbia, stereo)

Funny Girl: Original Cast Album Streisand sings Jule Styne and Bob Merrill's songs, including "Don't Rain on My Parade," "I'm the Greatest Star," and "People." (Capitol, stereo)

The Broadway Album Streisand's return to classic pop in 1985; Broadway musical songs include "If I Loved You" (*Carousel*), "Adelaide's Lament" (*Guys and Dolls*), and "Send in the Clowns" (*A Little Night Music*). (Columbia, stereo)

SELECTED VIDEOGRAPHY

Funny Girl Streisand won a Best Actress Oscar for her movie debut in the role that originally launched her on Broadway. The 1968 quasi-bio of comedienne Fanny Brice is really a vehicle for Streisand's theatrical-kook antics. Songs by Jule Styne and Bob Merrill include "People" and "Don't Rain on My Parade." Directed by William Wyler. (RCA/Columbia Pictures tape and laserdisc)

Hello, Dolly! 1969 effort (directed by Gene Kelly) to re-create the full-blown pizzazz of 1950s musicals feels forced, but Streisand holds her own as matchmaker Dolly Levi. Costarring Walter Matthau, Michael Crawford, and E. J. Peaker, with a score by Jerry Herman. (RCA/Columbia Pictures tape and laserdisc)

Funny Lady 1975 screen sequel to *Funny Girl* has Streisand as grown-up (and still confused) Fanny Brice, caught up with impresario Billy Rose (James Caan). The Kander-Ebb music outshines the scattershot script. Directed by Herbert Ross. (RCA/Columbia Pictures tape and laserdisc)

My Name Is Barbra Streisand's Emmy-winning first TV special, from 1965; includes more than twenty songs, including "People," "My Man," "Second-Hand Rose," and "Don't Rain on My Parade." (CBS/Fox tape and laserdisc)

Color Me Barbra Streisand's second TV special, from 1966; includes "Sam, You Made the Pants Too Long," "Try to Remember," and "Who's Afraid of the Big Bad Wolf." (CBS/Fox tape and laserdisc)

Putting It Together: The Making of the Broadway Album Streisand-supervised promo documentary about the recording of her 1985 *Broadway Album*; songs include "Putting It Together," "Something's Coming," "If I Loved You," and "Can't Help Lovin' That Man." (CBS/Fox tape and laserdisc)

SYLVIA SYMS

SELECTED DISCOGRAPHY

. . . Then Along Came Bill 1990 tribute to Bill Evans on CD; includes "Like Someone in Love," "My Foolish Heart," "Polka Dots and Moonbeams," and "My Romance." (DRG, stereo)

Sinatra and Syms 1983 LP produced and conducted by Frank Sinatra for his longtime friend; includes "Them There Eyes," "That Old Devil Moon," "I Thought About You," and "Hooray for Love," with arrangements by Don Costa and Vinnie Falcone (available on CD and LP). (Reprise, stereo)

SELECTED VIDEOGRAPHY

Buddy Barnes Live from Studio B 1983 performance by singer/pianist Barnes, with guest appearance by Sylvia Syms singing "My Ship" and "Pick Yourself Up." (Sony tape, import)

MEL TORMÉ

SELECTED DISCOGRAPHY

'Round Midnight: A Retrospective CD compilation of recordings from 1956 to 1968; includes "Quiet Nights of Quiet Stars," "Fascinatin' Rhythm," " 'Round Midnight," and "I'll Be Seeing You." With the Marty Paitch Dektette, the Basie and Woody Herman big bands, others. (Stash, stereo)

Mel Tormé Sings of New York 1983 album includes "Autumn in New York," "Forty-Second Street," "Lullaby of Birdland," and "Harlem Nocturne" (available on CD and LP). (Atlantic, stereo)

George Shearing/Mel Tormé: Top Drawer 1983 jazz trio session on CD and LP; includes "A Shine on Your Shoes," "Stardust," and "Smoke Gets in Your Eyes." (Concord, stereo)

Mel Tormé Swings Shubert Alley CD reissue of 1960 album of Broadway songs, with the Marty Paich orchestra; includes "Too Close for Comfort," "All I Need Is the Girl," "A Sleepin' Bee," and "Old Devil Moon." (PolyGram, stereo)

The London Sessions CD reissue of 1977 album with symphonic orchestra conducted by Chris Gunning (featuring jazz saxophonist Phil Woods); includes "Send in the Clowns," "When the World Was Young," and "Yesterday When I Was Young." (DCC Jazz, stereo)

SELECTED VIDEOGRAPHY

Mel Tormé and Della Reese in Concert 1978 concert in Edmonton, Canada. Tormé and Reese duets include "Ordinary Fool" and a blues medley ("C. C. Rider" and "Stormy Monday"). Tormé solos on "When I Found You," "A Nightingale Sang in Berkeley Square," and "When the World Was Young." With the ITV Concert Orchestra. (MCA laserdisc)

RUDY VALLEE

SELECTED DISCOGRAPHY

Rudy Vallee, Sing for Your Supper CD compilation of eighteen original '30s recordings; includes the title song, "The Whiffenpoof Song," "I'm Just a Vagabond Lover," and "This Can't Be Love" (with Frances Langford). (Conifer, mono)

Heigh-Ho Everybody, This Is Rudy Vallee Selections from 1930s radio broadcasts on LP; includes "Heigh-ho Everybody, Heigh-Ho," "Betty Co-ed," "If I Had a Girl Like You," and "Let's Do It." (Olympic, mono)

Rudy Vallee and His Connecticut Yankees LP compilation of '30s recordings; includes "Deep Night," "The Stein Song," "St. Louis Blues," and "Life Is Just a Bowl of Cherries." (Halcyon, mono)

How to Succeed in Business Without Really Trying Original-cast LP of the 1962 Broadway production of the Frank Loesser musical, with Vallee and Robert Morse. Vallee performs "Grand Old Ivy" and "The Yo Ho Ho." (RCA, stereo)

SELECTED VIDEOGRAPHY

The Vagabond Lover Vallee virtually plays himself in this light romantic musical about an orchestra leader who falls for a client's niece, from 1929. He sings "I'm Just a Vagabond Lover," "If You Were the Only Girl in the World," and "I Love You, Believe Me, I Love You." (RKO/Video T.E.N. tape)

The Palm Beach Story 1942 Preston Sturges screwball comedy with Vallee hilarious in nonsinging role as millionaire half-wit. With Claudette Colbert, Joel McCrea, and Mary Astor. (MCA tape and laserdisc)

Unfaithfully Yours 1948 Sturges classic about suspected infidelity and murder, with Vallee at his comedic peak. Costarring Rex Harrison and Linda Darnell. (CBS/Fox tape)

DINAH WASHINGTON

SELECTED DISCOGRAPHY

The Complete Dinah Washington on Mercury Seven-volume set with three CDs boxed in each volume, comprising Washington's complete output for Mercury records; includes newly discovered, previously unreleased sides and rare singles. (PolyGram, mono and stereo):

Vol. 1: Selections from 1946 to 1949, including "Embraceable You," "The Man

I Love," "Ain't Misbehavin'," "Record Ban Blues," "How Deep Is the Ocean," and "It's Funny."

Vol. 2: Selections from 1950 to 1952, including "Harbor Lights," "Cold, Cold Heart," "Saturday Night," "Trouble in Mind," "Stormy Weather," and "My Devotion."

Vol. 3: Selections from 1952 to 1954, including "Don't Get Around Much Anymore," "TV Is the Thing," "A Foggy Day," "Crazy He Calls Me," and "You Go to My Head."

Vol. 4: Selections from 1954 to 1956, including "Teach Me Tonight," "A Cottage for Sale," "I Could Write a Book," "There'll Be Some Changes Made," "Let's Do It," and "Willow, Weep for Me."

Vol. 5: Selections from 1956 to 1958, including "Caravan," "Makin' Whoopee," "Honeysuckle Rose," "The More I See You," "Crazy Love," and "Lover Come Back to Me."

Vol. 6: Selections from 1958 to 1960, including "What a Diff'rence a Day Makes," "Cry Me a River," "Unforgettable," "This Love of Mine," "I Concentrate on You," and "Stardust."

Vol. 7: Selections from 1961, including "Without a Song," "Blue Skies," "Green Dolphin Street," "Blues in the Night," "Mood Indigo," and "If I Should Lose You."

Dinah James Clifford Brown, Clark Terry, Junior Nance, and other jazz musicians back Washington on "You Go to My Head," "I've Got You Under My Skin," medley of "Along Together"/"Summertime"/"Come Rain or Come Shine," and others (available on CD and LP). (PolyGram, stereo)

SELECTED VIDEOGRAPHY

Jazz on a Summer Day Bert Stern's classic documentary about the 1958 Newport Jazz Festival, featuring Washington, Louis Armstrong, Gerry Mulligan, Thelonious Monk, and others. (New Yorker tape)

ETHEL WATERS

SELECTED DISCOGRAPHY

Ethel Waters on Stage and Screen Compilation of show and movie selections and recordings from 1925 to 1940 on CD and LP; includes "Am I Blue," "Memories of You," "Stormy Weather," "Cabin in the Sky," and "Taking a Chance on Love." Musicians include Benny Goodman, Tommy Dorsey, and Jimmy Dorsey. (Columbia, mono)

Ethel Waters' Greatest Years 1950s LP compilation of material primarily from the '30s; four sides include "Brother, You've Got Me Wrong," "Sweet Georgia Brown," "My Handy Man," and "You Brought a New Kind of Love to Me." (Columbia, mono)

Miss Ethel Waters Concert performance from the late '50s on LP; includes "Porgy," "Oh, Lady Be Good," "Happiness Is Just a Thing Called Joe," and "St. Louis Blues." With Reginald Beane on piano. (Monmouth Evergreen, stereo)

SELECTED VIDEOGRAPHY

Cabin in the Sky Outstanding musical performances—including Waters' "Happiness Is Just a Thing Called Joe" and "Taking a Chance on Love"—highlight this 1943 fable about good and evil vying for one man's soul. Director Vincente Minnelli's first movie features an all-black cast, including Eddie Anderson, Lena Horne, Louis Armstrong, and Duke Ellington as well as Waters. (MGM/UA tape)

MARGARET WHITING

SELECTED DISCOGRAPHY

Margaret Whiting, Collectors Series CD compilation of twenty-six of Whiting's original Capitol recordings from the 1940s and 1950s, including "My Ideal," "It Might As Well Be Spring," "Moonlight in Vermont," "Old Devil Moon," "Faraway Places," and "That Old Black Magic." (Capitol-EMI, mono)

Margaret Whiting, Then and Now CD mixing standards by Arlen, Berlin, Mercer, Whiting, Rodgers, and others, with new songs by Felicia Blumenthal, Ervin Drake, Brian Gari, and Amanda McBroom; includes new arrangements of such Whiting hits as "Moonlight in Vermont," "That Old Black Magic," and "It Might As Well Be Spring." (DRG, stereo)

The Lady's in Love With You Another recent mixture of old and new, this one from 1985; includes "Boy! What Love Has Done to Me," "Little Jazz Bird," "Being Alive," "Last Night When We Were Young," "Take a Bite," and "My Favorite Year." (Audiophile, stereo)

Too Marvelous for Words: A Tribute to Johnny Mercer & Richard Whiting Two-disc LP album recorded in 1980, with seventeen songs that Whiting and Mercer wrote together or with other songwriters; includes "My Ideal," "Guilty," "My Future Just Passed," "On the Good Ship Lollipop," "Blues in the Night," and the title song. (Audiophile LP, stereo)

Margaret Whiting Sings the Jerome Kern Songbook Two-disc LP album of twenty-four songs by the composer Whiting knew as Uncle Jerry; includes "I'm Old-Fashioned," "Remind Me," "The Touch of Your Hand," "Smoke Gets in Your Eyes," "Long Ago and Far Away," "Bill," and "Can't Help Lovin' Dat Man." (Verve LP, mono)

SELECTED VIDEOGRAPHY

No movies or television programs in which Margaret Whiting has appeared as a singer have yet been released on video.

LEE WILEY

SELECTED DISCOGRAPHY

Night in Manhattan with Lee Wiley Originally released as an LP in 1950 and digitally remastered for CD in 1990; accompanists include Bobby Hackett, Joe Bushkin, Stan Freeman, and Cy Walter; includes "Street of Dreams," "A Ghost of a Chance," "Anytime, Anywhere," and "Soft Lights and Sweet Music." (CBS/ Sony Special Products)

Lee Wiley—West of the Moon 1956 LP with orchestra led by Ralph Burns; includes "Can't Get Out of This Mood," "You're a Sweetheart," "My Ideal," "As Time Goes By," "East of the Sun (West of the Moon)," and "Limehouse Blues." (RCA Japan, mono)

Lee Wiley Sings the Songs of George & Ira Gershwin and Cole Porter 1985 LP reissue of the historic 1939–40 set of recordings, the first by a major singer devoted entirely to popular songs by specific songwriters; includes "Sweet and Lowdown," "But Not for Me," "My One and Only," "Easy to Love," "Let's Fly Away," and "Let's Do It." (Audio Fidelity, mono)

Lee Wiley Sings the Songs of Richard Rodgers & Lorenz Hart and Harold Arlen 1986 LP reissue of the historic follow-up to the set above; includes "A Little Birdie Told Me So," "Here in My Arms," "As Though You Were There," "Stormy Weather," "Moanin' in the Mornin'," and "Fun to Be Fooled." (Audio Fidelity, mono)

Lee Wiley on the Air 1979 LP compilation of fourteen air checks from mid-1940s broadcasts, with Jess Stacy, Joe Bushkin, Pee Wee Russell, Billy Butterfield, Tommy Dorsey, and Bobby Hackett among the sidemen; includes "Sweet and Lowdown," "The Man I Love," "I Can't Get Started," "A Ghost of a Chance," "When Your Lover Has Gone," and nine others. (Totem, mono)

SELECTED VIDEOGRAPHY

No movies or documentaries including Lee Wiley are known to exist.

ANDY WILLIAMS

SELECTED DISCOGRAPHY

Andy Williams—16 Most Requested Songs CD compilation of sixteen recordings from the late 1960s onward; includes "The Days of Wine and Roses," "Red Roses for a Blue Lady," "Moon River," "The Impossible Dream," "Born Free," and "Canadian Sunset." (CBS/Sony, stereo)

Andy Williams—Moon River & Other Great Movie Themes CD compilation of recordings from the 1960s onward, including the title song, "The Days of Wine and Roses," "Charade," "Love Is a Many-Splendored Thing," "The Second Time Around," and "As Time Goes By." (CBS/Sony, stereo)

SELECTED VIDEOGRAPHY

None of Williams' several movies nor any of his TV specials have yet been released on video.

NANCY WILSON

SELECTED DISCOGRAPHY

A Lady with a Song CD includes "Do You Still Dream About Me," "This Love Is What I Need," and "Now I Know." (Columbia, stereo)

Forbidden Lover CD includes "A Song for You," "I Was Telling Him About You," and "I Never Held Your Heart." Arranged by Masahiko Satoh. (Columbia, stereo)

Broadway—My Way Early 1960s LP of theater songs; includes "I Believe in You," "Make Someone Happy," "My Ship," and "You Can Have Him." Arranged by Jimmy Jones. (Capitol, stereo)

Hollywood—My Way Movie-song companion to Wilson's *Broadway* album and released the following year; includes "Dearly Beloved," "Moon River," "Days of Wine and Roses," and "The Second Time Around." Arranged by Jimmy Jones. (Capitol, stereo)

SELECTED VIDEOGRAPHY

Nancy Wilson Concert performance from the '70s features Chick Corea and Stanley Clarke; songs include "I Want to Be Happy," " 'Round Midnight," and "Take the 'A' Train." (Sony tape)

BIBLIOGRAPHY

For Further Reference and Reading About the Singers,
Their Lives, Their Work, and Related Background

BOOKS

ALEKSIEWICZ, LOUISE. *Louis Armstrong: Periodical Articles (1947–1977)*. Chicago: Chicago Public Library, 1979.

ANDERTON, BARRIE. *Sonny Boy! The World of Al Jolson*. London: Jupiter Books, 1975.

ARMSTRONG, LOUIS. *Louis Armstrong, A Self-Portrait*. New York: Eakins Press, 1971.

———. *Louis Armstrong Diaries*. Newark, N. J.: microfilmed for the Institute for Jazz Studies, Rutgers University, 1987.

———. *Satchmo*. New York: Prentice Hall, 1954.

ASTAIRE, FRED. *Steps in Time*. New York: Harper & Brothers, 1959.

BALLIETT, WHITNEY. *American Singers, 27 Portraits in Song*. Oxford/New York: Oxford University Press, 1988.

BARNES, KEN. *The Crosby Years*. New York: St. Martin's Press, 1980.

———. *Sinatra and the Great Song Stylists*. London: Ian Allan, 1972.

BAUER, BARBARA. *Bing Crosby*. New York: Pyramid, 1977.

BIGARD, BARNEY. *With Louis and the Duke*. New York: Oxford University Press, 1988.

BLESH, RUDI. *Combo, USA* (Billie Holiday). Philadelphia: Chilton Book Co., 1971.

BRADY, FRANK. *Barbra Streisand*. New York: Grosset & Dunlap, 1979.

BRITT, STAN. *Sinatra the Singer*. London: Macmillan London, 1989.

CHILTON, JOHN. *Billie's Blues*. New York: Da Capo Press, 1989.

CLARKE, DONALD, ed. *The Penguin Encyclopedia of Popular Music*. London: Viking Penguin, 1989.

CLOONEY, ROSEMARY. *This for Remembrance*. New York: Playboy Press, 1977.

COLE, MARIA. *Nat King Cole: An Intimate Biography*. New York: William Morrow, 1971.

COLEMAN, EMILY. R. *The Complete Judy Garland*. New York: Harper & Row, 1990.

COLIN, SID. *Ella*. London: Elm Tree/Hamilton, 1986.

COLLIER, JAMES LINCOLN. *Louis Armstrong, an American Genius*. New York: Oxford University Press, 1985.

CONSIDINE, SHAUN. *Barbra Streisand*. New York: Delacorte, 1985.

CORNELL, JEAN GAY. *Louis Armstrong: Ambassador Satchmo*. New York: Dell, 1972.

CROSBY, BING. *Call Me Lucky*. New York: Simon and Schuster, 1953.

DAHL, DAVID, and KEHOE, BARRY. *Young Judy*. New York: Mason/Charter, 1973.

DAHL, LINDA. *Stormy Weather: The Music and Lives of a Century of Jazzwomen*. New York: Pantheon Books, 1984.

DAY, DORIS. *Doris Day*. New York: William Morrow, 1976.

DI ORIO, AL, JR. *Little Girl Lost: The Life and Hard Times of Judy Garland*. New Rochelle, N.Y.: Arlington House, 1973.

DOUGLAS-HOME, ROBIN. *Sinatra*. New York: Grosset & Dunlap, 1962.

EATON, JEANNETTE. *Trumpeter's Tale* (Louis Armstrong). New York: William Morrow, 1955.

EDWARDS, ANNE. *Judy Garland: A Biography*. New York: Simon and Schuster, 1975.

EELLS, GEORGE. *Ginger, Loretta and Irene Who?* (Ruth Etting). New York: G.P. Putnam's Sons, 1976.

FINCH, CHRISTOPHER. *Rainbow: The Stormy Life of Judy Garland*. New York: Grosset & Dunlap, 1975.

FORREST, HELEN, with LIBBY, BILL. *I Had the Craziest Dream*. New York: Coward, McCann & Geoghegan, 1982.

FRANK, ALAN G. *Sinatra*. New York: L. Amiel Publishing, 1978.

FRANK, GEROLD. *Judy*. New York: Harper & Row, 1975.

FREEDLAND, MICHAEL. *Jolie: The Al Jolson Story*. London: Comet, 1985.

FRIEDWALD, WILL. *Jazz Singing, America's Great Voices from Bessie Smith to Bebop and Beyond*. New York: Charles Scribner's Sons, 1990.

GARROD, CHARLES. *Nat "King" Cole, His Voice and Piano*. Zephyrville, Fla.: Joyce Record Club Publications, 1987.

GEHMAN, RICHARD. *Sinatra and His Rat Pack*. New York: Belmont Books, 1961.

GELB, ALAN. *The Doris Day Scrapbook*. New York: Grosset & Dunlap, 1977.

GIDDINS, GARY. *Satchmo*. New York: Doubleday, 1988.

GILES, SARAH. *Fred Astaire, His Friends Talk*. New York: Doubleday, 1988.

GOFFIN, ROBERT. *Horn of Plenty* (Louis Armstrong). New York: Allen, Towne & Heath, 1947.

GOLDMAN, HERBERT G. *Jolson: The Legend Comes to Life*. New York: Oxford University Press, 1988.

GOLDSTEIN, NORM. *Frank Sinatra, Ol' Blue Eyes*. New York: Holt, Rinehart and Winston, 1982.

GOURSE, LESLIE. *Louis' Children*. New York: William Morrow, 1984.

——. *Unforgettable* (Nat "King" Cole). New York: St. Martin's Press, 1991.

GREEN, BENNY. *Fred Astaire*. New York: Exeter Books, 1979.

GREEN, STANLEY, and GOLDBLATT, BURT. *Starring Fred Astaire*. New York: Dodd, Mead, 1973.

HARDY, PHIL, and LAING, DAVE. *The Faber Companion to 20th-Century Popular Music*. London/Boston: Faber and Faber, 1990.

HARVEY, STEPHEN. *Fred Astaire*. New York: Pyramid, 1975.

HASKINS, JAMES. *Mabel Mercer*. New York: Atheneum, 1987.

——. *Nat King Cole*. New York: Stein and Day, 1984.

——. *Queen of the Blues* (Dinah Washington). New York: William Morrow, 1987.

HASKINS, JAMES, with BENSON, KATHLEEN. *Lena, A Personal and Professional Biography*. New York: Stein and Day, 1984.

HOLIDAY, BILLIE. *Lady Sings the Blues*. New York: Lancer Books, 1956.

HORNE, LENA, with SCHICKEL, RICHARD. *Lena: An Autobiography*. Garden City, N.Y.: Doubleday, 1986.

HOTCHNER, A. E. *Doris Day*. Boston: G. K. Hall, 1976.

HOWLETT, JOHN. *Frank Sinatra*. Philadelphia: Courage Books, 1980.

IVERSON, GENIE. *Louis Armstrong*. New York: Thomas Y. Crowell, 1976.

JABLONSKI, EDWARD. *The Encyclopedia of American Music*. Garden City, N.Y.: Doubleday, 1981.

JASEN, DAVID A. *Tin Pan Alley*. New York: Donald I. Fine, 1988.

JASPER, TONY. *Tony Bennett: A Biography*. London: W. H. Allen, 1984.

JONES, HETTIE. *Big Star Fallin' Mama* (Billie Holiday). New York: Viking Press, 1974.

JONES, MAX. *Louis, The Louis Armstrong Story*. New York: Da Capo Press, 1988.

JORDAN, RENE. *The Greatest Star* (Barbra Streisand). New York: Putnam, 1975.

KELLEY, KITTY. *His Way* (Frank Sinatra). New York: Bantam Books, 1986.

KIMBRELL, JAMES. *Barbra, An Actress Who Sings* (Streisand). Boston: Branden, 1989.

KLIMENT, BUD. *Ella Fitzgerald*. Los Angeles: Melrose Square Publishing Co., 1989.

KNAACK, TWILLA. *Ethel Waters, I Touched a Sparrow*. Waco, Tex.: Word Books, 1978.

LAFORSE, MARTIN W. *Popular Culture and American Life*. Chicago: Nelson-Hall, 1981.

LEE, PEGGY. *Miss Peggy Lee*. New York: Donald I. Fine, 1989.

LEES, GENE. *Singers and the Song*. New York/Oxford: Oxford University Press, 1987.

LEWINE, RICHARD, and SIMON, ALFRED. *Songs of the Theater*. New York: H. W. Wilson, 1984.

LONSTEIN, ALBERT I. *The Compleat Sinatra*. Ellenville, N.Y.: Cameron Publications, 1970.

MAST, GERALD. *Can't Help Singin'—The American Musical on Stage and Screen*. Woodstock, N.Y.: Overlook Press, 1987.

MAXWELL, GILBERT. *Helen Morgan, Her Life and Legend*. New York: Hawthorn Books, 1974.

MCCLELLAND, DOUG. *Blackface to Blacklist: Al Jolson, Larry Parks and The Jolson Story*. Metuchen, N.J.: Scarecrow Press, 1987.

MERMAN, ETHEL. *Who Could Ask for Anything More*. Garden City, N.Y.: Doubleday, 1955.

MERMAN, ETHEL, with EELLS, GEORGE. *Merman, An Autobiography*. New York, Simon and Schuster, 1978.

MEYER, JOHN. *Heartbreaker* (Judy Garland). Garden City, N.Y.: Doubleday, 1983.

MILLAR, JACK. *Born to Sing* (Billie Holiday). Copenhagen: Jazzmedia, 1979.

MORDDEN, ETHAN. *Broadway Babies: The People Who Made the American Musical*. New York/London: Oxford University Press, 1983.

——. *The Hollywood Musical*. New York: St. Martin's Press, 1981.

MORELLA, JOE, and EPSTEIN, EDWARD. *Judy*. New York: Citadel Press, 1969.

MORRIS, GEORGE. *Doris Day*. New York: Pyramid Publications, 1976.

MOSHIER, W. FRANKLIN. *The Alice Faye Movie Book*. Harrisburg, Penn.: A&W Visual Library/Stackpole Books, 1974.

NOBLE, PETER. *The Negro in Films*. London: Skelton Robinson, 1946.

OBERFIRST, ROBERT. *Al Jolson, You Ain't Heard Nothin' Yet*. San Diego: A. S. Barnes, 1980.

O'BRIEN, ED. *The Sinatra Sessions 1939–1980*. Dallas: Sinatra Society of America, 1980.

PETERS, RICHARD. *The Frank Sinatra Scrapbook*. New York: St. Martin's Press, 1983.

PICKARD, ROY. *Fred Astaire*. London: Hamlyn, 1985.

PINFORD, MIKE. *Louis Armstrong, His Life and Times*. New York: Universe Books, 1987.

PLEASANTS, HENRY. *The Great American Popular Singers*. New York: Simon and Schuster, 1985.

ROCKWELL, JOHN. *Sinatra: An American Classic*. New York: Rolling Stone Press, 1984.

RUST, BRIAN. *The American Dance Band Discography 1917–1942*. New Rochelle, N.Y.: Arlington House, 1975.

——. *The Complete Entertainment Discography*. New Rochelle, N.Y.: Arlington House, 1973.

SANFORD, HERB. *Tommy and Jimmy: The Dorsey Years*. New Rochelle, N.Y.: Arlington House, 1972.

SCIACCA, TONY. *Sinatra*. New York: Pinnacle Books, 1976.

SHAW, ARNOLD. *The Jazz Age, Popular Music in the 1920s*. New York/Oxford: Oxford University Press, 1987.

——. *Sinatra, The Entertainer*. New York: Delilah, 1982.

SHEPHERD, DONALD, and SLATZER, ROBERT F. *Bing Crosby, The Hollow Man*. New York: St. Martin's Press, 1981.

SHORT, BOBBY. *Black and White Baby*. New York: Dodd, Mead, 1971.

SIEBEN, PEARL. *The Immortal Jolson: His Life and Times*. New York: F. Fell, 1962.

SIMON, GEORGE T. *The Best of the Music Makers*. Garden City, N.Y.: Doubleday, 1979.

——. *The Big Bands*. New York: Collier Books/Macmillan, 1974.

——. *The Sights and Sounds of the Swing Era 1935–1955*. New York: Galahad Books, 1971.

SINATRA, FRANK. *Sinatra in His Own Words*. London: W. H. Allen, 1979.

SINATRA, NANCY. *Frank Sinatra, My Father*. Garden City, N.Y.: Doubleday, 1985.

SMITH, KATE. *Living in a Great Big Way*. New York: Blue Ribbon Books, 1938.

SPADA, JAMES. *Streisand, the Woman and the Legend*. Garden City, N.Y.: Doubleday, 1981.

STROFF, STEPHEN M. *Discovering Great Jazz*. New York: Newmarket Press, 1991.

SWENSON, KAREN. *Barbra, the Second Decade* (Streisand). Secaucus, N.J.: Citadel Press, 1986.

TEUBIG, KLAUS. *Straighten Up and Fly Right* (Nat "King" Cole). Metuchen, N.J.: Scarecrow Press, 1989.

THOMAS, BOB. *I Got Rhythm* (Ethel Merman). New York: Putnam, 1985.

THOMAS, TONY, with comments by Fred Astaire. *Astaire, The Man, The Dancer*. New York: St. Martin's Press, 1984.

THOMPSON, CHARLES. *Bing*. New York: David McKay Co., 1976.

TORMÉ, MEL. *It Wasn't All Velvet*. New York: Viking, 1988.

TOWE, RONALD. *Here's to You*. (Peggy Lee). San Francisco: R. Towe Music, 1986.

TYLER, DON. *Hit Parade, 1920–1955*. New York: William Morrow/Quill, 1985.

VALLEE, RUDY. *Let the Chips Fall*. Harrisburg, Penn.: Stackpole Books, 1975.

——. *Vagabond Dreams Come True*. New York: E. P. Dutton, 1930.

VALLEE, RUDY, with MCKEAN, GIL. *My Time Is Your Time*. New York: Ivan Obolensky, 1962.

WALKER, LEO. *The Big Band Almanac* (rev. ed.). New York: Da Capo Press, 1978.

——. *The Wonderful Era of the Great Dance Bands*. Garden City, N.Y.: Doubleday, 1964.

WATERS, ETHEL. *His Eye Is on the Sparrow*. New York: Doubleday, 1951.

——. *To Me It's Wonderful*. New York: Harper & Row, 1972.

WHITBURN, JOEL. *Pop Memories 1890–1954, The History of American Popular Music*. Menomonee Falls, Wis.: Record Research, 1986.

WHITE, JOHN. *Billie Holiday, Her Life and Times*. New York: Universe Books, 1987.

WHITING, MARGARET, and HOLT, WILL. *It Might As Well Be Spring*. New York: William Morrow, 1987.

WILDER, ALEC. *American Popular Song*. Oxford/London: Oxford University Press, 1972.

WILLIAMS, MARTIN T. *The Jazz Tradition*. Oxfordshire: Oxford University Press, 1983.

ZEC, DONALD. *Barbra* (Streisand). New York: St. Martin's Press, 1981.

ARTICLES

ALBERTSON, CHRIS. "Mel Tormé." *Stereo Review*, March 1987.
AMES, M. "Ethel Waters: Clearly One of the Greatest." *High Fidelity*, August 1968.
APONE, CARL. "After 30 Years Steve and Eydie Are Ready for More." *New Jersey Courier-Post*, August 16, 1985.
ARNOLD, ELLIOTT. "Shirley Ross Wiser But Not Sad as Play Ends" (interview). *New York World Telegram*, July 15, 1940.
BALLIETT, WHITNEY. "A Nice Place to Be" (Fred Astaire). *The New Yorker*, January 1, 1979.
————. "Survivors" (Barbara Lea). *The New Yorker*, Mary 20, 1985.
BERENDT, J. "Don't Worry 'Bout Me" (Billie Holiday). *Esquire*, October 1989.
BOSWELL, CONNEE, and BROOKS, MICHAEL. Untitled essay for *The Boswell Sisters 1932–1934* (LP). Canaan, N.Y.: Biograph Records, 1972.
BROOKS, MICHAEL. Untitled essay for *Bing Crosby: The Crooner* (CD). New York: CBS Records, 1988.
————. Untitled essay for *Nothing Was Sweeter Than the Boswell Sisters* (LP). London: Ace of Hearts/Decca, 1966.
BROSSARD, C. "Barbra Streisand: New Singing Sensation." *Look*, November 19, 1963.
BUDER, LEONARD. "About Jo Stafford." *The New York Times*, June 23, 1946.
CARR, LARRY. Untitled essay for *The Bing Crosby Story: The Early Jazz Years 1928–1932* (LP). New York: Columbia Records, 1967.
————. Untitled essay for *Lee Wiley Sings the Songs of Richard Rodgers & Lorenz Hart and Harold Arlen* (LP). Atlanta, Ga.: Audiophile Records, 1986.
CHAPMAN, MARY. "A Career for You Is OK with Me" (Dick Haymes interview). *New York Journal-American*, February 19, 1944.
"Clean-Cut Chip" (Jack Jones). *Newsweek*, December 14, 1964.
CLOONEY, ROSEMARY. "I Love to Eat, But I Hate to Get Fat." *Ladies Home Journal*, August 1959.
COLACELLO, BOB. "No More Blues for Liza" (Liza Minnelli). *Vanity Fair*, June 1987.
COLEMAN, WILLIAM G. "4 Girls 4—An Uncommon Denominator" (Rosemary Clooney, Helen O'Connell, Margaret Whiting). *After Dark*, September 1978.
CONATY, RICH. "Connee Boswell." Essay for *The Boswell Sisters—Okay, America* (LP). Greenport, N.Y.: Jass Records, 1986.
COUTROS, PETE. "Andy's Hardy" (Andy Williams). *New York Sunday News*, June 23, 1957.
————. "A Canary Builds a Nest" (Jo Stafford). *New York Sunday News*, November 6, 1953.
DANCE, STANLEY. "Rockin' Chair Lady, Barrelhouse Gal" (Mildred Bailey). *Saturday Review*, October 13, 1962.
DAVIDSON, B. "Tomato on Top Is Doris Day." *Look*, June 20, 1961.
DAVIS, F. "The Real Stuff in Life: Tony Bennett Brings Urgency, Not Nostalgia, to the Standards He Sings." *The Atlantic*, August 1990.
DEFFAA, CHIP. Untitled essay for *You're the Cats—Barbara Lea and the Legendary Lawson-Haggart Jazz Band* (CD). Atlanta, Ga.: Audiophile Records, 1990.
"Delicious, Delectable, Delovely" (Ethel Merman). *Time*, November 22, 1963.
DE TOLEDANO, R. "Perennial Ella." *National Review*, March 25, 1961.
DRIGGS, FRANK. Untitled essay for *Lee Wiley Sings the Songs of George & Ira Gershwin and Cole Porter* (LP). Atlanta, Ga.: Audiophile Records, 1985.
————. Untitled essay for *Lee Wiley Sings the Songs of Richard Rodgers & Lorenz Hart and Harold Arlen* (LP). Atlanta, Ga.: Audiophile Records, 1986.
"Durable Underground Doyenne" (Mabel Mercer). *Life*, October 15, 1965.

FLATLEY, GUY. "But Liza Refuses to Be Shocking" (Liza Minnelli). *The New York Times*, February 20, 1972.

FLIPPO, CHET. "On the Town with Tony Bennett." *New York*, May 11, 1981.

"Fog Lifts" (Mel Tormé). *Newsweek*, January 6, 1964.

FRIEDWALD, WILL. "The Dancing Man Who Also Sang" (Fred Astaire). *The New York Times*, June 11, 1989.

GEHMAN, RICHARD. "Lady (for a) Day." *Saturday Review*, August 29, 1959.

GILES, SARAH. "The Flair of Fred Astaire." *Vanity Fair*, December 1987.

GOODE, MORT. "Russ Columbo." Booklet included with *Russ Columbo, A Legendary Performer* (LP). New York: RCA Records, 1976.

GRATZ, ROBERTA BRANDES. "Steve and Eydie." *New York Post*, February 1, 1969.

"Greatest Pretender" (Nancy Wilson). *Time*, July 17, 1964.

"Gumm Sisters at Grauman's Chinese" (Judy Garland). *Variety*, November 6, 1934.

HAMIL, PETE. "Goodbye Brooklyn, Hello Fame" (Barbra Streisand). *Saturday Evening Post*, July 27, 1963.

HARRISON, BARBARA GRIZZUTI. "The Lies About My Mother—and Me" (Liza Minnelli). *McCall's*, May 1975.

HENTOFF, NAT. "Lady Be Good" (Lee Wiley). *Wall Street Journal*, April 2, 1986.

———. "Mature Mr. Bennett." *Holiday*, November 1965.

———. Untitled essay for *Barbara Lea, Do It Again* (LP). Atlanta, Ga.: Audiophile Records, 1983.

"Her Name is Barbra" (Streisand). *Life*, January 9, 1970.

HINCKLEY, DAVID. "Tony Bennett, Artist." *New York Daily News*, May 4, 1986.

HOLDEN, STEPHEN. "Peggy Lee at 67: Still in the Swingtime of Her Life." *The New York Times*, January 31, 1988.

"Hot as a Torch" (Peggy Lee). *Newsweek*, March 21, 1960.

HUBLER, RICHARD G. "When Jo Stafford Sings." *Coronet*, April 1955.

"In the Garden of Eden with Doris Day." *Look*, December 17, 1963.

"Jo Stafford: Her Fame Is Up, Her Weight Down." *PM* (New York), March 31, 1946.

KAHN, R. "Is There a Doris Day?" *Ladies Home Journal*, July 1963.

KATZ, RAYMOND. "Hello, Everybody!" Booklet with *Kate Smith, A Legendary Performer* (LP). New York: RCA Records, 1978.

KEATING, J. "Marathon Named Merman." *Theatre Arts*, September 1960.

KENNEDY, WILLIAM. "Under My Skin" (Frank Sinatra). *The New York Times Magazine*, October 7, 1990.

KERRISON, RAY. "Kate Smith—Ordeal of a Heroine." *New York Post*, May 19, 1986.

"King" (Nat Cole). *Time*, February 26, 1965.

KLEMESRUD, JUDY. "Dinah, Ageless, Is Reveling in Her 60s" (Dinah Shore). *The New York Times*, April 26, 1981.

KORALL, B. "Measure of Sinatra." *Saturday Review*, October 15, 1966.

———. "Realm of Mercer and Short." *Saturday Review*, April 12, 1969.

KREUGER, MILES. Untitled essay for *Bing Crosby in Hollywood 1930–1934* (LP). New York: Columbia Records, 1967.

LARDINE, BOB. "Two *Not* for the Road" (Eydie Gormé-Steve Lawrence). *New York Sunday News*, March 31, 1968.

LEES, GENE. "Consummate Artistry of Peggy Lee." *High Fidelity*, July 1968.

———. "Frank Sinatra: Confessions and Contradictions." *High Fidelity*, March 1969.

"The Life Story of Shirley Ross." *Picture Show* (London), July 28, 1938.

LISSNER, JOHN. "Lee Wiley's Back." *The New York Times*, November 26, 1972.

MANDEL, H. "Sparrow in the Sky" (Billie Holiday). *Down Beat*, July 1989.

MCANDREW, JOHN. Untitled essay for *Love Me or Leave Me—The Original Recordings of Ruth Etting* (LP). New York: Columbia Records, 1955.

MELCHER, TERRY. "Doris Day I Know." *Good Housekeeping*, October 1963.

MERYMAN, R. "Authentic American Genius" (Louis Armstrong). *Life*, April 15, 1966.

MICHENER, CHARLES. "Liza Minnelli—The Z is for Zap." *Cosmopolitan*, December 1974.

MOON, BUCKLIN, and TOWNSEND, IRVING. "Mildred Bailey: Portraits." Essay for *Mildred Bailey: Her Greatest Performances 1929–1946* (LP). New York: Columbia Records, 1981.

MOONEY, GEORGE A. "Musings of Connie" (Boswell). *The New York Times*, November 17, 1940.

MORDDEN, ETHAN. "I Got a Song" (Judy Garland). *The New Yorker*, October 22, 1990.

MORRIS, GERRY. "Dinah, There's Nobody Finer" (Dinah Shore). *The Friars Epistle*, April 1989.

———. "Liza with a Z—Afire with Zing" (Liza Minnelli). *The Friars Epistle*, September 1989.

MORRISROE, P. "Miss Peggy" (Lee). *New York*, April 30, 1990.

"Mother's at the Waldorf" (Rosemary Clooney). *Newsweek*, October 3, 1960.

MOTHNER, I. "Barbra: A Frantic, Brassy, Tender Funny Girl." *Look*, October 15, 1968.

NACHMAN, GERALD. "Eydie Gormé: The Sunshine Vitamin." *New York Post*, March 7, 1965.

———. "The 'Good Sound' of Jo Stafford." *New York Post*, November 15, 1964.

NASH, ALANNA. "Rosemary Clooney: I Figure If You Just Hang On Long Enough, You Get to Be Woven Into the Fabric of People's Lives." *Stereo Review*, March 1990.

NELSEN, DON. "Joltin' Jo" (Jo Stafford). *New York Sunday News*, May 19, 1957.

———. "Springtime at 61" (Helen O'Connell). *New York Daily News*, October 13, 1981.

———. "Whiling Away with Whiting" (Margaret Whiting). *New York Daily News*, September 30, 1982.

NEVILLE, MARA. "A Different Kind of Grandmother" (Dinah Shore). *New York Sunday News*, April 26, 1981.

NEWMAN, D. "Where the King of the World Goes" (Frank Sinatra). *Esquire*, December 1987.

"Now: Mermania" (Ethel Merman). *Newsweek*, March 2, 1964.

OKON, MAY. "Pop Okayed the Pops" (Steve Lawrence). *New York Sunday News*, December 1, 1957.

OKRENT, D. "St. Francis of Hoboken: Forget Everything You've Heard About Frank Sinatra—Just Listen." *Esquire*, December 1987.

"Out of the Fog" (Mel Tormé). *Time*, March 1, 1963.

"Parsimonious Peggy" (Lee). *Time*, November 3, 1967.

"Pops" (Louis Armstrong). *The New Yorker*, June 27, 1988.

"Recovering Vic Damone." *Time*, January 19, 1987.

ROBINSON, L. "First Lady of Jazz" (Ella Fitzgerald). *Ebony*, November 1961.

———. "Life and Death of Nat King Cole." *Ebony*, April 1965.

———. "Nancy Wilson." *Ebony*, December 1963.

"Rudy Vallee." *Esquire*, June 1962.

SANDERS, C. L. "Louis Armstrong, the Reluctant Millionaire." *Ebony*, March 1964.

———. "Requiem for Queen Dinah" (Washington). *Ebony*, March 1964.

"Sensible Art" (Mabel Mercer). *Newsweek*, January 27, 1964.

SHANAS, BERT. "Role as Stars Outshone Mom and Pop Roles" (Gormé/Lawrence). *New York Sunday News*, March 30, 1969.

SHELTON, PATRICIA. "This Is Eydie Gormé." *Christian Science Monitor*, December 16, 1969.

SHEPHARD, RICHARD F. "Two Who Sang Their Way Up" (Steve Lawrence, Andy Williams). *The New York Times*, August 24, 1958.

"She Who Is Ella" (Fitzgerald). *Time*, November 27, 1964.

"Shirley Ross Will Stay Retired." *New York Morning Telegraph*, July 14, 1959.
SIMMONDS, C. H. "Marvelous Miss Mercer." *National Review*, August 26, 1969.
SIMON, GEORGE T. "Bing Crosby." Booklet included with *Bing Crosby, A Legendary Performer* (LP). New York: RCA Records, 1977.
———. "Rockin' Chair Lady" (Mildred Bailey). *New York Herald-Tribune*, August 19, 1962.
SINATRA, FRANK. "Me and My Music." *Life*, April 23, 1965.
"Soft Answers" (Nat "King" Cole). *Newsweek*, March 1, 1965.
STANLEY, S. and H. "Lovelorn Lady" (Billie Holiday). *Saturday Review*, January 12, 1963.
STEIN, J. "An Evening with Louis Armstrong." *American Scholar*, Winter 1990.
"Storyteller" (Mabel Mercer). *Time*, January 18, 1960.
SULLIVAN, MARY X. "Because He's Just My Bill" (Helen Morgan). *Boston Sunday Advertiser*, October 12, 1941.
"The Survivors" (Ella Fitzgerald). *Ebony*, November 1990.
"Sweet Nancy" (Wilson). *Life*, June 14, 1966.
"Talk of the Stars" (Rudy Vallee). *Newsweek*, October 23, 1961.
TIEGEL, E. "Peggy Lee." *Down Beat*, June 1990.
"Tony's Second Time Around" (Bennett). *Time*, March 6, 1964.
ULANOV, BARRY. "Lee Wiley, an Inspired Singer and a Subtle One Too, Is Full of Musical Eloquence," *Metronome*, December 1952.
WAHLS, ROBERT. "Look Who's Back: Dick Haymes." *New York Sunday News*, August 8, 1960.
"Welcome Home, Bobby" (Short). *Ebony*, June 1964.
WHEELER, T. C. "Timeless Charm of Peggy Lee." *Saturday Evening Post*, October 10, 1964.
WILLIAMS, M. "Billie Holiday: Triumphant Decline." *Saturday Review*, October 31, 1964.
———. "Ella and Others." *Saturday Review*, November 28, 1964.
WILSON, EARL. "Harry's Girl" (Helen Forrest). *New York Post*, June 25, 1982.
WILSON, JOHN S. "Billie Holiday—Jazz Singer, Pure and Simple." *The New York Times*, July 6, 1958.
———. "Gravelly or Tender, It's All Mercer" (Mabel Mercer). *The New York Times*, January 19, 1969.
———. "Helen O'Connell Sings at Copacabana" (interview). *The New York Times*, October 5, 1964.
———. "Miss Whiting Happens to Like New York" (Margaret Whiting). *The New York Times*, August 19, 1977.
———. "Success Is No Surprise to Him" (Steve Lawrence). *The New York Times*, April 19, 1964.
WILSON, LIZA. "Nice Guys Finish First" (Andy Williams). *New York Journal-American*, April 28, 1963.
ZION, SIDNEY. "Outlasting Rock—Sophisticated Melody and Lyrics Make a Comeback." *The New York Times Magazine*, August 2, 1981.

INDEX

ABOUT THE AUTHORS

David Hajdu is a senior editor of Time Warner's *Entertainment Weekly*, a former New York music critic for the *Hollywood Reporter*, and a contributor to *Rolling Stone*. A pop composer himself, he has had his songs performed at New York jazz clubs and cabarets. He is a founding editor of *Video Review* magazine and the author of *How to Shoot Your Kids on Home Video*. An alumnus of New York University, he lives in New York City with his wife and two children.

Roy Hemming is reviews editor of *Video Review* and a longtime classic-pop reviewer for *Stereo Review*. He has hosted radio programs devoted exclusively to show music and classic pop, and also produced the New York Philharmonic's weekly broadcasts for ten years. He is a former editor of *Senior Scholastic* and *World Week* magazines, and the author of *The Melody Lingers On: The Great Songwriters and Their Movie Musicals* and *Discovering Great Music on CDs, LPs, and Cassettes*. A native of Connecticut and a graduate of Yale and Stanford, he lives in New York City.